An
EXPERIENCE-BASED
APPROACH
TO Language
AND READING

An EXPERIENCE-BASED APPROACH TO Language AND Reading

edited by

Carl Braun, Ph.D.
Professor, Faculty of Education
University of Calgary

and

Victor Froese, Ph.D.
Associate Professor, Faculty of Education
University of Manitoba

University Park Press
Baltimore • London • Tokyo

UNIVERSITY PARK PRESS
International Publishers in Science and Medicine
Chamber of Commerce Building
Baltimore, Maryland 21202

Copyright ©1977 by University Park Press

Typeset by Action Comp Co., Inc. and Alpha Graphics, Inc.
Manufactured in the United States of America by Universal Lithographers,
Inc., and the Optic Bindery Incorporated.

Library of Congress Cataloging in Publication Data
Main entry under title:
An Experience-based approach to language and reading.
Bibliography: p.
Includes index.
1. Language arts—Addresses, essays, lectures.
2. Reading—Addresses, essays, lectures.
I. Braun, Carl.   II. Froese, Victor.
LB1576.E94   372.6   77-6691
ISBN 0-8391-1146-0

Contents

Contributors

Carl Braun, Ph.D., Professor, Faculty of Education, University of Calgary

David Olshin, Ed.D. Associate Professor, the University of Calgary

Victor Froese, Ph.D., Associate Professor, Faculty of Education, University of Manitoba

Dianne Seim, M.A. Part-time reading instructor, the University of Manitoba

NCTE Committee on Guidelines to Evaluate the English Component in Elementary School Programs

Ves Thomas, Ph.D. Professor of Education and Associate Dean, the University of Calgary

Preface

Like most books in education, this one is directed to a target audience. We have attempted to speak to some of the needs frequently expressed by the undergraduate language arts student. We do feel, however, that there is much between these covers that will come as a welcome resource for the practicing teacher who is looking for alternative strategies for instructional improvement. The many comments from teachers who have read the manuscript bear this out.

Anyone faced with yet another book on language and reading is justified in raising his eyebrows because the proliferation and redundancy in the area are embarrassingly obvious. To make the claim that this volume lacks a measure of redundancy would be absurd. We do lay claim, however, to many programmatic suggestions that are underpinned by the pervasive link between feelings and thoughts that grow out of experience and the modes of communicating these feelings and thoughts. This, in our opinion, is the foundation of a language-reading program, and this premise, if present elsewhere, is far from explicit. We are convinced that a program built on such a premise has the advantage of flexibility necessary to meet the needs of all children, be they culturally and linguistically different or developmentally slow or fast. The total thrust is that teachers build programs on the combination of what the child brings experientially and linguistically and what his needs are, rather than on a blind list of curriculum objectives.

The volume is divided into five sections. Following a chapter outlining the rationale of the program, two chapters suggest sources of input that the teacher might employ to provide "grist" for the learner's language development. The four chapters dealing with diagnostic aspects of programming attempt to aid the teacher in identifying specific needs to consider intervention strategies in a total language context. Three chapters focus on various aspects of "integration." We recognize that the term is frequently misconstrued because of the varying contexts within which it is used. In this book integration denotes two things. First, it implies capitalizing on common experiences to develop and refine language skills in a way that will bring about mutual facilitation of listening, speaking, reading, and writing. Second, it denotes a cross-fertilization of the language arts with other subject areas to facilitate language development but also to facilitate mastery of content areas through improved communication competency.

In answer to the need for a system of monitoring progress, the final section pinpoints some of the pitfalls commonly encountered in language programs. Furthermore, it suggests ways of keeping records of children's competencies and needs.

We sincerely hope the teacher will find between these covers some guidelines and some inspiration to program for a richer language environment for today's children. If this hope is met even in small measure, our efforts have been amply rewarded.

An
EXPERIENCE-BASED
APPROACH
TO Language
AND READING

PART I
RATIONALE

chapter 1

Experience:
The Basis for
Communication
Skills
Development

Carl Braun

Faced with a plethora of theories (and platitudes) about the impact of certain learning experiences on children's development, it is not surprising that some teachers find themselves in a state of bewilderment. Part of this bewilderment, no doubt, stems from some uncertainty regarding *how* learning is best effected, and part from their exposure to the compromise between what is known about learning and what commercial interests often promote.

Perhaps the most crucial problem is the uncertainty about the theoretical basis or rationale underlying the approaches and methods teachers attempt to employ. This state of uncertainty can be interpreted in at least two ways. First, if the teacher wavers about whether or not her treatment of children (including methods and organization) best meets their cognitive, social, and emotional needs, her instruction will lack conviction. It is well known that without optimism and a corresponding conviction, even the best designed methodology is doomed to failure. (Not all that surprising is the fact that, given some degree of conviction, some generally considered poor methodologies seem to "work.") Second, and equally pertinent, a lack of understanding of a theoretical basis for instruction denies the teacher the opportunity to exploit in the fullest sense a particular approach. This often results in "dead ends" in instruction.

This chapter discusses the rationale of one aspect of the child's world in relation to the development of communication skills: his experience. We all glibly assent to the need for a rich experiential base but frequently fail to consider *why* and to *what* ends this expeience is to be applied in the classroom.

A CASE IN POINT

To illustrate the impact of experience on the production of language, note the spontaneity and richness of the chart dictated by Miss Miller's first-grade class. This was only one of a series of episodes communicated by the children after a visit to ice caves about 20 miles from the school.

> We went into the ice cave. It was so dark we had to use our flashlights. All the kids were as quiet as mice. It was slippy and real real spooky. Nobody was real scared—just a little. Miss Miller yelled "Don't go farther." We could of slipped and felled right off the end of the cave and plumped into millions of dark and real dangerous caves under the world.

There is no intended implication that experience must originate 20 miles from the school. Experiences, equally rich, can often be provided right within the classroom. These may include (as will be noted in subsequent chapters) a science experiment, observation of plants or animals in the classroom, an applied mathematical problem, music and art activities, creative drama, and so on and on.

Whatever the source, what rationale is there for providing for experience as a basis for instruction? To hark back to the ice cave episode, perhaps what is most striking is the obvious and natural link between what children have experienced, what they have thought and felt, what they have spoken, what the teacher has written, and, finally, what they are now able (with varying degrees of success) to read. The reader will recognize this as basic to Allen's (1964) premise for the language experience approach to reading. There is no need here to elaborate on the issue that such an approach can and should proceed far beyond an "approach to reading" to include all aspects of language development (receptive and expressive) and concept development. We need to remind ourselves, though, of the advantages of such an approach. For one thing, flexibility is the key. It can be used successfully with beginning readers, remedial and corrective readers, culturally disadvantaged children, and, additionally, in conjuction with any other approach. The fact that the teacher accepts the learner's existing language to create his own personal reading materials is in itself a tremendous plus. The goal of such an approach is, indeed, to "develop the ability to communicate in all facets of language" (Hall, 1970). The goals include development of word attack skills, wide reading vocabulary, comprehension, and a permanent interest in reading. A strong case can be made for the approach in that it ensures success and confidence rather than bewilderment and frustration, particulary at the beginning reading stage.

Certainly, these first-graders reading the "ice cave" story are thinking, speaking, listening, and reading about ideas and feelings that are deeply couched in meaning. The ideas are real; consequently, the language used to talk and read about these ideas is real-life language. It is, perhaps, this element of realism rather than artificial or contrived language that forms the basis for a successful, meaningful, communications experience.

Apart from the aspect of realism, a word is interjected here about the need to integrate the teaching of the language arts: listening, speaking, reading, and writing. The interrelationships between oral language and reading competence are well documented (Clay, 1968; Loban, 1963; Ruddell, 1965; Strickland, 1962; Tatham, 1970). While research regarding the interrelationships of listening and writing with the other language arts is less conclusive, the plea for integration can certainly be made on the premise that it promotes an understanding of the function of reading and writing and the relationship of all the language arts to learning. Such integration against a backdrop of meaningful experience is one of the surest guarantees of a successful learning experience.

COMMUNICATION ABOUT THE REAL WORLD

The aim of any language-reading program is to help children communicate lucidly and concisely with others whether the medium be print or speech. One could argue that to develop this competence some knowledge of the physical properties (squiggle and sound) is useful. Certainly, learning to become aware of the physical properties is within the realm of the abstract. If one adds to this a message (content) that is contrived or artificial, the learner is likely to remain in a state of "cognitive confusion" (Downing and Oliver, 1974) certainly with regard to the physical properties of written language.

Perhaps the most vivid documentation of breaking the barrier between the physical properties of language and the property of language that communicates is the case of Helen Keller's language development (Keller, 1958). She describes how her teacher gave her a doll and spelled the word "d-o-l-l" in her hand. She describes the flush of childish pleasure and pride in her success in spelling the word correctly. She admits that she did not know that she was spelling a word "or even that words existed; I was simply making my fingers go in monkey-like imitation..." (p. 28). She goes on to describe how, while she was playing with her new doll, her teacher placed her big rag doll into her lap in an attempt to have her grasp the notion that "d-o-l-l" applied to both. She further describes the tussle she and her teacher had over "m-u-g" and "w-a-t-e-r" and the problem Helen encountered in confounding the two. The teacher despaired awaiting an opportunity for her to try the lesson with modified teaching strategies.

> We walked down the path to the well house attracted by the fragrance of the honeysuckle with which it was covered. Someone was drawing water and my teacher placed my hand under the spout. As the cool stream gushed over one hand she spelled into the other the word water, first slowly, then rapidly. I stood still, my whole attention fixed upon the motions of her fingers. Suddenly I felt a misty consciousness as of something forgotten—a thrill of returning thought; and somehow the mystery of language was revealed to me. I knew then that "w-a-t-e-r" was the wonderful cool something that was flowing over my hand. That living word awakened my soul, gave it light, hope, joy, set it free! There were barriers still, it is true, but barriers that could, in time, be swept away (p. 28).

The teaching strategies employed to teach Helen Keller the relationship between the physical properties and the communication function of language would, indeed, seem exaggerated for normal children. However, what does become salient is the fact that without real experience she would not have developed the concept of language. Her case demonstrates "on a magnified scale the emotional and intellectual implications of the mastery of language related to experience for all human beings" (Goddard, 1974, p. 10).

Let us relate this briefly to the ice cave episode. Obviously, the children were impressed with the quietness of the confines of the cave. To say simply that the kids were "quiet" was not enough. There was a need to communicate exactly how quiet they were. The feelings of the children are reflected in the words, "Nobody was real scared—just a little," an acceptable way of expressing fear with just a little hedging. The fact that they have a real context around which communication centers sets the stage for communication of both thought and feelings—something impossible in a vacuum.

In Keller's case, she learned that "w-a-t-e-r" spelled on her hand was a physical way of representing the "wonderful cool something...." Normal first-graders know what the utterance "water" represents, i.e., they have established the relationship between the physical properties of speech and communication. What many of them have not accomplished is an understanding of the link between the physical properties of written language and communication. A healthy classroom climate will often reveal questions that children use in the process of clarifying the relational properties. In the early stages questions such as, "Is that a word?" "Is that word 'spooky'?" are typical of this unraveling mystery of the conventions of written language in relation to speech and ideas. Later the teacher finds extensions like, "I didn't know 'flashlights' was one word" or, "I didn't know 'dark' and 'dangerous' start the same." The probability of these kinds of queries and discoveries occurring is much greater in the context of experience than in an artificially contrived context.

It may seem redundant to emphasize that basing what is taught on experience aids in eliminating, at least to a degree, the difficulty that children encounter who come to school with a "non-school" language repertoire. This applies equally to children who come either from basically "nonverbal" or "non-English" homes. (Chapter 6 provides many examples of activities to aid the teacher in helping children from such backgrounds.)

Finally, then, an experience-based approach reduces the hazard of the child's "thinking" in fragmented thoughts and reading the artificial language of "non-ideas" as opposed to the kind of language that communicates ideas and feelings — love, hate, joy, sadness. There is likely no stronger defense one could make for the provision of a rich and varied experience base.

Thorn (1974) believes that a major cause of reading disability can be traced to school practices in which reading is taught in a program divorced from experience and the totality of language.

> For the first time, children meet language that does not communicate in a meaningful way and that is not a natural part of their attempts to interpret and organize their environment. For the first time they see language as something that is artificial and imposed and as something

that causes uncertainty and brings in its wake disapproval. This should not, and need not, be so if written language is introduced as a natural extension of oral language, and children from the beginning recognize it as a tool for organizing their own reality, serving their needs as surely as oral language (p. 26).

PROVISION FOR VARYING LEVELS OF DEVELOPMENT

A further case for provision for and capitalization on experience can be made on the basis of the varying levels of development represented in any classroom. Piaget has suggested that the child at beginning school age is an intuitive thinker whose perception is centered (i.e., the tendency to center attention on one detail at a time) rather than decentered. This strong tendency to be tied to one dimension of thought at a given time would suggest a system for beginning reading with an absolute minimum of detailed analysis. This connotes reading words as rich as possible in imagery to obviate unnecessary analysis. The only guarantee of accomplishing such an image intensity is to base the written language on the child's experiences and interests. This does not mean that available printed materials cannot be used if the materials can, in fact, be "hooked up" with the child's interest and experience. Froese (1976) has suggested such materials. Thorn (1974) relates a teaching episode in which the teacher introduces the theme, "We should be responsible for our own things." The teacher took the group on a cloakroom tour to collect an assortment of abandoned balls, mitts, and other items. The group recalled an instance when a classmate had lost her lunch. It had been found on the playground where she had left it while watching a ball game. The class talked, wrote, and read about lost-and-found experiences. The next day they read a published story in which three children claimed that "somebody" was responsible for their lost mitts, while their mother insisted that "You had your mitts, not somebody!"

> One of the first comments of the group was 'They're just like us! Bet they left those things at school!' A sympathetic but critical discussion of the children's behavior followed. The teacher contrasted this group's reaction with that of another group which she had asked to read the story without any preparation. They finished and their attitude was "So what?" and "What's wrong with them always losing their things? . . ." If teachers want children to relate an author's ideas to their own experience, it is sometimes necessary to raise that experience to a level of consciousness so that it is readily available to them as they read (p. 28).

In instances such as this, the reader is already "centered" on a theme leaving his resources free to deal with the written language with a minimum of problems. Certainly, the need for detailed visual analysis is reduced because he is already "tuned in" to the theme.

A program based on experience, then, does not imply that the classroom functions only within the range of the immediate interests that the child brings to school. It is the function of the school to enrich and extend the existing interests and to stimulate new interests and to provide experiences, real or vicarious, to give depth and reality to these interests.

While children go through identifiable stages of cognitive development, they do so at varying rates. A program based on experiences and interests of children provides flexibility that can be used to capitalize on these varying rates of development. A common experience may have elements to develop oral language-listening skills for some, reading skills for some, and spelling-writing skills for others. Even within these global areas, the specific skill needs will vary. Chapter 10 illustrates how a common experience can be used to achieve skill improvement for children at varying stages of development.

Goddard (1974) illustrates how such flexibility can, and should, be extended into what is known as an "undifferentiated" curriculum which connotes a whole experience that becomes the focal point for overlapping areas of knowledge.

> For example, within the area of mathematics, language is included; and in constructing and creating with materials of many kinds children may build mathematical concepts and extend their command of language. In other words, if children are able to have enriching experiences, language ability is developed among a great number of other skills. Learning is not fragmented but comes from the totality of a child's experiences (p. 37).

A pervasive dilemma facing the school relates to the question of *when* children are ready to benefit from formal reading instruction. It is known that in a classroom of 25 to 30 children around 6 years of age, there is an astounding spectrum of stages of readiness. Again, giving the instructional program an experience base and developing oral and written language from this base allows the flexibility of providing for children who are already reading, those who need further development in some of the auditory-visual readiness skills, as well as those who are ready to begin transcribing their own thoughts and feelings on to paper. Some examples from the ice cave episode might be helpful here. Suppose some children need emphasis on auditory aspects of language development. The teacher might use the oral output of the children to build these skills. For example, if rhyming elements need to be developed she may take examples from the story. "I am thinking of a word that rhymes with 'ice.' The clue is, 'The kids were as quiet as _____.'" Or, "We couldn't see a spark, it was so _____." Other examples of auditory skill development might be, "Show me how many parts you hear in the words I say: 'nobody,' 'flashlights,' 'spooky,' 'dark,' 'scared.'" (The teacher would likely ask the children to say each word to themselves and clap for each part or feel how many times the jaw dropped as they said the word.)

Another group is already at the reading state, but the teacher is concerned about the lack of fluency. She prepares phrase strips or overhead transparencies of meaning units from the story, e.g., "into the ice cave," "as quiet as mice," "real real spooky," "end of the cave," etc. The children are encouraged to read each unit as one rather than as isolated words. The teacher might aid this by sweeping her hand quickly underneath the units or even providing meaning clues such as, "This (into the ice caves) tells us *where* we went." Later, she might put these meaning units into a new sentence context.

One could go on and on and extract material from one experience to aid in fostering skill development in listening, oral language development, any aspect of decoding or comprehension or writing. The ensuing chapters provide numerous illustrations of how this can be accomplished. The inference here, then, is not at all that skill development is to be left to incidental as opposed to systematized skill instruction. It means, simply, that the group is comprised of children at widely varying developmental stages and that an experience shared by the children can be capitalized upon to extend communication skills commensurate with these varying stages.

READING AS A PSYCHOLINGUISTIC PROCESS

Much has been said in the past decade about the nature of the reading process. The most pervasive, and probably the most persuasive, theme has been that of reading as a pycholinguistic process (Smith 1975; (Goodman, 1967; Pearson, 1967a; Smith, 1975). It is not within the scope of this chapter to elaborate on a psycholinguistic theory of reading; however, because little has been said elsewhere regarding the theory in relation to experience, a brief exposition is provided here.

Basically, the psycholinguistic theory of reading holds that the reading process is first and foremost language-based. The reader has available a vast resource of language cues based on his knowledge of language. These cues include *graphophonic* elements (the sounds and patterns of sounds of the oral language and the squiggles and patterns of squiggles of the written language), *syntactic* elements (the ordering relationships among words in sentences), and *semantic-associational* elements (knowledge of what words refer to in the real world and how words are hierachically related). According to the theory, the reader uses, in concert, the array of graphophonic, syntactic, and semantic-associational cues to derive meaning from the printed page. Efficient reading demands that a sufficient "mix" of syntactic and semantic-associational cues are available so that graphophonic analysis can be minimized. According to the theory, the reader *predicts* what is coming in print and uses graphophonic information to *verify* the predictions. According to Pearson (1967a):

> Novice or poor readers are so bound up in their search for phonic information that they have little chance to attend to meaning. Good readers, on the other hand, because they attend to meaning, may often make unimportant errors in decoding words accurately (p.310).

This is no more than a skeletal structure of the theory. The justification for a discussion of theory here is the fact that the semantic-associational cues are often not rich or at all available for the reader. This is particularly true for material that is dull in the first place and outside the realm of experience for a particular reader. As a result, the reader must rely on syntactic and graphophonic cues only (often the latter). This carries strong implications not only for the decoding aspects of reading but also for the development of comprehension skills. Certainly, a dearth of experience relevant to a reading selection reduces seriously the amount of prediction possible, thus increasing the load of graphophonic information (and the amount of analysis) required. It becomes abundantly clear, then, that a solid experience base for reading is not only justifiable for but absolutely essential to the development of proficiency.

MOTIVATION AND EXPERIENCE

"Purpose and incentives play a part in the achievement and mastery of any skill" (Goddard, 1974, p. 23). Reading and writing are no exceptions. As Goddard has stated, "The more reading and writing is incorporated into a social context, the more quickly the linguistic conventions of that society will be grasped by children" (p. 27). This can be explained, at least in part, by the fact that if a written message with a degree of meaningfullness is produced before the child's eyes, he is more likely to focus attention on *how* the message is being presented than if meaningless verbiage is imposed on him. This early attention to the conventions of language will aid the learner whether the task be reading or writing. The same motivational benefits are likely to accrue with respect to the content of the material as well. In other words, the activity has a chance of becoming goal-oriented in terms of both medium and content. Teachers and parents are equally concerned that positive attitudes toward reading and writing should be acquired; this long-term goal can be attained only if the short-term goals attend to the basic need of a purpose for communication.

Sylvia Ashton-Warner (1964) demonstrated in the extreme sense the benefits of capitalizing on the interest-experience dimension in her work with Maori children in New Zealand. As she gathered the children around her, she would try to determine which words had intense meaning at the time. She would write these words of personal interest and meaning on cards for the children to take home. If the children were able to read the words the next day, the choices had been good ones and were added to each child's bank of "key" words. If not, the words were discarded. What is central to Ashton-Warner's program is that words children initially read and write come from within themselves, from their feelings of love, hate, joy, disgust, and fear and are connected with their interests and experiences.

The motivational benefits are likely to be revealed most readily in the success of the learner. However, if a program, is indeed based on interest and experience, the motivational aspect should go even further. Because the content of reading and writing is grounded in familiar experience, the learner is most likely to share with others what he can produce orally, what he can read, or what he can write. The content of *his* communication is essentially an extension and exteriorization of himself and, thus, worthy of communication.

The need to take into account interest and experience in teaching disabled readers is documented by Neilsen and Braun (1976). They report a program of instruction for an adult non-reader. All the material for instruction was relevant to the learner's experience and interests.

> ...words employed to teach specific skills were chosen on the basis of Lorne's interests: hockey, baseball, community places and events, cars, etc....Initial words were selected on the basis of need (e.g. street signs,

billboards) experience and interests...the authors photographed everything in Lorne's community from street signs to the boarded beach cottage. These photographs were mounted on sheets of paper, some in isolation, others in series. Expository materials were written based on these photographs employing names of local places and people. This technique offers the advantage of adding relevance to the reading material. Further, it can be used for reading for detail, sequencing, supplying titles (main ideas), and basic critical reading skills (pp. 278-280).

"EXPERIENCE": FOUNDATION FOR CONCEPT ACQUISITION AND COMPREHENSION

No doubt the reader has decided by this time that the importance of providing experience stops at the prereading and early reading stages, or, at best, can be used with illiterate adults. Certainly, the need for direct experience is much more important at early levels than it is at later levels for reasons already discussed. However, the benefits of direct experience extend far beyond the beginning reading level. For one thing, direct experience is the key source of information required for the acquisition of concepts that are brought to bear in listening, speaking, reading, and writing. It is, to a large degree, the development of a wide range of concepts that determines the reader's depth of comprehension in his reading at early, as well as later, reading levels. No one can argue against the impact of experience on comprehension. Pearson (1976b) has stated:

> Experience is at the heart of comprehension...Experience is what we are referring to when we say that a person is good at reading "between the lines" (p. 18).

Not only does the background of experience provide the "content" to be applied in comprehension, but, perhaps equally important, it provides the reader (or listener) with the notion of *how* to apply this experience (and to extend experiences vicariously) at later levels.

Pearson (1976b) makes a strong case for using concepts already known by students to approach the teaching and learning of unfamiliar concepts:

> Of those concepts related to the concept I want to teach, which ones do the children already possess (and maybe even have a set of direct experiences for)? ... What are the anchor points that I can use to assess the new concept? ... to assist the students in assimilating the new information into their pre-existing body of meaning (pp. 9-10).

The reader, for example, is confronted with a passage like the following:

> One of the most interesting characteristics of amphibians, such as the frog, toad, newt and salamander, is that they are cold-blooded animals (Thorn, Braun, and Richmond, 1973, p. 26).

The reader has a limited schema for amphibians consisting, perhaps, of a few of the chief properties (where they live, body covering, etc.) and knows a limited number of examples from direct experience, e.g., the toad and frog. These are his anchor points in his pre-existing store of information. The teacher's task is to attempt to help the learner "identify the critical properties that distinguish the concept she/he already possessed from the one you were trying to explain" (Pearson, 1976b, p. 10).

In the "amphibian" example, the teacher can help the learner capitalize on the pre-existing information, but the learner may also have developed strategies to apply independently the anchor points he already possesses.

SUMMARY

This chapter has attempted to underpin the need for experience as a basis for the development of communication skills. The rationale included the fact that experience offers a position from which to develop these skills in a real rather than contrived context, that it fosters flexibility to take into account varying stages of development, that it provides maximum input for the development of semantic-associational cues in reading and listening, that it has motivational benefits, and finally, that experience provides a solid foundation for concept acquisition and comprehension generally.

The ensuing chapters provide numerous examples of *how* experience can be provided and capitalized upon in the classroom to enhance acquisition of communication skills.

LITERATURE CITED

Allen, R. V. 1964. The language experience approach. In: W. G. Cutts (ed.), Teaching Young Children to Read. United States Office of Education, Washington.

Ashton-Warner, S. 1964. Teacher. Simon and Schuster, New York.

Clay, M. 1968. A syntactic analysis of reading errors. J. Verb. Learn. Verb. Behav. 7: 634–638.

Downing, J., and Oliver, P. 1974. The child's conception of a word. Read. Res. Q. 9: 568–582.

Froese, V. 1976. The teaching of reading in a Piagetian way. Manitoba J. Educ. 11(2):15–17.

Goddard, N. 1974. Literacy: Language-experience Approaches. Macmillan Education, Ltd., London.

Goodman, K. S. 1967. Reading:A psycholinguistic guessing game. J. Read. Spec. May.

Hall, M. A. 1970. Teaching Reading as a Language Experience. Charles E. Merrill, Columbus.

Keller, H. 1958. The Story of My Life. Hodder and Stoughton, London.

Loban, W. 1963. The Language of Elementary School Children. National Council of Teachers of English, Research Report, No. 1 Champaign, Ill.

Neilsen, A. R., and Braun, C. 1976. Teaching the drop-out to read—A case report. Acad. Ther. XI(3): 275–281.

Pearson, P. D. 1976a. A psycholinguistic model of reading. Lang. Arts 53: 309–314.

Pearson, P. D. 1976b. The nature of comprehension. Paper presented at the National Reading Conference. Atlanta, Georgia, December.

Ruddell, R. B. 1965. The effect of four programs of reading instruction with varying emphasis on the regularity of grapheme-phoneme correspondences and the relation of language structure to meaning on achievement in first grade children. Report of Cooperative Research Project No. 2699. University of California at Berkley.

Smith, F. 1975. Comprehension and Learning. Holt, Rinehart and Winston, New York.

Strickland, R. G. 1962. The language of elementary school children: Its relationship to the language of reading textbooks and the quality of reading of selected children. Bulletin of the School of Education, Indiana University, Bloomington, Indiana.

Tatham, S. M. 1970. Reading comprehension of materials written with selected oral language patterns: A study of grades two and four. Read. Res. Q. 5: 402–426.

Thorn, E. A. 1974. Integration of the language arts and the prevention of disability in beginning reading. Manitoba J. Educ. 24–28.

Thorn, E. A., Braun, C., and Richmond, I. 1973. Practice Strategies II. Gage Educational Publications, Toronto.

Part II

INPUT
Factors

chapter 2

Facilitating Experience-based Language Development

Carl Braun

One of the dilemmas pervading educational practice is the degree to which instruction in language should be structured. The controversy has spanned the full gamut from promotion of intensive drills on isolated skills to programs totally without form or structure that leave development of language skills to incidental learning. This controversy has perhaps been more lively with regard to written language than to oral language instruction. However, determining the optimum degree of structure in both aspects poses a persistent pedagogical problem.

The position taken in this chapter is that the degree of structure in and of itself will not create or necessarily solve any instructional problem. The thrust of instructional planning, rather, must come from attention to specific objectives, which provide a focus for language-development activities. These objectives, then, in relation to broader goals of language development form the structural framework for curriculum planning and instruction.

In Chapter 1 a strong case was made for ensuring that the reader has available (and uses) semantic-associational and syntactic cues in addition to graphophonic cues. One of the broad goals of language-development activities, then, involves providing the child with a language base (semantic and syntactic) that he can use effectively in the reading act. The activities outlined in this chapter,

19

taken as a whole, reflect such a broad goal. The subheadings under which these activities appear reflect the more specific goals of language instruction. While many of the activities suggested here appear geared toward oral (expressive) or listening (receptive) goals, most if not all activities can be transferred without modification to a reading and/or writing context depending on the level and needs of the learner.

In accordance with statements made in Chapter 1, the activities here are developed through experience—both real and vicarious.

VOCABULARY DEVELOPMENT

Vocabulary Breadth and the Language Environment

There is perhaps no better way of facilitating a rich repertoire of basic vocabulary items than to provide the child with an environment rich in sound and sense. This implies, as indicated in the previous chapter, that experience underpins what the child hears and reads and what he talks and writes about. This is another way of saying that concrete examples form the basis for the most successful language learning environment.

Another requirement for a language environment is that the child hears language related to his experience and, further, that he is stimulated to use language in a real audience situation in a nonthreatening atmosphere. This stimulation and consequent feedback are probably the best means to ensure that the child will acquire not only labels but the requisite relationships among labels.

A number of nonlinguistic factors must also be considered in developing a fruitful language environment. Certainly, a wealth of manipulative materials must be available to stimulate a wide range of sensitivities to sight, sound, smell, taste, and texture. Too often the need for a heightened sensitivity to things in the environment is not seen as relevant to language development. It is perhaps the aspect of sharpened sensitivity, heightened powers of observation, and a concomitant curiosity about things that is at least as important in language development as the language the child hears.

The range of experiences to be used in developing a breadth of vocabulary is as wide as the teacher's imagination. Observations and discussions about the weather, for instance, might be stimulated by questions such as: "Is the *temperature* today cold or warm?" "How do we find out what the *temperature* is?" (Go outside and see if you get cold; listen to the radio; ask someone who can read a *thermometer*, etc.) "What does the sky look like this morning?" (*Clear; sunny; cloudy; overcast; gloomy;* etc.)

The example illustrates how observations about weather can provide a good basis for vocabulary growth, e.g., "temperature," "thermometer," "overcast," etc. Furthermore, this might lead to development of labels related to more specific aspects of weather. For example, after the ideas regarding cold, hot, warm, etc., have been grasped, this might be extended to "How cold?" "How hot?" etc. This would logically lead to an introduction of adjectives and later to the development of concepts and terms related to specific measurement of temperature and precipitation.

The amount of learning that will occur from incidental discussions about topics such as weather will depend on the kind of learning "climate" within the classroom. If the teacher displays enthusiasm and gives encouragement to respond spontaneously, the probability is that children will become interested in the topic and make observations outside of the classroom context and engage in discussion with their peers and family.

The topic of "weather" is used here only for illustrative purposes. Equally worthwhile observations may center around "the local grocery store," "birds in our community," "our families," "growing things," "things we ride in," etc. Chapter 10 gives examples of topics that can be used to good advantage in developing the notion of reading and writing as communication skills. Any of the topics can be used simply to develop oral language (vocabulary) skills.

The sensitive teacher will recognize that children's books provide a fantastic resource for language development generally and particularly for vocabulary extension (see Part VI, Appendix A). While it may be difficult at times to locate the kinds of books that extend specifically the experiences from classroom or community observations, field trips, etc., most children's books are so well illustrated that these illustrations provide the kind of "experiential" background that enhances vocabulary development. This is true especially if the teacher capitalizes to the fullest extent on intonation patterns and kinesics (gestures and facial expressions). A few excerpts are included here to illustrate some of the possibilities.

An example of a children's favorite that readily comes to mind is Lynd Ward's *The Biggest Bear*. The opening statement sets the scene not only for an exciting story but also for words that are loaded with meaning and ready to be "picked up" by the keen listener:

> Whenever Johnny went down the road to the store for a piece of maple sugar or something, he always felt humiliated. The other barns in the valley usually had a bearskin nailed up to dry. But never Johnny's barn (p. 4).

The story unfolds as Johnny's befriended bear makes a nuisance of himself in the community by drinking milk meant for calves, raiding smokehouses for bacon, and raiding cornfields at night. It is not surprising to learn that the bear grows quickly to an enormous size when he goes as far as to drink up the McLean's store of maple syrup. Indeed,

> ... What they had to say about Johnny's bear was plenty. He was a trial and a tribulation to the whole valley (p. 46).

The vividness of the illustrations accompanying the text add considerably to the excitement and meaning of the selection. What is noteworthy in an example such as *The Biggest Bear* is that sensitive reading will bring out a depth of feeling that becomes a most critical component of the words that children will focus attention on. There will be little doubt about how Johnny feels when he feels "humiliated"; there will be even less doubt about what is meant when the author relates that the bear was "a trial and a tribulation."

Equally rich resources for vocabulary extension are found in books like Marcia Brown's, *Once a Mouse* ... and John Langstaff's, *Frog Went A-Courtin'*. (Annotated bibliographies of selected children's books are provided in Part VI, Appendix A.) The teacher who prepares children for the reading of a book, reads it effectively, and reflects appreciation and enjoyment herself is providing children with an "experience" in the truest sense. The need to select books judiciously, to read them and read them well to and with children, and to do this on a continuing basis cannot be over-emphasized in providing for a rich vocabulary development environment.

Vocabulary Growth and Concept Development

The foregoing section has dealt with the need to provide an atmosphere and activities that promote vocabulary breadth. It is possible, even highly probable, that children will learn to "mouth" many words that have limited meaning for them. Even in the case where a concrete experience accompanies language production, a child often focuses his attention on aspects of the referent not intended by the teacher. There is no suggestion here that the experience has been wasted. However, as far as is possible, the teacher will want to provide experiences that relate language labels to concepts which the labels represent. The implication, of course, is to base concept development in concrete experiences.

DeCecco (1968) has made a strong case for the need to ensure that children are given instruction that enables them to give attention to the relevant attribute of a concept. Among the nine steps that DeCecco outlines, at least one needs to be highlighted here: the need to provide the child with nonexemplars as well as exemplars of the concept he is to learn. This aids the learner in making the necessary discriminations between "what is" and "what is not," helping him to abstract the specific attributes that comprise the concept. For example, suppose the objective is for the child to be able to identify examples of the concept "triangle." The teacher presents exemplars including equilateral, scalene, and isoceles triangles and triangles of varying sizes so that size is eliminated as an attribute of triangularity. It is certainly possible for the child to abstract the relevant attributes of triangles (three sides joining; three angles) from these exemplars, particularly if attention is directed to the attributes. However, one is likely to find children who, when presented with a trapezoid or parallelogram, will label these as triangles. For this reason it is sound teaching practice to present some nontriangular shapes (nonexemplars) in the teaching cycle so that the abstraction of the "three-angle" attribute becomes highlighted.

At least two other factors need to be taken into account in instruction in vocabulary and concepts. First, there is a need to provide opportunities for the child to relate the newly acquired concept to aspects of his environment that are already familiar to him whether in the form of concrete objects or pictorial and/or story representations. For example, the child who has acquired the basic concept of "triangularity" might be asked to find shapes in the classroom or home that are triangular. He might find a picture of a kite and discover triangular shapes within it. This follow-up learning experience aids the learner not only in making finer discriminations but also helps him to generalize to new situations that are different from the instances presented in the initial learning situation. The other consideration relates partly to the notion of generalizability but includes active use of language in the presence of, and as an aid to, concept development. For instance, questions like "What does this remind you of?" or, "It is as large as a _____" will aid the learner in relating a newly acquired concept to what he already knows. Furthermore, it will help in developing the kinds of language forms that are essential to effective communication as in the case of similies: "large as a whale," "red as an apple," "soft as a pillow," etc.

Concept of Shape and Form   There is no suggestion here that children do not learn many concepts and vocabulary referents in unstructured natural communication situations. The store of concepts they come to school with certainly attests against such a notion. The intent here is simply to suggest a few activities and guidelines to aid in instructing children who have not developed some of the basic concepts necessary for effective communication.

Concrete Level   Collect as many objects (home and classroom) of the concept you feel needs teaching, e.g., roundness. Allow children to feel and to talk about the shapes. Be sure to include objects of varying sizes and colors so that size and color are immediately eliminated as attributes of roundness. Include one or two shapes (triangle or square) that clearly are not round and have children discuss the differences between round and other shapes. Encourage children to think of all the round shapes they can on their way to and from school and at home.

An extension activity might well include asking children to form a large circle, pointing out that there is no beginning or end to the line of children. Then ask them to form three or four rows and have these rows gradually join hands to form three or four smaller circles.

Other extension activities might include making circles with pieces of string, modeling clay, etc. Arts and crafts activities as well as physical education activities can be productive in developing these basic concepts.

Pictorial Level   Encourage children to look for pictures that include round shapes in catalogs, magazines, advertisements, and picture books. Also, have them draw round shapes such as clocks, faces, balls, and balloons.

The need to use picture books for the development of any concept cannot be over-emphasized. Only a few examples of such books are used for illustrative purposes here. Others are annotated in Part VI, Appendix A. The *Starters Maths* series (published by MacDonald and Company) have excellent pictures with accompanying activities to aid children in developing basic concepts. For example, *Playground Maths* include a series of illustrations of parks and playgrounds followed by simple problem-solving tasks such as:

> Look at the shapes in the park. Can you find the round shapes? Are there any other shapes you can see? (p. 10)

Another title in the series is *Circus Maths.* Pictures of various circus acts are presented and children attempt to identify shapes. For example:

> The trapeze is swinging from side to side. Show how it moves? What pattern does the smoke make? What other patterns can you see? (p. 11)

In the same book acrobats are pictured in triangular shoulder-stand formations. The task is:

> What shape have the acrobats made? How many acrobats are in each row? (p. 13)

Symbolic-Verbal Level   There is no doubt that communication is present at the concrete level; it is absolutely essential at the pictorial level. However, it is well to consider at least briefly how the acquisition of basic concepts can aid in expanding communication skills at the symbolic-verbal level. For example, encouraging children to make comparisons (or simile constructions) with the acquired concept as the base is useful. For example, children might be asked to brainstorm in response to "round as __ _____." You would expect responses such as "round as a ball," "round as a balloon," "round as a face," etc.

More and more teachers are beginning to elicit such responses orally and then to transcribe the responses onto chart paper long before children are actually able to read the words. This activity is to be commended because children see what they have said in print, and some of them begin to make independent discoveries such as, "'round' looks the same each time you print it."

Again, the use of carefully selected poems and children's stories can be used to excellent advantage. For example, Joan Sullivan's *Round Is a Pancake*, a vividly illustrated book, presents the concept of "round" in inverted sentence patterns as well as patterns with compound elements. The delightful rhythm aids in children's repeating the patterns.

> Round is a daisy
> And a fisherman's reel,
> Round is a hamburger,
> Round is a cake,
> Round is a cherry,
> And the cookies we bake,
> Round is a puppy,
> Curled up in a rug,
> Round are the spots
> On a wee ladybug (pp. 17–23).

Further annotated examples of children's books to aid in using the language of shape and form are found in Part VI, Appendix A.

The concept of "roundness" has been used here to illustrate activities useful in facilitating concept development and its accompanying vocabulary. Space does not permit a detailing of activities for other "shape" concepts. One further point needs to be made, however, with regard to the teaching of these concepts. The teaching of language should be extended from these basic concepts to include elements such as "long," "thin," "straight," "curve," "squiggly," "slant," etc., because these words can be used to good advantage in directing attention to the main attributes of the major concepts.

Concept of Time   The basic principles of instruction considered under "Concept of Shape and Form" apply to most other concepts. In many instances, using the heading "Concrete Level" means no more than that concepts are introduced in the presence of concrete experience.

Concrete Level   Understanding time and the related concepts of sequence presents difficulties for many children. Part of the problem stems from the fact that for most of the concepts it is difficult if not impossible to illustrate with concrete objects. The difficulty is often compounded by adult attempts to force children into using the language of time and sequence without the requisite basis in experience.

It is often considered wise to approach the teaching of time and sequence by beginning from "times" that have special significance to children. Young mid-Western rural children in the 1940s and 1950s typically anticipated the time for the beginning of school as, "When the grain is ripe." Preschool children often identify their birthdates by statements such as, "When Santa comes," "When the flowers bloom," "When the snow comes," etc. By the same token, children at a very early age associate special times of the day with events. Times for special television shows, snack time, and story time soon become associated with a particular time of day. Whether or not these kinds of responses reflect children's natural ways of thinking about time or whether they reflect adult assumptions about how they *should* think about time, associations with special events appear to be a more effective means of identification than attempts to force specific calendar day labels.

It would appear that discussion about time and sequence with young children produces effective results if associations are encouraged in communications about special days and seasons. This is essentially the same as saying that experiences which the child has found interesting can be used effectively as an association point with a new concept. For this reason, the commonly used time concepts and vocabulary associated with seasons, days, months, even minutes and hours are not the most difficult to teach.

The problem arises more frequently with the relational concepts and their referents: long, longer, longest; soon, before, after, finally; etc. Again, perhaps the only sound basis for assisting children in using these words meaningfully is to permit them to hear them in a wide variety of experiential contexts. There is much to be said for bombarding them with these words (and encouraging them to use them) *during* the experience. The example offered here relates an experience of a first-grade butter-making activity in a classroom on an Indian reserve school. The teacher, fully aware of children's deficits in many of the time-relational words, emphasized these throughout the activity. Statements such as:

> *First,* we must clean the jar ... *before* we pour the cream, the jar must be spotless .... *Soon* we will be ready .... Does the jar look clean *now*? ... *Soon* Janice can come and pour the cream .... *Then* we will have to shake the jar vigorously .... All right Janice come *now* and pour the cream .... *Now* we will take turns shaking the jar .... Watch what *will* happen to the cream *while* we shake the jar .... Can you see something *beginning* to happen? ... Very *soon* the butter should be finished .... Finally! Finally! This took a long time!

Included in the teacher exposition were varied questions also stressing time-relational words such as, "What should we do next?" "How *long* do you think we have been shaking this jar?"

It should be noted here that the teacher's ability to identify children's language needs is of utmost importance. Furthermore, because relational words have no concrete referent, not only is the point in time related to the experience crucial but it is also related to the teacher's stressed intonation on the "key" words to be emphasized. Intonation communicates much of the meaning of relational words.

Pictorial Level   In many instances it is useful to refer back over and over again to events of a field trip or classroom experience to lend opportunity to use the concepts in the absence of the actual experience. It is one thing to talk about the sequence of a process (as in the experience of butter-making) in retrospect but quite another to have pictorial reference available to aid recall and to clarify thinking. In the classroom experience cited earlier, the teacher used a Polaroid camera to take pictures of each stage of the butter-making process to provide useful input for follow-up activities at a later date. These pictures were mounted on an oak tag. These were particularly valuable for some of the slower children. The teacher would place the pictures in jumbled order on the chalkboard ledge and ask children to sort them into the right order. To aid recall and to use some of the relational words used earlier, she would ask questions such as, "Why do you place this picture *before* that one?" "Which picture *follows*?"

Other pictorial aids to enhance time concept learning include the use of large homemade classroom calendars with ample space to record important events that have happened as well as events that are approaching. For children who are unable to read, it is important to represent some of the events with pictures. This makes handy reference for discussion of things that happened "yesterday," "last week," "last Friday," etc.

Symbolic-Verbal Level   Again, the justification for discussion of time concepts under "Symbolic-Verbal Level" is justified only by the fact that some activities are carried out with less directly related concrete experience than others. This certainly does not exclude discussion of activities experienced earlier. Furthermore, extension activities that are primarily verbal in nature often aid in achieving a level of automatic language use.

Brainstorming activities to stimulate children to associate concepts of time with activities and objects in the environment is at least one means of aiding transfer of skills developed. For example, children may name all the things they can think of that are slow: donkey, beat up car, elephant, granny, etc. These responses, then, can be used to develop simile constructions, "as slow as a donkey," and so forth.

The use of children's stories and poems comes readily to mind. For example, poems like the following (Marshall, 1970) are found in most children's anthologies:

> Solomon Grundy
> Born on Monday
> Christened on Tuesday
> Married on Wednesday
> Took ill on Thursday
> Worse on Friday
> Died on Saturday
> Buried on Sunday
> That is the end
> Of Solomon Grundy (p. 6).

This is the kind of activity children engage in for sheer pleasure. However, "rattling off" the sequence of days bring to a level of automaticity a sequence they are familiar with on the basis of experience.

Many children's storybooks have a very clear sequence, as in Lynd Ward's *The Biggest Bear*:

> He (the bear) likes pancakes on Sunday Morning .... In the *fall* Mr. McCarroll got pretty upset *when* the bear spent a night in his corn-field .... In the *winter* he had a wonderful time with the bacons and hams .... But it was worse *later* .... Finally Mr. McLean started talking to Mr. Pennell .... *After* the neighbors had left .... So the *next morning* ... (pp. 30–54).

The whole story is literally "glued" together with words depicting time and sequence. If one wished to be technical, one could say that these words represent the basis of the structure or organization for the entire story. Again, the teacher's effective use of intonation and juncture is important in aiding children in relating (consciously or unconsciously) the main events to the time element.

Song activities and recordings are also valuable aids in extending language skills and concepts. As an example, *Learning Basic Skills through Music* (Educational Activities, Inc.) is a recorded version of songs and games to supplement language and concept instruction. The slow, ponderous music accompanying the following words emphasizes "slowness":

> The elephant moves very slowly
> Oh, so very slowly
> He doesn't like to move too fast
> Because he is so big and fat ....

This slowness is contrasted with increased tempo (nonexemplar) in the music because:

> ... should he see a tiger,
> Or spy a mean old hunter
> He will start to run and shake the ground
> And make them all fall down,
> Rumble, rumble, rumble ....

It is one thing for children to grasp concepts and to communicate them orally but quite another to apply the same concepts effectively in reading and writing. It appears that "language experience" types of activities go a long way in filling this gap. However, to accomplish this goal, it is essential that the teacher differentiate instructional activities to meet the needs of children with varying abilities. For example, the teacher who capitalized on the butter-making experience used picture stimuli to aid the language of sequence for one group of children. Another group of children were ready to function at a vastly different level. She asked the group to tell her all the things that they had done. Each response was listed on chart paper. The next task was for the children to sort the activities into the right order. She transcribed these on a new chart. Then she proceeded to construct a paragraph with the group by taking each step of the process at a time. She elicited from the pupils the time-sequence words that she might use as "cement to fill all the cracks in the list." Not only did the children experience the process of constructing a paragraph, but they also became keenly aware of the function of these key time words in both writing and reading.

The sample activities for developing concepts of "shape" and "time" should suffice to demonstrate some general principles involved in teaching and extending concepts and the language used to communicate these concepts. Because the same general principles apply to the development of concepts such as "number," "space," etc., further activities are not presented here. However, because classification competence is such an asset to most learning in school, a separate discussion on classification activities is included here (Note: in a very true sense, development of basic concepts already involves a classification of stimuli.)

Classification Schemes

Concrete Level The basic learning principles emphasized regarding the development of concepts apply to learning of classification competencies. It is certainly not necessary to document the need to begin from a base of concrete experience. For this reason, again, the classroom should abound in concrete materials exemplifying a wide variety of shapes, colors, sizes, sounds, and textures.

To aid the child in bringing some order into his environment is perhaps the most useful contribution the school can make. The child needs some way of "putting together" the bits of learning he gains from his experiences. Yardley (1970) emphasizes the need to help the child to organize cognitively:

> Grouping and classification lead to generalizing or abstracting that which holds these experiences together as a class. The name doesn't necessarily stand for any single idea but rather for the idea of all similar ideas. When using it the child has pooled a number of sense impressions. His sense impressions have grown into clear ideas. The quality of these ideas depends on the intensity and variety of the experiences which preceded them and with which they continue to be associated (p. 13).

Yardley's statement holds strong implications for basing the teaching of classification skills in concrete experience.

As an example of a classification activity, the teacher might place on a table things to eat (banana, orange, candy, peanut, soda cracker) and things to play with (toy car, truck, ball, crayons). The task would be for children to sort them into two separate groups of things. For very young or slow learners, prompting questions might be essential, e.g., "What is this for?" What the teacher is attempting to do is to aid the child in focusing on the *use* as a means of classification. After the sorting is completed the teacher might say, "All these things (foods) are things to _____," and, "All these things (toys) are things to _____ with."

It is desirable to include a lot of verbal interaction with activities of this nature. In the example given above, for instance, function or use is the basis for classification. Questions should be employed constantly to bring to a level of awareness the "function," e.g., "Why did you put this (object) on this pile?" A good variation of the activity is to place things of one class together with a few nonexemplars and ask the child to pick out the ones that do not belong and then ask for justification of the selection.

Practical experience-type activities to extend thinking and speaking in terms of classes may involve short field trips. For example, a trip to a grocery store might well be used to point out that groceries are organized according to subclasses. The children may be led to generalize that all the products in one aisle are frozen products. Again, it is important that they are led to make this generalization. The teacher might ask them to list the various products: ice cream, peas, corn, meat pies, etc., and then ask, "Why do you think all these things are together in this aisle?" "Why is ice cream kept here?" Then the teacher might emphasize, "In this aisle we find only *frozen foods*." A similar activity to extend this from the "recognition-identification" levels to a "production" level would be to simulate a small store in the classroom and emphasize putting things of the same general class together. For young children, a simulated general store will be more successful than a grocery store as the classes of products will be more distinguishable. There are many natural classroom situations that lend themselves well to the teaching and application of classification competencies.

There is a need to give attention to learning multiple classifications. For example, objects of varying sizes and colors might be displayed. Children might be asked to sort them into piles of "large" and "small" objects, then into "red" and "green," and finally into "large red," "large green," "small red," and "small green." Again, it is important to stimulate thinking by asking appropriate questions and to insist on children justifying their classification schemes. Not only does this aid in providing the teacher with diagnostic feedback, but it also gives the child the opportunity to use immediately the language of concepts in a real communications context.

Some teachers very successfully provide practice in the use of multiple classification by having children put objects that belong together inside two hula hoops lying on the floor, e.g., things to work with and things to play with. Then after some discussion they lead children to see that some things, such as crayons and books, can be used for both work and play. These things, then, belonging to both classifications are placed into the overlapping area when one hoop is placed partly over the other to become an "intersecting set" (McCracken and McCracken, 1972, p. 62).

To illustrate further, sounds of various types might be recorded for children to classify in various ways. For example, initially they might classify according to "highness" or "lowness" of pitch, then according to "loudness" or "softness." Following this, they might reclassify according to "loud-high" "low-soft," etc. A further classification might include whether they would expect to hear the sound "indoors" or "outdoors."

Pictorial Level There is no suggestion here that there should be clearcut boundaries between the concrete level and pictorial level in teaching classification skills. Certainly, some pictures are very easy to classify and some objects are very difficult to classify, depending to a large degree on the dominance of the attributes of the examples and, at least as much, on the child's background of experience relevant to the "things" being classified. After all, it is largely the experiences that aid in gaining initial familiarity with the "uses," "shape," "size," or whatever concept determines the classification.

All this said, it is still useful to provide considerable experience at the pictorial level. This might include a lot of cut-and-paste activities. Children might be provided with large sheets of paper, catalogs, and magazines and given directions like, "Find pictures of circus animals." "Find pictures of farm animals." "Find pictures of winter clothing." "Find pictures of things that go on water." Other activities might include construction of simple picture graphs showing, for example, how many children in the class have "pets that fly" and how many have "pets that swim" or "pets that run." The graph would simply have a title for each category (or a picture representing the classification for non-readers) and stick figures representing the number of children under each category.

Activities like the one in Figure 1 are also of value. The task is for children to identify the "things" that belong together. If they have trouble determining the classification, questions should be used to trigger the "class," e.g., "What can the little bird do that the rabbit can't do?"

Symbolic-Verbal Level The number of ways of stimulating verbal skills related to classification is limited only by the teacher's imagination. In the discussion of concrete and pictorial levels, references were made to the need for teachers' effective use of questioning strategies. This applies both to the development of classification schemes and to the ability to use language related to the classifications. For example, in an activity suggesting recording of sounds for classification, the teacher might extend the child's language by suggesting similies:

Figure 1. Exercise for the pictorial level of the classification scheme. (Printed with permission from Downing, J., Braun, C., Evanechko, P., and Ollita, L. *The Canadian Readiness Test*, unpublished manuscript.)

Soft as a (*hum*)
Squeaky as a (*mouse*)
Loud as (*thunder*)
Low as a (*bass fiddle*)

This is the level at which classifications of more abstract ideas should occur. The teacher might have a large cutout of a clown and ask children to brainstorm for all the circus words they can think of: "menagerie," "trapeze," "sideshow," "merry-go-round," etc. The teacher might do well to print these words on the clown as they are being suggested. She might have a large cutout of Noah's ark on water and ask for all the animals the children can think of. She might print the names of land animals on the ark and names of swimming animals on the water. Pictorial-verbal charts like this around the room become useful sources for words children like to use in their own attempts at writing. Use of a pictorial thesaurus with words classified within pictures is a good follow-up to this type of activity. *Words We Use* (Gage Educational Publications) is a good example of such a thesaurus.

Further exploration into abstract classes of words like adjectives promotes good vocabulary extension. For example, following an activity related to weather, the teacher might, with the suggestions from the class, produce a chart with "weather words." If she wishes to focus on adjectives, she might say that the word has to say something about "What kind of days we can have"—cloudy days, foggy days, etc. Charts of this nature might include "funny words," "sad words," "hospital words," "vacation words," "tired words," and so on.

Sorting written words into appropriate classifications is an exercise not only to extend the ability to classify but also to review words encountered in previous experiences (either real or vicarious). For example, the class may have discussed "ranching," "circuses," and "sports." The teacher might randomly list words such as "roundup," "brand," "sideshow," "trapeze," "bowling," "lariat," "hiking," "baseball," "stampede," etc. The class might then be asked to list these under the classifications "sports," "ranching," and "circus." For younger children, the words might be written on cards and the cards placed under the appropriate classes in a pocket chart or in boxes. This type of activity can be used to good advantage in the middle grade content areas. It can be used to good advantage also in extending synonyms. For example, the scrambled words might be "giant," "petite," "minute," "enormous," "miniature," "diminutive," "gigantic," etc. The task is to sort them into classes "large" and "small." The activities described can be used equally advantageously at a listening, reading, or writing level.

The activities described above are logical preludes to the development of personal word banks or word books in which children keep words important to them under specific classifications. These activities also become a useful "lead in" into the level where children classify words by various phonemic or structural elements. This might include "words beginning the same as *monkey*," "words beginning the same as *clock*," "words ending in -tion," and so on.

Language Cues and New Meanings

In Chapter 1 reference was made to "anchor points" that are available for the listener or reader to assess new information. In a sense the ability to use these anchor points requires that the listener or reader have an awareness of how language works with respect to the interrelatedness of sentence elements. The following examples illustrate how the reader can and should use anchor points to at least estimate meanings of new words:

> Most marsupials, such as the kangaroo, wombat, the bandicoot, and the koala, live in Australia and New Guinea. They vary in size from the seven-foot-tall kangaroo to the tiny marsupial mouse, only inches in length (Thorn, Braun, and Richmond, 1974, p. 26).

The child, either listening to this passage or reading it to himself, depending on his experience, should be able to use either "marsupial" or "kangaroo" or both to generalize some meaning to "wombat," "bandicoot," and "koala" if these are unknown items for him. It is noteworthy that either the classification (in this case marsupial) or one of items in the class (e.g., kangaroo) can be used mutually as anchor points.

Deriving new meanings is not restricted to classification schemes. Note that in the following example it is possible to derive the meaning of a foreign word embedded in English discourse from words surrounding the foreign word.

> Every morning before school, Rowena delivers a *Zeitung* to many houses in her neighborhood. To others, she delivers a *Zeitung* only on Saturday. After delivering her Saturday *Zeitungen*, Rowena goes from house to house collecting the money for the *Zeitungen*. Rowena and her customers know that reading a *Zeitung* helps them to know what's going on in the world. Rowena herself enjoys the sports pages in the *Zeitung* best of all (Thorn, Braun, and Richmond, 1973, p. 36).

The child should be made keenly aware of the elements of language that signal meaning. For example, the "a" and "the" noun signals in the discourse above leave no doubt as to the grammatical class the word belongs to. Semantic-associational clues such as "going from house to house," "collecting money," "reading," and "sports pages" are further clues the child should be encouraged to focus on either in listening or reading.

SYNTACTIC DEVELOPMENT

In the earlier discussion about vocabulary development the importance of an environment conducive to such development was underlined. This is equally important with regard to symtactic development. For such development to occur the program must be rich in experiences, good language models must be present, and the atmosphere must be such that the child feels free to use language, even risking language that does not always fit the adult model.

The vocabulary activities described above are certainly to be employed in the presence of "whole language"; that is, to divorce the teaching of vocabulary from syntactic context would be difficult and, if it were possible, utter stupidity. Indeed, the suggestions for "using cues for new meanings" involve syntactic cues to a very significant degree. However, depending on individual and group needs, the accent and focus will sometimes be on specific vocabulary-related objectives and sometimes on syntactic-related objectives. For this reason, the two major areas are discussed under separate headings.

Exposure to Varied Syntactic Patterns

It is easy to reach agreement on the fact that the teacher needs to accept the kinds of language patterns children come to school with. This is true in oral discourse including times when children relate their experiences for the teacher to record. This is good; however, the goals of the classroom must include instructional activities that help to extend the kinds of syntactic patterns children use and perhaps aid them in becoming more aware of the patterns they are already using. Below are suggestions for these kinds of extension and awareness activities.

Stories, Poems, and Songs There is perhaps no principle more important in selecting these activities than to base them on the child's natural interests and the universal appeal for rhythm. An environment "thick" with story, verse, and song is probably the best guarantee that this interest and appeal will be satisfied. Library shelves are filled with stories waiting to be read, chanted, and listened to. Many of these are particularly useful in aiding the development of patterns of varying structures. It is important to note here that the emphasis at the beginning is on listening—listening to the ideas and the vehicles that carry these ideas. Children will become sensitized to the peculiar intonation patterns that characterize certain syntactic elements, the junctures, and the stresses that are as essential to the meaning as the arrangement of the words themselves. There are many stories that will only be listened to. However, there are many that children will want to hear often enough for them to memorize and to chant along as the teacher reads. This is excellent. The sound patterns they have listened to are becoming the sound patterns of their own productions. A few examples of

good sources of such stories and poems are given here. Additional
annotated references appear in Part VI, Appendix A.

For example, Leland Jacobs' poem "Old Lucy and the Pigeons"
(in Martin, 1966) not only uses varied and recurring sentence
patterns, but it also expands these same patterns with phrases,
adjectives, and adverbs so that the kernel sentence repeats with
one variable added:

> Old Lucy Lindy lived alone.
> She lived alone (in an old stone house).
>   . . .
>
> She didn't like dogs.
> She didn't like cats.
> And (especially) she didn't like pigeons.
> All day she was busy.
> She was busy (with a hammer).
> She was busy (with nails).
> She was busy (with a brush) (pp. 16–17).

The poem illustrates well how sentence patterns (and corresponding
rhythmic patterns) repeat and how the basic pattern can repeat
but at the same time be expanded with an additional rhythmic and
meaning element. It is often valuable to have children add
their own expansions simply to add to the fun and their linguistic
awareness. For instance, they might be encouraged to add to the
following:

> Go away, pigeons.
> Go away (from my fence).
> Go away (from my yard).
> Go away (from my house).

If children are unable to add additional elements (phrases),
discussion will produce the basic ideas necessary for such expansions.
The teacher might ask, "Where else might Old Lucy Lindy find
pigeons?" It is likely that responses such as "On the grass," "On
the roof," "On the gate" will emerge. These, then, become the
source for the expansions.

There are many children's books that use effectively the
cumulative recurring sentence pattern to build up a sequence of
events. Barbara Emberley' *Drummer Hoff* illustrates the notion
well. The events leading up to Drummer Hoff's firing off the
cannon begin with, "Private Parriage brought the carriage."
Each soldier appearing brings one part of the remarkable machine.

One event per page is added, so that on the last page the whole series is repeated:

> General Border gave the order,
> Major Scott brought the shot,
> Captain Bammer brought the rammer,
> Sergeant Chowder brought the powder,
> Corporal Farrell brought the barrell,
> Private Parriage brought the carriage,
> but Drummer Hoff fired it off (p. 22).

Another brand of verse-type literature with high appeal for children has repeating nonsense elements. Cazden (1975) makes a convincing case for this type of "language play." She hypothesizes that language play aids in developing metalinguistic awareness ("the ability to make language forms opaque and to attend to them in and for themselves," p. 4). She believes the step toward literacy will be easier if the child's attention has been focused on the *means*, the *forms*, of language rather than only on the ends (the content communicated). Cazden strongly advocates word games. It would seem that much of the literature written for young children, if chanted, would serve this function. Edna Preston's delightful *Pop Corn and Ma Goodness* comes readily to mind.

> Ma Goodness, she's coming a-skippetty skoppetty
>   skippetty skoppetty
>   skippetty skoppetty
>
>   . . . .
>
> Pop corn, he's a-coming a-hippetty hoppetty
>   hippetty hoppetty
>   hippetty hoppetty
>
>   . . . .
>
> A-chippetty choppetty
>   mippetty moppetty
>   snippetty snoppetty
>   Bippetty boppetty
>   Flippetty floppetty
>   Together they go a-lippetty loppetty . . . (pp. 1–20).

The examples of verse-type literature illustrated above incorporate patterns that, for the most part, children already use to some degree. There is a need to read to them a lot of literature that introduces (at the listening level) language that they do not use at the speaking level. Lynd Ward's *The Biggest Bear* cited earlier in the chapter is a good example. Virginia Lee Burton's *The Little House* is another:

... At first the Little House was frightened, but after she got used to it she rather liked it. They rolled along the big road, and they rolled along the little roads, until they were way out in the country. When the Little House saw the green grass and heard the birds singing, she didn't feel sad anymore (p. 37).

There are many children's songs that can be used in similar fashion to develop, first, a sensitivity to the sound patterns and then to have children sing along and produce these patterns themselves. An example should suffice.

> This old man
> He played one,
> He played nicknack on my thumb.
> Nicknack paddywack
> Give the dog a bone!
> This old man came rolling home.

The advantage of using the natural rhythmic impulse of children to aid language development cannot be over-emphasized.

Sensitization to the Meaning Signals in Language

Mention was made earlier in this chapter of the importance of emphasizing intonation patterns where reading to children as a means of vocabulary development. The intonation cues carry a large portion of the relational meanings. For example, in *The Little House*, just cited "At first," "but after," "until," and "When" are very significant words that trigger an essential aspect of meaning—the sequence of events. In speech, intonation gives the listener clues as to what to anticipate. This should happen when children listen to stories. Hopefully, this will aid them not only to use these sequence signal words effectively when they speak but also to anticipate what will happem in print as they later apply this language base to reading. The ultimate goal is for these signal words to be applied as they organize their own writing.

Comparison signals can be developed in similar fashion. Apart from using stories and poems, the teacher might start with the language that children have produced, as in the earlier example of the butter-making experience. Imagine the production went like this:

Mr. James has a big truck on his farm. Mr. Jones has a big truck on his farm. Mr. James' truck is blue. Mr. Jones' truck is green. Mr. Jones uses his truck to carry cattle. Mr. James uses his truck to carry grain.

The teacher *might* demonstrate how signal words can be used to show relationships among ideas, or with more advanced children she might elicit suggestions from them, e.g., "Let's put the first two sentences together. I'll start and see if you can finish. 'Mr. James has a big truck on his farm *and* . . . .' " The "and" should signal what might follow. Another alternative would be, "Mr. James *and* Mr. Jones *both* . . . ." In this case the two words "and" and "both" trigger the comparison signal. To carry the exercise further, "Mr. Jones' truck is blue, *but* . . . ." Again, the intonation of "but" should be emphasized as a signal of what is going to follow. There is absolutely no need to stress with young children that these are "comparison-contrast" signals. It is simply a matter of sensitizing the children to these signals at a listening level and gradually teaching for transfer at the other communication levels. Other comparison signals such as "different," "however," etc., should be stressed as the needs and competencies of children suggest.

Other areas for "signal" instruction include "classification" and "causation." Again, the best approach is to use such teaching aids as extensions of the children's experiences and own language output as well as literature and song selections. Classification signals emphasized in the primary grades include "several," "some," "others," "still others," "besides," "many," "for example," "also," "in addition." Cause-effect signals include words such as "therefore," "as a result," "because," and "reasons."

The important issue in all such teaching is the realization that meaning is complete only as interrelationships among words and among sentences are understood. For this reason, the emphasis must always be on teaching signal elements in context.

Stress on the connection between the intonation patterns of oral language and the punctuation conventions of written language requires special attention. In the primary grades there are many games and activities that can be used effectively to develop this. For example, the teacher might ask a question and stress the rising pitch at the end, then ask the children to respond by holding up a paper bag puppet with question marks for ears. For statements and exclamations, appropriate paper bag puppets would be used. Many of the children's literature references in Part IV, Appendix A are rich in the variety of sentence types that should be used in aiding a keen awareness of the oral-written relationship.

At the more advanced levels, exercises like the "Comedy of Commas" in Nurnberg (1970) are helpful. The examples below illustrate:

Which will require a lot of postage?
  a) Shall I stick the postage on myself?
  b) Shall I stick the postage on, myself? (p. 34)
Both may be bad table manners, but which is harder to do?
  a) Do not break your bread or roll in your soup.
  b) Do not break your bread, or roll in your soup (p. 36).
Which headline has a suggestion of cannibalism about it?
  a) SENATE GROUP EATS CHICKEN; CABINET WIVES,
     SWEETBREADS.
  b) SENATE GROUP EATS CHICKEN, CABINET WIVES,
     SWEETBREADS.

The emphasis in exercises like these focuses sharply not only on the interrelatedness of the oral-written conventions but also on this relationship to meaning.

Reinforcing Word Order Awareness

The discussion so far has dealt with activities that should heighten syntactic awareness. However, for some children additional instruction appears to be necessary, particularly instruction that employs activities requiring active involvement of the children. For instance, word play and word order manipulations help children build structures and "see" the relationships among syntactic elements.

A trip to the zoo might stimulate an activity like the following. The teacher might ask, "What can monkeys do?" Typical responses would be:

> Monkeys chatter
> Monkeys leap
> Monkeys tease
> Monkeys whimper
> Monkeys tumble
> Monkeys scamper, etc.

The teacher might record these so that the children can see the spatial relationship of the noun and verb as well as hear it. It is a good practice, and fun for children, to chant these patterns rhythmically and quickly as the teacher sweeps her finger under the lines.

Following extensive play and practice with noun-verb practice, children might be aided in filling adjective slots. The teacher might initiate this by asking, "What kinds of monkeys did you see?" Typical responses would be:

> Tricky monkeys
> Baby monkeys
> Silly monkeys
> Tired monkeys

> Sleepy monkeys
> Hungry monkeys, etc.

Again, these can be read and chanted. The next stage is to combine the responses from the verb slots with the responses to the adjective slots so that they would chant:

> Tricky monkeys chatter,
> Baby monkeys leap,
> Silly monkeys tease, etc.

At these stages it is valuable to put the words on cards, using different colors for nouns, verbs, and adjectives. In this way children can manipulate the cards to produce a large variety of combinations. Children who cannot read the words might be teamed with a child who can. Once they have played with the different combinations, they should be encouraged to check each combination as to whether it "makes sense" as well as "sounds right." For example, "Sleepy monkeys leap" sounds right but makes little sense.

The kind of syntactic manipulation described above can be extended to include any syntactic element. For instance, phrases might be introduced. The teacher might ask, "Where can we find monkeys?" Responses would likely include "in the park," "in the zoo," "in the cage," etc. These can then be further incorporated in extensive chants:

> Skinny monkeys climb in the cage.
> Hungry monkeys eat in the zoo.

After some of this practice, "when" phrases might be added, and so on and on. This can be extended to practice with compound elements, auxiliary verbs, etc. A variation of manipulating cards on the desk or in a pocket chart includes using clothespins to pin words and phrases on a line strung across the room.

SUMMARY

This chapter has provided one approach to sequencing learning-teaching strategies for vocabulary development. These sequences involve concrete, pictorial, and verbal-symbolic presentation of material. Emphasis in teaching should be on a close relationship between the development of concepts and the language used to communicate these concepts. Teaching techniques and materials to enhance syntactic development should be selected so that rhythm, sound, and sense of the language, in concert, are maximized in the communication process.

APPENDIX:

CHILDREN'S BOOKS

AND RECORDING REFERENCES

Books

Brown, M. 1961. Once a Mouse .... Charles Scribner's Sons, New York.
Burton, V. L. 1942. The Little House. Houghton Mifflin Co., Boston.
Emberley, B. 1971. Drummer Hoff. Prentice-Hall, Englewood Cliffs, N.J.
Foster, L. 1974. Circus Maths. MacDonald and Company, London.
Foster, L. 1974. Playground Maths. MacDonald and Company, London.
Jacobs, L. 1966. Old lucy and the pigeons. In: B. Martin, Sounds of the Storyteller, pp. 12–17. Holt, Rinehart and Winston, New York.
Langstaff, J. 1955. Frog Went a-Courtin'. Harcourt Brace and World, New York.
Preston, E. M. 1953. Pop Corn and Ma Goodness. The Viking Press, New York.
Sullivan, J. 1963. Round Is a Pancake. Holt, Rinehart and Winston, New York.
Ward, L. 1952. The Biggest Bear. Houghton Mifflin Co., Boston.

Records

Learning Basic Skills though Music. 1972. Educational Activities Inc., Freeport, N. Y.

LITERATURE CITED

Cazden, C. B. 1975. Play with language and metalinguistic awareness: One dimension of language experience. In: C. Winsor (ed.), Dimensions of Language Experience, pp. 3–19. Agathon Press, New York.
DeCecco, J. P. 1968. The Psychology of Learning and Instruction. Prentice-Hall, Englewood Cliffs, N.J.
Marshall, S. 1970. Expression. Vol. 4. Granada Publishing Ltd., St. Albans.
McCracken, R. A., and McCracken, M. J. 1972. Reading Is only the Tigers Tail. Leswing Press, San Rafael, Cal.
Nurnberg, M. 1970. Fun with Words. Prentice-Hall, Englewood Cliffs, N.J.
Richmond, I. 1971. Words We Use. Gage Educational Publications, Toronto.
Thorn, E. A., Braun, C. and Richmond, I. 1973. Practice Strategies for Something to Remember. Gage Educational Publications, Toronto.
Thorn, E. A., Braun, C. and Richmond, I. 1974. Practice Strategies for How Many Miles. Gage Educational Publications, Toronto.
Yardley, A. 1970. Reaching Out. Evans Bros., London.

chapter 3

Child Authorship: Process and Product

Victor Froese

> We are shaped
> and fashioned
> by what we love.
> J. W. Goethe

This quotation adorns my office wall in the form of a commercial poster. Its message is universal and clearly illustrates for me the process and product of child authorship.

In this chapter I intend to present a rationale for child authorship, acquaint the reader with some sources of published children's work, suggest some procedures for stimulating authorship, and outline some techniques for bookbinding. "Authorship" is naturally used in the most general sense because it includes any work, not necessarily published or printed, that the child has created.

RATIONALE

Child authorship is a total and indelible experience. Why?

> What students do in the classroom is what they learn (as Dewey would say), and what they learn to do is the classroom's message (as McLuhan would say) (Postman and Weingartner, 1969, p. 19).

Books are everywhere in the school (or should be), but the relationship of these books to live people is often lost. The permanence of print seems to convey the omnipotence of the author. This necessitates the need for author sincerity and an exposé of the process of writing. An eminent author of books for children confirms this:

> Children are demanding. They are the most attentive, curious, eager, observant, sensitive, quick and generally congenial readers on earth. They accept, *almost without question,* anything you present them with, as long as it is presented honestly, fearlessly, and clearly (E. B. White, 1940, p. 140).

Children obviously have the "stuff" or content required for authorship, but they must engage in the process to understand it. In fact, that may be the only procedure that will allow them to question the fallibility of an author.

Above all, authorship nurtures the creative process—a process lauded by most curriculum builders and teacher training institutions.

> It is the supreme art of the teacher to awaken joy in creative expression and knowledge (A. Einstein, from Logan and Logan, 1971, Introduction).

Knowledge about ourselves, our universe, and our capabilities must be discovered through the interaction with "things": books, people, ideas, and dreams. No one has more aptly stated this view than Jean Piaget:

> Knowledge is not given to a passive observer; rather, knowledge of reality must be discovered and constructed by the activity of the child (J. Piaget, from Ginsburg and Opper, 1969, p. 14).

Child authorship encourages this bold, experiential type of learning. Cognitive, affective, psychomotor, and conative learning are involved. In *From Cover to Cover*, Joy Hebert supports this notion most eloquently: children whose writing is published see themselves as *creators* of ideas, as *producers* of language, as *functioning members* of the language community.

From a more impersonal research perspective, the same support for child authorship may be generated. Children obviously have considerably more language facility orally than in the written mode. However, the transfer principle may readily provide the answer to how one might capitalize on this discrepancy. Ruddell's investigation of the structure of oral and written language confirms the above conjecture, especially as it relates to understanding the written message.

> Reading comprehension is a *function of the similarity of patterns* of language structure in the reading material to oral patterns of language structure used by children (R. B. Ruddell, 1965, p. 273).

Authorship then may be a means of utilizing the oral (and more advanced) structures not readily found in most basal readers which constitute a large portion of the child's reading diet. Thereby his level of written language usage may be elevated to nearer his oral language complexity.

In his summary of readability research, George Klare (1963) refers to a related issue; that is, the relationship of experience to understanding a written message. Klare states: *"The greater a reader's background* and experience with a given topic, and *the greater the redundancy* of the writing, *the less effect an increase in readability will have"* (p. 16). It appears, then, that through personal authorship exists a means by which children may aspire to new heights in language experience; through new language experience, language develops into the more complex structures of mature writing.

Child authorship rests on sound psychological, physiological, rational, and pedagogical bases. It is an avenue for developing the "whole child" in an integrated, naturalistic, and humanistic manner. With that caliber of involvement most anything is possible:

> Your heart will always be where your riches are (Matthew 6:21).

SOURCES OF PUBLISHED CHILDREN'S WRITING

Below are listed some selected and annotated sources of children's writing. An attempt has been made to present a variety of writing types (there are many more sources of children's poetry available than any other type of writing): captions, anecdotes, letters, stories, paragraphs, and even a dictionary. At least two sources describe in sensitive detail the bookmaking approach to teaching children the joy (and frustration) of authorship. Stegall, in *The Adventures of Brown Sugar,* relates her experiences in writing a book with a whole class of fourth-graders as an alternative to "doing grammar." She describes in detail the process of selecting a topic or theme, the planning and outlining of chapters, the actual writing and selection of sentences and paragraphs (the editing process), and the final outcomes. The text is presented in its entirety for our enjoyment.

Another author, Arnstein, in *Children Write Poetry,* presents a unique approach to involving children in writing poetry. First, the teacher entices the children into constructing a book by surrounding them with the basic materials. The book is left momentarily while the teacher introduces short but captivating poems. Naturally the favorites are eventually mounted in each child's book. Next, a poem by a young author is introduced (*Poems by a Little Girl* by H. Conkling), and soon the children wonder why they cannot do the same. Presto, the stage is set. Of course, much more input follows, but for that the reader should refer to the original work.

As mentioned in the introductory paragraphs, children often fail to see themselves as producers of language: authors. Frequently, that realization alone actualizes the child's desire to write, and for that reason the following children's works are presented.

A further reason for presenting the sources below is to sensitize the teacher to other children's writing. It can also be observed that the freshness and honesty in these works is not affected by political boundaries, continents, or language differences. Children are children are children with all that this expression connotes. Children's work must be recognized as an art form just as adult verse and prose are recognized.

The following annotated references are roughly grouped into four categories for easy reference: prose works, mixed forms (prose, poetry, etc.), art forms (includes poetry or prose), and poetry collections.

Prose Works

Stegall, Carrie. 1967. The Adventures of Brown Sugar: Adventures in Creative Writing. NCTE, Champaign, Illinois.

Mrs. Stegall, the teacher, explains how her 40 fourth-graders produced the book *The Adventures of Brown Sugar*. A 10-page introduction describes the procedures, the remainder is the children's work.

Children of the Kingfisher Indian Day School. Our Cree Dictionary.

Grades Two and Three, St. Philip's School, Fort George, P.Q., Canada. We Live at Fort George.

The Children of Years One and Two, Kettle Point Indian Day School, Forest, Ontario. We Visit the farm. These little volumes are published by the Education Division, Indian Affairs and Northern Development, 1849 Yonge St., Toronto 295, Ontario.

Hildes, Joey. How the Pelican Got Its Baggy Beak.

MacDonald, Kendall James. 1974. Patrick the Diesel. Peguis Publishers, Winnepeg.

Both books are written and illustrated by the authors, who are elementary school students (10 and 9 years old, respectively).

Lewis, Richard. 1969. Journeys, Prose by Children of the English-speaking World. Simon and Schuster, New York.
An international collection of elementary school-aged children's work.

Mixed Forms

Hazzard, Russ (editor). 1974. It's Not Always a Game. All About Us, Box 7000, Ottawa.
This is a collection of poetry and prose by 6-to 18-year-olds from across Canada. Only minor editing was done. A number of French pieces are included, as well as one in braille.

Joseph, S. M. (editor). 1969. The Me Nobody Knows. Avon Books, New York.
These are the writings of mostly Black or Puerto Rican elementary school children. Included are poems, diaries, letters, and paragraph stories about their environment, their fears, their fantasies, and their hopes. A filmstrip and record interpretation (by white children) of some of these works is available from the *New York Times.*

Art Forms

Pellowski, A., Sattley, H., and Arkhurst, J. (editors). 1971. Have You Seen a Comet? Children's Art and Writing from Around the World. John Day, New York.
This is a collection of stories, letters, and anecdotes by children from 75 countries.

Holland, J. (editor). 1969. The Way It Is. Harcourt, Brace and World, New York.

Vogel, R. (editor). 1969. The Other City. David White, New York.
Both of these books contain photographs and descriptions or captions and are the results of an experimental project of Kodak and Teachers College, Columbia University. The first book deals with neighborhood, beaches, and parks, the second with people, shopping, school, and jobs. These books exemplify the work of teenagers.

Poetry Collections

Lewis, Richard. 1966. Miracles: Poems by Children of the English-speaking World. Simon and Schuster, New York.
The Wind and the Rain: Children's Poems. 1968. Simon and Schuster, New York.

These are truly international collections of elementary school-aged children's work. This book also contains fine, large photographs by Helen Buttfield.

Thompson, Denys. 1972. Children as Poets. Heinemann, London.

As the title suggests, this collection of poems by British writers ages 5 to 18 features the children's work *first*. An 11-page postcript follows.

Schaefer, C. E., and Mellor, K. C. (collectors). 1971. Young Voices. Collier Books, New York.

This is a collection of poems by children in grades 4 to 6 in New York City sponsored by the Creativity Center at Fordham University. The 122 poems were selected by judges from over 20,000 entries.

Froese, Victor (compiler). 1974. Century of City: A Poetry Project. University of Manitoba, Winnipeg.

This book contains a variety of poetic forms—shape poems, catalogue verse, cinquain, diamante, etc.—by poets aged 7 to 15 from metropolitan Winnipeg, Manitoba.

Articles about Child Authorship

Hall, Mary Anne. 1972. "Children As Authors," Elementary English 49 (October): 889–893.

Miner, M. E. 1972. "Books by Kids—for Kids," Elementary English 49 (October):894–896.

"Bookmaking by Grants." 1974. In Review: Canadian Books for Children. (Summer): 10–12.

Brennan, S. W. 1976. "Publishing children's writing," Reading Teacher 29 (February): 447–449.

Young, V. M., and Young, K. A. 1968. "Special education children as the authors of books," Reading Teacher 22 (Nov): 122–125.

SITUATIONS TO STIMULATE WRITING

Most attempts at creative writing lack the "warm-up" time and the "input" time required to produce successful results. Creativity can not be turned on instantaneously. The previously mentioned child-authored books can serve as motivators. However, much more input and involvement are required to stimulate good writing; hence, a few suggestions are listed below along with some references that present other ideas in more detail. Following these motivators is a further list of ideas for bookmaking.

Primary

Use a "magic net" made from 36″ × 72″ nylon netting. While wearing the net, let several children select a role (animal, toy, person) and move (walk, dance, stand) accordingly. The remaining children may compose the story while the teacher records it on chart paper or chalkboard.

Use Mary O'Neil's *Hailstones and Halibut Bones* as an avenue for creating associations with colors (feelings, things, sounds). Allow children to select construction paper in a color of their choice and mount on it their list of associations printed on a separate sheet.

Intermediate

Try the "memory writing" writing technique. Have students look around the room for some object that reminds them of something from their own past. Does the first "memory" remind them of some other memory? Give children a limited amount of time to record as many associations as possible. These can then be arranged as notes for a composition.

Students enjoy imitating other styles of writing or speech such as is found in primers, in Dr. Seuss books, or as is used by sportscasters. Bring in an armful of primers or Dr. Seuss books and allow them to read several. Tape record a portion of a hockey game, football game, or basketball game to play to the class. Ask students to copy the style but substitute their own content.

Secondary School

Use the "Grouptalk" and other procedures demonstrated in the film "Strategies of Small Group Learning" distributed by the I/D/E/A Corporation. The procedures can be used effectively to stimulate ideas for subsequent writing.

Write a menu for a restaurant (short-order, drive-in, night spot). Select appropriate items, use terse but enticing language, include sketches if desired. Design a cover. It may be wise to collect sample menus to post in the room.

SPECIFIC IDEAS FOR MAKING BOOKS

The ideas for bookmaking listed below may be adapted to many levels. They are "starters" only and most teachers will undoubtedly think of many other ideas or adaptations.

Collections of Pictures

Each child draws a picture on some aspect of a story; these are then mounted. Sequence of events can easily be taught this way.

Collections of Poems

A variety of poetic forms may be introduced to children, e.g., catalogue verse, shapepoems, diamante. Each form could make up a book, or a variety of forms could be collected over a period of time.

Collections of Textures and Shapes

Materials such as sandpaper, cloth, vinyl, sponge, etc., may be mounted on each page. A variety of concepts may be taught this way.

Collections of Experiments or Recipes

Instructions developed as charts for a science unit (measurement, observation, etc.) may be compiled into a book along with the findings. Alternately, favorite recipes might be collected and classified into chapters, e.g., cookies, desserts, drinks.

Collections of Prose

The beginning of a story followed by a variety of endings is a popular approach. This allows the teacher to structure the type of writing that will follow: dialogue, description, exposition.

Collections of Anecdotes, Puns, or Cartoons

Often "elephant" jokes, "knock-knock" jokes, "moron" jokes, or other trends catch the children's fancy. Collect and write or print them. Children may bring their favorite cartoons and mount them. They may explain why they find them enjoyable or funny. Alternately, the "balloons" containing the dialogue might be blotted out and substituted by their own suitable dialogue. (Liquid paper works well for that purpose.)

Collections of Words

Putting together dictionaries, thesaurus, etc., children may experiment with the graphics of word making:

THIN, LONG, ZIGZAG, SQUEEZE, fancy.

Newspaper advertisements use many styles of type and may be a source of letters. Collections of "soft" words (fluffy), "nice" words (exquisite), "long" words (electromagnetic), "color" words (magenta), etc., make fine books.

Collections of Stories

Single stories from unused primers may be rebound as "easy readers." New covers may be designed in art class using a variety of artistic styles: potato printings, collages, finger paintings. In the intermediate grades, children are often interested in writing their own stories for younger children and should be encouraged to do so.

Collections of Puzzles and Riddles

Constructing crossword puzzles is one of the easiest ways to teach dictionary skills. The dictionary of synonyms and antonyms (or thesaurus) as well as crossword dictionaries are almost essential and may be introduced naturally through this activity. A variety of subject area vocabularies can be integrated by requiring 10 words from the science unit or social studies unit to be worked into the puzzle as a start.

Collections of "Beefs and Bouquets"

In these collections, students can vent their feelings about pet topics: school, sports, newscasters, T.V. programs, music, etc.

BOOKBINDING

The binding of a book adds considerably to the pride of the author and also gives the work a more "professional" look. While standard bookbinding methods are not easily mastered by elementary school students, some modified methods suitable for a variety of age levels are outlined below.

For primary-grade children, a parent helper or teacher's aide might produce the "empty book" described below, or the accordian book could be used to combine a class project. For intermediate grades and middle schools, the standard bookbinding method might be used with the aid of the art teacher (techniques for designing cover, etc.) or the industrial arts teacher (help with clamps and presses, etc.). It is *essential* (not only suggested) that the teacher attempt the particular procedure selected before using it as a class project. While the product is self-rewarding, much student frustration can be avoided by anticipating problem areas and planning for a variety of contingencies.

"Empty Books"

Empty books are most easily constructed from standard 8½" × 11" paper because that size will easily pass through a normal sewing machine. For the primary grades approximately three sheets plus a construction paper cover is adequate (that will result in 12 sides if every side is used, or six sides if only one side is used).

1. Assemble three or more 8½" × 11" papers.

2. Fold the papers to get the center line.

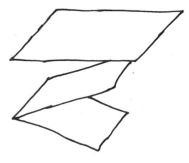

3. Select a 9" × 12" construction paper sheet for the cover.

4. Fold it to get the center line.

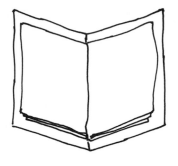

5. Place the pages on the cover, aligning them on the center fold.

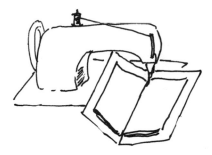

6. Sew through the center line with the longest stitch set on the sewing machine.

"Accordion Books"

This type of book folds like an accordion and is read first from one side, flipped over, and then read from the other side. Because of its continuous nature, illustrations or writing may extend over several pages. It is wise to construct the book shell separately; do the writing on separate sheets of suitably sized paper, and then mount the final products on the book shell. This procedure avoids wasting the more expensive materials. Naturally, the accordion book may be of any length, depending on the size of the group producing it.

1. Cut the appropriate number of "pages" from heavy cardboard. Remember to allow for the front and back covers. Six pieces result in 10 pages plus front and back covers.

2. Place the pages approximately ¼" apart and connect with cloth tape with adhesive-back (as used in book repairs, etc.), preferably from both sides. If the space is not left, the pages will not fold properly.

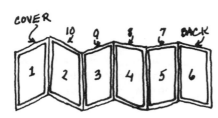

3. Prepare the work to be mounted on regular paper. Use rubber cement for the mounting because the excess may be easily removed. It is, of course, possible to mount work over several pages (over the taped joints).

Modified Bookbinding

To bind a book of this type, a commercial metal strip fastener is used. This book has the advantage that pages may be added (or removed) at any time. Often students like to use potato printing or object printing to decorate the cover before assembling the book.

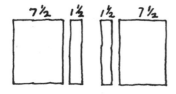

1. Using two pieces of heavy 9" × 12" cardboard, cut a 1½" strip from each.

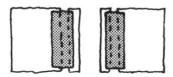

2. Place the strips approximately ⅛" from the larger sheet and use cloth tape with adhesive-back to fasten them together. This will provide the necessary hinge to allow the cover to open easily.

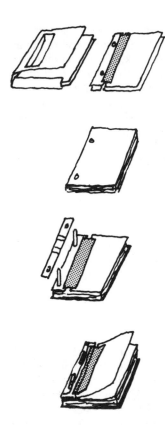

3. Using a paper punch, punch holes through both covers simultaneously, if possible, because this ensures better alignment.

4. Punch 8½″ × 11″ pages on which the actual writing or illustrating is done.

5. Using a metal fastener inserted through the holes, fasten the pages and cover together.

6. Carefully open the cover and fold over. Repeat the same procedure with the pages.

Standard Method of Bookbinding

While the procedure described may at first appear complicated, it is nevertheless manageable. The first attempt may not be perfect but it will be rewarding! Be sure to check out the required materials and the procedures before attempting it with the class.

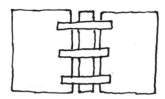

1. Cut two pieces of heavy cardboard slightly larger than the pages to be used. Also cut a narrow strip approximately the *thickness* of the book. Join all three pieces with cloth tape (with adhesive back). Allow ⅛″ between pieces to allow the cover to fold easily.

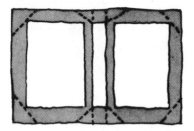

2. Select material, paper, or adhesive-backed vinyl to cover the book. It is recommended that "white glue" be thinned (1 part glue to 2 parts water) and spread with a paintbrush on the covering material. (This is not necessary if adhesive-backed vinyl is used.)

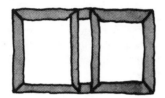

3. Trim as indicated in diagrams 2 and 3.

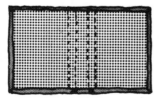

4. Use normal construction paper over the inside of the cover. It is advisable to insert the whole cover assembly between two pieces of plywood; clamp and allow to dry over night. Alternatively, cover the assembly with protective paper and stack books on it for the necessary pressure.

5. Assemble the selected number of pages. A heavy-duty stapler is required for more than 20 pages. Staple three or four times along the edge.

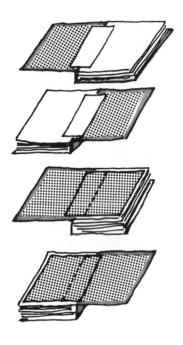

6. Fold cover as in diagram and attach pages to cover, using adhesive-backed cloth tape. Repeat on other side. Spread glue over the strips of tape. Using the same color of construction paper as in step 4, cover the tape as indicated in the diagram. Allow to dry. Repeat the procedure on the reverse side. Allow drying time before attempting to fold the cover.

LITERATURE CITED

Ginsburg, H., and Opper, S. 1969. Piaget's Theory of Intellectual Development. Prentice-Hall, Englewood Cliffs, N.J.

Goethe, J. W. 1960. This is actually a loose paraphrase of the German: Man lernt nichts kennen als was man liebt. In: Seldes, G. (compiler), The Great Quotations. Lyle Stuart, New York.

Klare, G. R. 1963. The Measurement of Readability. Iowa State University Press, Ames.

Logan, L. M., and Logan, V. G. 1971. Design for Creative Teaching. McGraw-Hill, New York.

Postman, N., and Weingartner, C. 1969. Teaching as a Subversive Activity. Delacorte Press, New York.

Ruddell, R. B. 1965. The effect of oral and written patterns of language structure on reading comprehension. Teacher 18:273.

Weiss, H. 1974. How to Make Your Own Books. Crowell, New York.

White, E. B. 1973. On writing for children. In: Haviland, V. (ed.), Children and Literature: Views and Reviews. Scott, Foresman, Glenview, Ill.

PART III
DIAGNOSTIC ASPECTS

chapter 4

Diagnostic Teaching of Composition

Victor Froese

While visting a primary classroom recently, I found one of the teachers frustrated—ready to "scream and pound something"—because her writing lesson was unsuccessful in her opinion; children who were expected to complete a story about a haunted house (which had been discussed and read) simply recorded expressions like: ghosts, a creature, etc. She was expecting sentences, modifiers, and creative responses. Was she expecting too much? What was wrong with her methods? What could be done?

This chapter does not answer those questions specifically but it does generally examine the underlying issues and assists the teacher in teaching composition diagnostically. More specifically, an attempt is made to explain why problems like these arise, what some of the procedures and mechanics of writing are, what a typical skills list might consider, and how to evaluate formatively for teaching purposes.

WHY ARE THERE PROBLEMS WITH TEACHING COMPOSITION?

An important reason for children not writing well is that they have not been taught the skills we expect them to exhibit. The last two decades have seen an emphasis on creative writing, often with the assumption that freeing children to write would result in improved composition. Preceding that trend was an over-emphasis on mechanics, usage, and syntax. Neither extreme has been successful in producing good writers, but as a result of these unfortunate emphases, many teachers are not adequately prepared to handle both tasks, textbooks are often inappropriate, and, to make matters worse, theories have changed again.

Terminology has changed, too, to the chagrin of many, yet it must be mastered to fully grasp the significance of current trends. What follows might be considered a language experience for the teacher. One crucial word is necessary to begin—the word grammar, a study of the structure and operation of language. It is a generic term and is not synonymous with *usage*, e.g., whether one should use "may" or "can" in a particular context. Pooley (1963) has provided an analogy that helps to understand the distinction: "Change is to grammer what etiquette is to behavior. Behavior simply notes what people do, etiquette sets a stamp of approach or disapproval upon actions, or sets up standards to guide actions" (p. 66). Essentially, grammar as defined here may be justified in the curriculum because it helps the student to understand how language is used in communication. As a result, the rote learning of somewhat inconsistent rules does not help, but the formulation of generalizations based on experience with language does help. It is, from a psychological perspective, a cognitive approach (Henderson, 1973).

Table 1 contrasts some aspects of traditional and contemporary grammar. It can be seen that the contemporary approach is in keeping with the assumptions underlying the language experience program; that is, it attempts to describe the language already used by students and bring that understanding to a conscious level.

A further problem of considerable vexation to teachers is the fact that research has not clarified which composition or grammar skills should be taught nor at which grade level. Some useful grade placement practices have been presented by Hochstetler (1971), but there is hardly complete agreement on these practices across states or provinces, or even school divisions. An example of a comprehensive language skills check list is found in Part VI, Appendix C to illustrate the range of problems involved in organizing composition, usage, and mechanical skills as well as the group processes involved. The skills check list may also be used as an evaluation device.

A further source of confusion results from uncertainty about the place of creative writing, expository writing, rewriting or revision, and when mechanics or usage should be taught. While no definitive answer exists, it may be stated that transfer of learning is dependent on the similarity of the training task to the transfer task. This should indicate that composition is best learned through writing—but writing with a purpose and with assistance on the mechanics and techniques

Table 1.   A contrast of some aspects of traditional and contemporary grammar

Traditional grammar	Contemporary grammar
Emphasis on words: 　Each part of speech is identified as well as its relationship to other words ↓	Emphasis on word groups: 　Basic sentence patterns are studied to show how words work in context. ↓
Parts of speech are categorically defined: 　Nouns are the names of persons, places, or things. ↓	Word classes: 　Each word class is signaled by its *form* or *function* and is taught inductively. ↓
Sentences are defined: 　A sentence is a complete thought. ↓	Sentences are identified by reason of physical characteristics: 　Word order, intonation, subject-predicate structure. ↓
Different types of sentences are defined: 　A sentence that asks a question is an interrogative sentence. ↓	Basic sentences are transformed: 　Question transformations, negative transformation, etc., are performed in predictable ways. ↓
Certain expressions are considered proper or improper: 　may—can 　in-into 　between—among	Usage is determined by purpose, place, and population: 　Goodness or "properness" is relative.

deemed to be important. It is wise to separate for teaching purposes the creative process from the more mechanical aspects of writing. Even then it is advisable to use actual errors exhibited by students' writing as a basis for instructional decisions rather than introducing hypothetical examples only. Because a composition is rarely completed in one period anyway, the following sequence is recommended and supported by several sources (Smith, 1973).

1. First period—the focus is on recording ideas as rapidly as possible
2. Second period—this is the proofreading and editing session where mechanics, spelling, and syntax are corrected; oral reading in pairs or small groups is helpful (Burns and Broman, 1975)
3. Third period—teach important skills based on observed errors; practice and drills should be related back to students' work

STAGES IN WRITING COMPOSITION

The language experience approach implies a method of language learning closely tied to the child's cognitive development that avoids verbal labeling and chaining without concomitant meaning associations. Loban's (1964) work also helps one to recognize the interdependency of writing, speaking, reading, and listening. Strong supportive programs are required in all the language arts to produce good composition; but more than that, conscious provision of *transfer* opportunities is necessary. That is, the relationship between oral language and writing, between listening and writing, and between reading and writing must be capitalized on to transfer skills already present in the more developed modes to the less developed modes. Only the teacher, through diagnostic teaching procedures, can make that procedure relevant and effective. In this section both the procedures and the mechanics of progressing from the writing readiness, to the dictation, to the independent writing, to the experimenting stage are developed.

STAGE I: WRITING READINESS

Writing readiness is one component of the basic literacy training begun (formally) in kindergarten and the first grade. Downing (1969) has summarized a number of classical studies into the understanding of literacy concepts and concluded that it is the *abstract quality* of written language and the *vagueness of its utility* that cause difficulty for the child. It is clearly the teacher's function to assist the young student in understanding both the *concepts* of literacy, the *vocabulary* of literacy, and the usefulness of *language* (in addition to the nonverbal) in communication. These basic facets of comprehending language are common to oral and written expression (Harris, 1973). The writing readiness stage capitalizes on that fact.

The basic tenet of the language experience approach as expressed by Lee and Allen (1963) is:

> What I can think about, I can say
> What I can say, I can write
> I can read what I have written
> I can read what others have written for me (p.46).

The teacher in helping the child to understand these relationships can engage in the following types of activities (Table 2) that may lead to successful writing and that consequently may be thought of as *writing readiness* activities.

STAGE II: DICTATION

The second stage, dictating a composition to a recorder (parent volunteer, teacher, older student), is elaborated here. This does not imply that students do no writing of their own, it simply means that encoding in written form is still difficult for them while they have many ideas to express and they can express them orally to someone else. Dictating to a volunteer simply eliminates the physical and mechanical procedures required for writing, which the student has not developed fully at this point.

Furthermore, the literacy concepts alluded to in the writing readiness stage are extended and reinforced. The dictation phase focuses on refining ideas orally before recording, on the transfer of language from oral to written form, on the purpose of written language, on the rudiments of word recognition, and on building the child's confidence in using oral and written language to communicate and to remember ideas.

Teachers and student-teachers first attempting to write experience charts have often expressed the difficulties encountered and the lack of information on specific procedures to follow. An excellent source to begin with is Ashland's (1973) article, but additional information is necessary (as identified by student-teachers attempting the precedure) and will subsequently be elaborated.

Table 2. Types of activities the teacher can use to help a student understand certain relationships

Relationship	Activity
A. What I can think about, I can say.	1. Have child explain to an adult how to draw something. 2. Have children reach into a bag and describe objects by feel only. 3. Tape-record a child's voice and play it back. 4. Look into a mirror while speaking. Note what happens to lips, teeth, and tongue, e.g., use words such as bat, shoot, this. 5. Have the child explain the sequence of activities that got him to school.
B. What I can say, I can write.	1. Child prints her/his own name on notebooks, rulers, etc., to identify the object as hers/his. 2. Verbal labels or captions are affixed to things. 3. Use words as group signifiers, i.e., round objects, red beads. 4. Read picture books and have children point to "what it says." 5. Draw attention to punctuation marks that can be identified by ear. Read to them; have them point to the symbols on a chart. 6. Learn letter "names" and uses for them. Learn to discriminate letter "names" from letter "sounds."
C. I can read what I have written.	1. Write and read key words. 2. Compose individual and group experience charts. 3. Focus attention on upper and lower-case letters. 4. Develop some spelling sense by identifying letter combinations that go together. 5. Read acceptable and unacceptable sentences and have students identify them, e.g., "They saw a car." "They car is blue." 6. Match individual word cards with words in an experience story. 7. Discuss how one decides where to put emphasis in a choral reading piece and how one might indicate it in print, i.e., compare oral to written emphasis cues.

Continued

Table 2. *Continued*

Relationship	Activity
D. I can read what others have written for me to read.	1. Read alphabet and simple picture books. Emphasize the difference of pictures and words. 2. Discuss examples of words written in manuscript and cursive forms; upper and lower case letters, written (manuscript or cursive) and printed (as in books). 3. Read class-compiled books for sharing; newspaper headlines for news; informational books for facts.

Types of Experience Charts

It is useful to consider a variety of types of experience charts because the underlying purpose will differ and also because it gives the teacher several alternative procedures to use when appropriate. Lee and Allen (1963), for example, discuss four types: personal language charts, work charts, narrative charts, and reading skill charts.

Personal Language Chart   The purpose of the personal language chart is to allow the child to express himself without concern for being able to read every word. In fact, it is a direct follow-up of drawing an idea in pictorial form. It allows him to experiment with words, sounds, and expressions. The payoff is seeing his own language in print and enjoying the experience; the chart is personal and·is not intended for sharing nor necessarily needs to be kept. In fact, it may be recorded on the chalkboard and then erased. Later on, when the child is able to write himself, this chalkboard exercise is often made a daily experience to allow the child to "write himself out."

Work Chart   As suggested by the title, the work chart is of a more utilitarian nature. The teacher and students may plan their activities for the period, for the morning, or for the day. These activities are then recorded on a chart or chalkboard and accompanied by picture clues, a diagram, or rebus-type symbols (available from American Guidance Service, Circle Pines, Minnesota). Other variations of the work chart would be recording a recipe with ingredients and instructions; writing up the steps in an experiment or the results from it; listing the monitors for various chores; summarizing safety rules or drill directions; sequencing procedures for making a puppet; or agreeing on rules for show and tell. Work charts are functional and should be revised if the first draft does not work or if the procedure can be improved. They are in a sense the forerunners of notetaking and summarizing.

Narrative Chart   The narrative chart is the best known and often is a recording of the actual or imaginary experiences of the narrator(s). It is more this chart's purpose than its nature which distinguishes it from work charts. The language lends itself to more repetition, more personal expression, and more colorful language. Often narrative charts are collected, duplicated, and assembled into books for the classroom library. Because they contain common experiences, they are easily read and provide easy (yet important) reading practice.

Reading Skills Chart   A fourth type of chart, the reading skills chart, is only mentioned briefly because its purpose is more for developing reading than writing skills. The reading skills chart develops skills *diagnosed* as necessary to a number of children. That is, the children may not recognize words representing necessary concepts (i.e., measure, opposite, etc.), or they may not recognize certain numbers accurately, or they may not identify important sight words quickly.

Problems in Writing Experience Charts

As mentioned earlier, certain procedural problems arise when writing experience charts. Some of these key problems are discussed below, along with some suggestions for overcoming them.

How Are the Contents of the Chart Formulated?   When a group of 10 children have had a common experience (e.g., baking cookies, visiting the nurse) they naturally all wish to talk and to present their varied reactions, opinions, and feelings. Not everything can be recorded on the chart. Consequently, it is suggested that a full discussion of the event occurs before any recording is attempted, even for individual charts. After the discussion, the teacher tells the student(s) that some of what they have said will be recorded.

How Are Multiple Responses Handled?   When the composing is done in a spontaneous manner, often more than one child responds simultaneously or says nearly the same thing. It is suggested that all responses be accepted but that the group must decide which one to record. Judicious guidance by the teacher ensures that the most sensible statement is selected rather than the response from the more popular child.

How Can the Ideas Discussed be Remembered for Recording Purposes? Because many ideas are brought up during the oral phase, some are not necessarily directly related, and because it is often difficult to recall the best points, a type of notation system is recommended for the recorder. Sawicki et al. (1969) refer to these notations as "caption" words. Through the use of "caption" words the flow of ideas is not interrupted (i.e., by the teacher's writing) and later these main ideas may be expanded into sentences.

How is Wandering Attention Coped with While Writing Group Charts? Those students not directly contributing often cannot read the sentence being recorded and hence lose interest. It is suggested that the teacher or recorder say each word as it is written and then have the group read each sentence when it is completed to preserve the flow of its language. Often it is wise to indicate the student's name in parentheses after the statement hc has dictated.

Should the Exact Words of the Speaker be Recorded? This question often arises because dialect or nonstandard English responses are commonly observed. Ruddell (1974) suggests accepting nonstandard dialect in oral and written expression with regular spellings at the beginning stages but recommends a gradual transition to standard English in written expression. For teachers having to deal with dialect or second-language problems the reading of Ruddell's chapter on "Non-Standard Dialects and Second Language Learning: The Instructional Program" is recommended.

Why Can't Some Students Read the Experience Chart? At the beginning stages children are more accurately "role-playing" the reading act and their recognition of words relies heavily on memory and other global cues. Word recognition is not as important at this stage as feeling successful at "reading."

As a result, a gradual withdrawal of teacher assistance is recommended. That is, first the teacher reads smoothly while pointing to words in a sweeping left-to-right motion; then the children read together with the teacher; only then is personal reading *offered.* If the individual contributors have been identified then those children could be given first opportunity as an intermediate step to other children reading the chart independently.

There are no foolproof guidelines to the length of the chart but frequently dictated short charts (perhaps up to four sentences) seem preferable to long ones. Even then, some children will only recognize a few words on the chart, but that should be an encouraging sign to the teacher. These recognized words should be recorded on individual cards and made part of a "word bank."

What Does the Teacher do about Unusual or Difficult Words?
It is wise for the teacher to have a dictionary handy that can be consulted for difficult words like triceratops, cicada, Sei Whale, licorice (or liquorice). In fact, it would be quite unrealistic to communicate the idea that adults know how to write *all* words correctly. Naturally, the necessity for using a dictionary is communicated in this way and a situation requiring the dictionary could easily lead into the construction of personal dictionaries.

STAGE III: INDEPENDENT WRITING STAGE

The beginning of independent writing is a slow yet rewarding process. It is a difficult transitional stage as well, and it is well for the teacher to know some of the reasons. Lundsteen (1976) suggests that children must make the transition from sensory to imagined and symbolized images, and they must do this without immediate feedback or response from an audience or there may be no real audience at all. Children, in shaping their compositions, must also analyze what they are doing while they are writing; this is a process that has not yet been habituated and is difficult even for mature writers. Furthermore, the child must produce a much more complete message in writing than in speaking (the reason for the frustrated teacher in the example at the beginning of this chapter). As a consequence of these changes, the introduction of independent writing must be a gradual one fostered by much teacher support, absence of criticism, and accompanied by much success on the student's part. Some procedures and mechanics for accomplishing the transition from dictation to independent writing are outlined below.

In the 1970s, attention of research in language development has increasingly focused on "the interaction of the child's perceptual and cognitive development with linguistic and nonlinguistic events" (Bloom, 1975, p. 291). Knowing something about the child's development helps the teacher both to appreciate the intricate balance of cognitive/linguisic development and to understand why his production (actual writing) appears far less sophisticated than oral use of language or his language competence (or understanding) would lead one to believe.

Two very inportant cognitive-developmental changes occur in most children during their elementary school years. Between the ages of 5 to 7 years, approximately, the child makes the transition to using symbolic thought. That is, the child is capable of representing ideas in some symbolic form—iconic or verbal. He can now deal with ideas more adequately on a mental rather than physical level. The child is able to imitate models even when they are not present, and he is able to more readily separate himself from his immediate environment (Ginsburg and Opper, 1969). Obviously, these cognitive abilities affect (or, more accurately; interact with) the child's writing and composition. For example, teachers often note faulty pronoun use, incorrect ordering of ideas, and omission of assumed ideas. The teacher, in fact, can use simple, classroom-like activities to check on the child's transition from what Piaget identified as sensorimotor and preoperational periods. The well know "conservation" experiments can be used even informally to ascertain how the child thinks about things and how he explains them. "Conservation" ability is the ability to transform the shapes of balls of clay and to understand that they remain invariant or to understand that several objects (buttons, coins) arranged close together or far apart still represent the same quantity. This ability signals the preoperational stage.

The second important cognitive-developmental change often occurs in the upper elementary grades, somewhere between ages 7 and 11 when the child progresses to what Piaget referred to as the concrete operational stage. Smith, Goodman, and Meredith (1976, p. 146) suggest that "the language of the dialogue at this stage should teem with 'becauses,' 'althoughs,' 'ifs,' 'givens,' and 'supposes,' provided the teacher keeps in mind what is 'concrete' in the mental operations of his learners." The child is also able to take a point of view different from his own. His vocabulary is rapidly expanding because he is able to classify on several dimensions and be aware of subsets of ideas, but these abilities are still largely perception bound and direct experiences lie at the basis of most thinking and language in children at this stage of development. That gives rise to what to adults may be illogical "becauses" and "ifs."

Transitions to Independent Writing

Teachers are often disappointed with children's first writing because much spelling is "phonetic," sentences are incomplete, and punctuation and capitalization are imperfect. These matters should not be discouraging. On the contrary, when one considers the cognitive-developmental aspects of the above abilities, one must marvel that the child can do so much.

Several activities already mentioned in previous chapters—word banks, bookmaking, and labeling—can provide some transfer at this juncture. The teacher should make a point of printing key words on the board or experience chart after a story has been read or discussion has taken place. Also, many objects should be labeled in the classroom. Even simple sentence frames can be displayed. At the initial stages of writing the recombining of words and sentence frames should be expected; in fact, it is a creative act for the child. Picture books with simple texts (see Part VI, Appendix A) as well as class-made books are other sources of words. Collections of art work with attached labels can be collated to form new books for sharing (or if put on stencils for taking home).

Most writing at this stage should be sensory, experiental, or utilitarian because concreteness and immediacy are important. The reader is encouraged to consult Moffett (1968) for detailed analyses and descriptions of various writing tasks attempted with children at various age levels. Because much variety and much writing are a demanding challenge for the teacher as well, sources of ideas such as Moffett's book and Carlson's (1970) are recommended.

Needless to say, much individualization of instruction is necessary. Total class introduction of most skills is probably wasteful of both energy and time. Consequently, the teacher needs some guidelines for analyzing children's written work in order to determine *who* needs *what*.

The writer has found that both student-teachers and teachers become better observers when analyzing children's compositions with the help of a scale like Sundbye's (1973) or an adaptation of it. It should be immediately emphasized that items on the scale should not be used for writing comments on students' papers. By constructing a table (Table 3) of the elements on the scale against each student's paper, a diagnostic profile may be compiled. Even a cursory glance will identify weak areas, and a detailed analysis provides much insight into the individual student's performance. Caution should be immediately suggested because each analysis relates only to the type of writing undertaken (narrative, descriptive, etc.) and cannot be generalized. For example, a scenic picture will not result in many "action" words. On the other hand, a teacher may structure several writing situations to get a more generalizable profile. The following two profiles, one for grade three, one for grade six, indicate the type of information that may be derived from using a scale. The teacher's comments and children's work are included in unedited form. The present author is indebted to the students in the 1976 School Centered Elementary Program (University of Manitoba) for the following examples.

Table 3. Evaluation of a third-grade creative writing assignment

					Children				
Skill area	Karen	Robert K.	Robert A.	Leslie	Kenton	Darren	Derrol	Brenda	Eddie
1. Complete sentences	Yes	Sometimes	Sometimes	Yes	No	No	Yes	Yes	Yes
2. Capital letters	Yes	Yes	Mostly	Yes	Yes	No	Sometimes	Yes	Yes
3. Periods and question marks	Mostly	Sometimes	Mostly	Yes	No	No	Sometimes	Sometimes	Yes
4. Related ideas	Yes	Yes	Yes	Yes	Yes	Yes	Yes	Yes	Yes
5. Time sequence	Yes	Yes	Yes	Yes	Yes	Yes	Yes	Yes	Yes
6. Modifiers for nouns and verbs	Sometimes	Yes	Sometimes	Yes	Sometimes	No	Sometimes	Sometimes	Yes
7. Title	Yes	Yes	No	Yes	Yes	Yes	Yes	Yes	Yes
8. Variety in sentences	Yes	Yes	Yes	Yes	No	No	Yes	Yes	Yes
9. Coordinators to combine	Mostly	Sometimes	No	Yes	Sometimes	No	Yes	Sometimes	Yes
10. Sounds and rhythms of words	Yes	Yes	Yes	Yes	No	No	Yes	Sometimes	Yes
11. Third person	Yes	No	Yes	No	No	No	No	No	No
12. Imaginative ideas	Mostly	Yes	Mostly	Yes	No	No	Yes	Yes	Yes

Yes, consistently uses; no, not at all; mostly, usually uses; sometimes, occasionally uses.

Analysis of Primary Writing—Example

Considerations for Marking   The motivation for a creative writing assignment affects the resultant writing. In this case the assignment involved topics that were inspired by the Christmas season through Christmas books (*Charley Mouse Finds Christmas*), songs ("Rudolf the Red-nosed Reindeer"), and records ("The Christmas Carol"). The extent of imaginative ideas was restricted in that the topics involved familiar tales. I modified my evaluation of imaginative ideas by considering the extent to which the child expanded upon or viewed differently the topic. Since topics were given, these invariably became the titles, so that no original titles were created.

Consideration was also given to the brevity of the compositions. I did not ask for a specific length but had given them half sheets of foolscap which they assumed meant a short story. Evaluation of sentence variety was limited in some cases where the story was only three sentences long.

The third person did not apply to obvious topics—"I worked as one of Santa's helpers."

I allowed for the variants "mostly" and "sometimes" because I felt the need for more flexibility in order to give an accurate diagnosis. "Mostly" indicates strength in an area and "sometimes" indicates weakness.

As is suggested by Sundbye's (1973) scale this evaluation should not be applied in isolation but on repeated occasions.

Diagnosis as a Group

Strengths:	Appropriate use of capital letters
	Enumeration of related ideas
	Maintains simple time sequence
	Imaginative ideas
Weaknesses:	Complete sentences
	Appropriate use of periods and question marks
	Modifiers for nouns and verbs
	Proper use of co-ordinators to combine sentence elements

NOTE: Kenton, Darren and Robert A. (Table 3) appeared to have been at a loss for imaginative ideas and this seemed to affect the quality of their writing. In general, these three had difficulty expressing themselves. In future, I would try to use different means to stimulate these boys and evaluate again to see if they were still weak in these areas.

I definitely feel that this scale has merit in that its criteria evaluates basic elements of writing that add to the clarity of expression as well as including basic style regularities. If used on repeated occasions, I feel that it would be helpful in indicating where the child has difficulty in expression. I would use this scale as an indicator to each child's particular needs. When the child is beginning to write I would help him individually with his weak areas and would try different ways to stimulate creative ideas.

Samples

CHRISTMAS

Once upon a time a rabbit named rudolph. Had 5 sisters and 5 bothers. But the bothers and sisters were mean to him. They wouldn't let him play with them. then one foggy hristman eve santa came to say its off why said the rabbits? rudolph don't shine that nose no bright rudolph with that nose will you guide my sleigh tonight then all the rabbits love him as they sounted out with glee rudolph the red nosed rabbit you go down in history.

Robert A.

I worked as one of Santa's helpers!

I'm a little mouse,
and I live in a little store,
So when Christmas comes,
I don't have much fun,
and I don't like it any more!

One night it was Christmas
it was very quiet in the store,
then all of a sudden, I head
something coming near me!
Then a big red mitten reached down and picked me up!
Then I knew it was Santa Claus. He took me to the
north pole and thats how I worked as one of Sants helpers.

Leslie

Meet my dog Humbug!

Once apoun a time my friend cam over.
She said who's that I said that's Humbug
What a werd looking Humbug
It's a dog I named him Humbug
She was going to stay for lunch
So Humbug jumped up and ate her dinner.
She would not play with me again! and she ran away.

Brenda

Analysis of Imtermediate Writing—Example

Methods   The material used for this exercise was gathered from a Year 6 class. The recording "The Marvelous Toy" (from the "Peter, Paul and Mommy" album) was used to stimulate them: it was played twice and then we discussed it together. Descriptions of its sounds, movements, colors, etc., were received from the class and written on the chalkboard. After listening to the recording once more, the chalkboard was erased and the students were told to write a composition about the toy. I felt I limited their creativity by asking them to write about *the* toy rather than *a* toy, and writing their descriptions on the board (this seemed to give them the idea that there was a correct description of the toy). If I were doing this again I would correct these two things.

In spite of this the stories written were on the whole quite creative and imaginative. Although the class had done some creative writing earlier in the year, they had not been exposed to such a method of stimulation and seemed to enjoy it. I am looking forward to trying something like this again later in the year.

Analysis and Discussion of Results   To analyze the compositions using Sundbye's (1973) 25 elements, I chose to use a range of 1–3 rather than a simple yes or no decision (Table 4). I also wanted to keep the range narrow to facilitate the evaluation of the compositions, some of which were quite short and thus did not have that much to work with. A wider range would allow more flexibility, but would prove unwieldy to determine the students' capabilities. A score of one indicates the pupil is completely ignorant of the concept or that he is very weak in using it; a score of two indicates an acceptable level of use but improvement is desirable; finally, a score of three means the student is competent in that skill.

I also added two other categories: NA for "not applicable" where I felt the format of the composition did not allow for some of the elements. For example, elements 5 and 11 often fell into this category. I don't feel that a time sequence should be a part of every composition, nor that the writer always use the third person. I used NE to indicate insufficient evidence to make a judgment. In this respect I simply did not want to state that a student was weak in a category just because he did not use it in this composition; if another composition were analysed at a later date then this score could be clarified. For example, elements 8 and 15 were exclusively "NE" except where the student used the idea showing that he was thinking of it at the time. I feel that these two elements are governed by the format of the whole composition and if the student is not using that format then he should not be identified as being weak in that element.

The results show some interesting facts. Very few of the 25 elements were done suitably by all or almost all students: 4, 5, 6, and 7 were the only ones done consistently well. It is interesting to note that even at a Grade 6 level many students are still having trouble with the "basics"—complete sentences, capitalization, punctuation. An examination of the analysis of Dean's work (9) is interesting: he is obviously weak in the very basic skills that he should have gained at the primary level, but often shows a grasp of the elements that Sundbye classifies as advanced. Bruce (8), who is also weak in the basics, does not show the same competence as Dean in the higher skills. Valerie (10) ranks the highest of all students, having scored 3 in all elements except the two deemed as NE. If, as Sundbye states, the elements are listed according to advancing skills, then the analysis of a "typical" student should have shown competence from 1-12 (the primary grades) and then tapered off from 13-25. This is indeed true for 5 of the 12 students: Graham (1), Laurie (2), Paula B. (3), Joyce (4), and Mike (12). Those students not yet discussed showed a mixture of weaknesses at the elementary and intermediate skills level. However, it is not the purpose of this examination to investigate all errors noted, but rather to focus on those elements in which groups of students were negligent. Several categories stand out in this respect (1, 16, 17, 18, 19, 21, 22, and 23) and on Sundbye's scale all but 1 are the more advanced elements. My follow-up to this exercise would be to focus on these areas, especially 1, in an attempt to bring them up to a more acceptable level. While working on these with the class I would also mention the other elements that could be improved so that the students who were already competent in the basic ones could sharpen up the finer skills.

The Wonderful Toy

The wonderful toy made many sounds. When it stoped in made a big POP sound. When it started it made a fast ZIP sound and when it stayed still it made a soft, but long PURR sound. It also made sound like WHIP. I think it made it when the toy was in a hurry. It made sounds like a soldier when he is marching. Also like a train, chuga, chuga. But the best sounds I like are POP, ZIP, WHIP, and PURR. The toy went all over the hous making th sounds it did. What a sonderful toy.

Paula B.

Table 4. Use of Stindhye's 25 elements to analyze the compositions of a grade six class

Skill area	Graham	Laurie	Paula B.	Joyce	Heather	Paula R.	Sandra	Bruce	Dean	Valerie	Lisa	Mike
1. Uses complete sentences	3	3	2	3	1	1	2	1	1	3	2	1
2. Uses capitals	3	3	3	3	3	3	3	2	1	3	2	3
3. Uses periods and question marks	3	3	3	3	1	3	3	1	1	3	3	3
4. Enumerates ideas, related	3	3	3	3	3	3	3	3	3	3	3	3
5. Maintains time sequence	3	3	NA	3	3	3	NA	NA	NA	3	3	3
6. Uses modifiers for nouns or verbs	3	3	3	3	3	2	3	3	3	3	3	3
7. Gives story a title	3	3	3	3	3	3	3	3	3	3	3	3
8. Inserts questions to vary sentences	NE	NE	NE	2	NE	NE	NE	NE	3	NE	NE	NE
9. Uses coordinators to combine sentence element	3	1	3	1	2	2	2	2	2	3	3	3
10. Manipulates sounds and rhythms of words	1	3	3	1	3	2	2	2	3	3	3	3
11. Uses third person	NA	NA	NA	NA	3	3	3	2	2	2	2	2
12. Uses imaginative ideas	3	3	3	3	1	2	2	3	3	3	2	2

13. Includes emotions and personal reactions	NA	NE	2	1	3	1	3	1	2	3	3	3
14. Uses a concluding sentence	3	3	3	1	2	1	1	3	3	3	3
15. Uses direct discourse	NE	NE	NE	NE	2	NE	NE	NE	NE	NE	NE
16. Uses original figures of speech	1	3	2	1	1	1	1	1	2	2	1
17. Uses repetition for effect	NA	3	2	1	1	1	1	1	3	2	1
18. Uses subordinate clauses and phrases	1	2	3	1	2	2	2	3	2	3	3
19. Inverts sentences	1	2	3	1	1	1	1	1	3	3	1
20. Places modifiers appropriately	3	2	3	2	2	2	2	2	3	3	3
21. Expresses humour	3	2	2	1	1	2	1	1	2	2	1
22. Expresses theme or symbolism	NA	NA	1	1	2	1	2	1	2	2	2
23. Uses punctuation to separate ideas	NE	3	3	2	1	3	1	1	3	1	1
24. Adds descriptive passage	NA	3	2	1	2	2	2	2	3	3	2
25. Expresses times sequences subtly	NA	3	2	2	2	2	2	2	3	3	2

1, ignorant of concept or very weak; 2, acceptable but improvement is desirable; 3, competent; NA, "not applicable"—format of composition did not allow for this element; NE, not sufficient evidence for an evaluation;

A Marvelous Toy

This toy goes pop! whirl! wiz! And when you pick it up it's got two big green glassy eyes and it got arms and legs. It goes backwords and foreword and goes up the stairs and down the stairs and stands still it canfit under a chair. It is one feet by five inches, is it a bike, a toy car, do you know wat it is.

Dean

Sounds of a Wonderful Toy

The wonderful toy made sounds such as; a soft wizzing sound as it marked past the boy. When it stopped it made short BOPs; when it started up again it made fast ZIPs!! and then as its lid bobbed up and down it gave out long loud POPs. And as it wen up the stairs it purred like a lost lonley cat. But when it came down agian it made a sound nobody had heard before, it sounded like all the WIZZes, BOPs, ZIPs, POPs put together in one happy tune.

Valerie

Category 12 on the scales—using imaginative ideas—is generally commented on by teachers. There is a general feeling that it should be expanded and somehow given more weighting. It should be noted that other categories—10, 13, 16, 17, 21, 22, and 25—also assess "imaginative" or creative ideas. One should in fact *resist* the urge to quantify these items and sum them for an overall score. The intent of the scale is to pinpoint areas that may require direct teaching, not to assign a grade to a student.

STAGE IV: LANGUAGE EXPERIMENTING STAGE

As can be seen from the intermediate (grade six) class profile, many students have not mastered all the normally observed elements of children's writing, and a considerable task still remains for the teacher. In this, the fourth stage of writing, elements such as symbolism, manipulating sounds, using humour, direct discourse, and subordination should be experimented with. Ruddell (1974, pp. 93–96) has neatly summarized research in the development of speech and writing through the school years. Two of Ruddell's conclusions are particularly germane:

The child's grammatical system is influenced by the language in his environment but his ability to generalize about his morphological and syntactical system appears to be central to his rapid acquisition of language.

The development of control over syntactic complexity in oral language and written language appears to be closely related.

The first statement is naturally the basis for writing in this stage, the experimenting stage. The second statement suggests how teaching might proceed: through much discussion, experimentation with language, and through literature and reading. The present author (Froese, 1975, pp. 68–74) has suggested a number of experiments in language that help to motivate language learning and that help the student to become an amateur linguist, in a sense. Approaches like these should be considered by the teacher.

The study of semantic development (word meaning) is still in its infancy (Bloom, 1975, pp. 273–276) and does not provide much help to the teacher of composition. But recent work in information processing (Norman and Lindsay, 1972) appears to provide, with considerable interpretation, some usable strategies for developing word meaning through various classification schemes. Naturally, this does not take the place of building word banks, class dictionaries, reading widely, and other techniques for expanding word knowledge. The above work suggests that words have at least three types of attributes: they have features or properties, belong to a class, and examples are possible. Figure 1 provides one scheme for teaching a rather complicated classification scheme for expanding meaning.

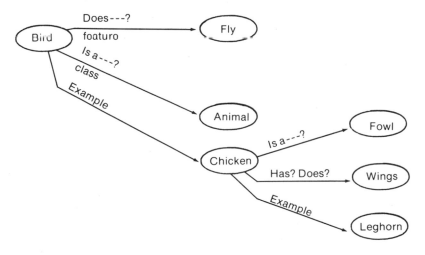

Figure 1. A scheme for teaching a rather complicated classification scheme for expanding meaning.

The teacher may try this procedure with a class or student when a word is partially known or if extension of meaning seems appropriate. Another technique to help more advanced students to understand how the test questions are generated (how words "mean") is to have them engage in free-association tasks (Figure 2), then group the association by category.

The teacher may also want to develop exercises in which colors are associated with moods or ideas. O'Neil's *Hailstones and Halibut Bones* provides many examples to get started. Much can be learned about children by having them explain what common words mean to them: big, nice, beautiful, etc. The literature on language development documents many interesting changes with age (Erwin and Foster, 1960; Maratsos, 1973). Another way of approaching the same matter with older children is to build and uses a thesaurus. Naturally, the intent of all these activities is to develop more precise expressions to use in speaking and writing.

Research over the past decade indicates that emphasizing sentence combining (O'Hare, 1973), sentence expansion, sentence transformation, and sentence types could be useful in developing students' language competence. While some changes in linguistic theory are appearing (Fillmore, 1968), the above ideas still prove useful in generating teaching, materials, and ideas. Essentially, the assumption is that all sentences spoken or written are based on one of several basic patterns (Roberts, 1958; Stageberg, 1971), which may be characterized in the following ways:

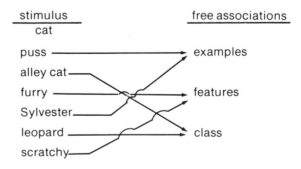

Figure 2. A free-association task in which associations are grouped by category.

1. N-V
2. N-V-N
3. N-V-N-N
4. N-LV-N
5. N-LV-ADJ

Where N means noun or noun phrase, V means verb or verb phrase, and LV means linking verb. These same patterns may be expanded by adding single or multiple modifiers or phrases. Precision and interest are enhanced through expansion of sentences. In order to gain further variety, these basic patterns are transformed by rearranging words to produce questions, inverted sentences, negative statements, commands, or passive sentences.

The importance of these types of activities is to help the student understand consciously what he has been doing intuitively and thereby give him considerably more control over his language. The Appendix to this chapter lists a number of sources of activities for accomplishing much of stage IV composition.

SUMMARY

This chapter began with an explanation of problems in written composition, then four stages or steps to writing were elaborated and procedures or materials suggested. Two important cognitive-developmental stages of children in the elementary grades were identified and their relation to language development suggested. Included were examples of evaluative profiles for the teacher to develop in order to accomplish diagnostic teaching. While definitive research is not available in all aspects of teaching children's composition, sources of support were indicated where applicable. It was recommended that experimentation in language (as in science, or in social studies courses) can be an effective and motivating manner of learning more about man's most unique ability: language.

APPENDIX:
SKILLS OF
COMPOSITION AND GRAMMAR—
SOME IDEA SOURCES

Boyd, G. A. 1970. Grammar and usage. In: Teaching Communication Skills in the Elementary School. Van Nostrand, New York. Classroom activities, pp. 164–172.

Carlson, R. 1970. Writing Aids Through the Grades. Teachers' College Press, New York.

Dallmann, M. 1971. Guiding growth in written expression, and Guiding growth in skills common to oral and written communication. In: Teaching the Language Arts in the Elementary School. Wm. C. Brown, Dubuque, Iowa. Capitalization, punctuation, sentence structure, paragraph structure, note-taking, outlining, grammar and correct usage.

George, M. Y. 1970. Skills. In: Language Art. Chandler Pub., Scranton, Pa. Spelling, capitals, dictation, summaries and outlines, letters, introductory sentences, quotation marks, etc.

Hurwitz, A. B., and Goddard, A. 1969. Grammar and Sentence Games. In: Games to Improve Your Child's English. Simon and Schuster, New York. Grammer Rummy, Sentence-forming fun, Verb Charades, Frantic Semantic Antic, etc.

Logan, L. M., Logan, V. G., and Paterson, L. 1972. Linguistics, usage and grammar. In: Creative Communication. McGraw-Hill Ryerson, Toronto.

Peck, R. L., and Peck, H. E. 1969. Art and Language Lessons for the Elementary Classroom. Parker Pub. Co., West Nyack, N.Y. 80 Lessons (with objectives) using learning, seeing, tasting, smelling and touching as avenues to writing.

Reeves, R. E. 1966. Ideas for Teaching English: Grades 7-8-9. N.C.T.E., Champaign, Ill.

Smith, J. A. 1970. The mechanics of written expression. In: Creative Teaching of the Language Arts in the Elementary School. Allyn and Bacon, Boston. Creative teaching of capitalization, punctuation, word usage, forms of written expression, sentence structure, etc.

Tiedt, S. W., and Tiedt, J. M. 1970. Writers at work. In: Elementary Teacher's Complete Ideas Handbook. Prentice-Hall, Englewood Cliffs, N.J. Parts of speech, verbs, spelling unfamiliar words, practising punctuation, constructing sentences, etc.

Wagner, G., Hosier, M., and Blackman, M. 1970. Language Games: Strengthening Language Skills with Instructional Games. Teachers Pub. Corp., Darien, Conn. Originality in speech and writing, dictionary and spelling power, correct usage, etc. (also a list of commercial games).

Willcox, I. 1963. Language Arts Activities for the Independant Work Period. Teachers Practical Press, New York.

Wilson, G. E. 1966. Language study. In: Composition Situations. N.C.T.E., Urbana, Ill. Grammar, usage, written representation, etc. (assignment suggestions are given for each).

LITERATURE CITED

Ashland, L. C. 1973. Conducting individual language experience stories. Read. Teacher 27(November):167–170.

Bloom, L. 1975. Language development. In: F. D. Horowitz (ed.), Review of Child Development Research, Vol. 4. University of Chicago Press, Chicago.

Burns, P. C., and Broman, B. L. 1975. The Language Arts in Childhood Education, pp. 285–287. Rand McNally, Chicago.

Carlson, R. K. 1970. Writing Aids Through the Grades. Columbia University Press, New York.

Downing, J. 1969. How children think about reading. Read. Teacher 23(December):217–220.

Erwin, S. M., and Foster, G. 1960. The development of meaning in children's descriptive terms. J. Abnorm. Soc. Psych. 61:271–275.

Fillmore, C. J. 1968. The case for case. In: E. Bach and R. T. Harms (eds.), Universals in Linguistic Theory, pp. 1-88. Holt, Rinehart and Winston, New York.

Froese, V. 1975. Exploration with language. In: O. H. Clapp (ed.), On Righting Writing, pp. 68–74. N.C.T.E., Urbana, Ill.

Ginsburg, H., and Opper, S. 1969. Piaget's Theory of Intellectual Development, pp. 66–71. Prentice-Hall, Englewood Cliffs, N.J.

Harris, S. G. 1973. Reading methodology—What's radical, what's traditional? Read. Teacher 27(November):135.

Henderson, E. H. 1973. Group instruction in a language-experience approach. Read. Teacher 26(March):590.

Hochstetler, R. 1971. Facets of language-grammar and usage. In: P. Lamb (ed.), Guiding Children's Language Learning, pp. 312–315 Wm. C. Brown, Dubuque, Iowa.

Lee, C. M., and Allen, R. V. 1963. Learning to Read Through Experience, pp. 46, 48–58. A-C-C, New York.

Loban, W. 1964. The Language of Elementary School Children, p.74. Champaign, N.C.T.E., Champaign, Ill.

Lundsteen, S. W. 1976. Children Learn to Communicate, pp. 230–231. Prentice-Hall, Englewood Cliffs, N.J.

Maratsos, M. P. 1973. Decrease in the understanding of the word "big" in preschool children. Child Dev.

Moffett, J. 1968. A Student-Centered Language Arts Curriculum. Houghton-Mifflin, Boston.

Norman, D. A., and Lindsay, P. H. 1972. The structure of memory. In: Human Information Processing. pp.375–433. Academic Press, New York.

O'Hare, F. 1973. Sentence Combining: Improving Student Writing Without Formal Grammar Instruction. N.C.T.E., Urbana, Ill.

Pooley, R. C. 1963. A perspective on usage. Language, Linguistics and School Programs, p. 66. N.C.T.E., Champaign, Ill.

Roberts, P. 1958. Understanding English. Harper and Row, New York.

Ruddell, R. B. 1974. Reading-Language Instruction: Innovative Practices, p. 281. Prentice-Hall, Englewood Cliffs, N.J.

Sawicki, F., Barnette, E., Blakely, J., and Elliot, G. 1969. Key Words to Reading: The Language Experience Approach Begins, p. 58. Mimeographed.

Smith, E. B., Goodman, K. S., and Meredith, R. 1976. Language and Thinking in School, p. 146. 2nd Ed. Holt, Rinehart & Winston, New York.

Smith, J. A. 1973. Creative Teaching of the Language Arts in the Elementary School. pp. 197, 296–297. Allyn & Bacon, Boston.

Stageberg, N. C. 1971. An Introductory English Grammar. Holt, Rinehart & Winston, New York.

Sundbye, N. W. 1973. Evaluation of children's compositions. In: King (ed.), A Forum for Focus, pp. 223–230. N.C.T.E., Urbana, Ill.

Veatch, J., Sawicki, F., Elliot, G., Barnette, E., and Blake, J. 1973. Key Words to Reading. Merrill, Columbus, Ohio.

chapter 5

Diagnostic Teaching of Reading in a Language Experience Context

Carl Braun

Most teachers readily come to the defence of a program with a heavy "language experience" emphasis when particular criteria are considered. For example, most will nod approval at the notion that such an approach recognizes our awareness of a need to integrate the language arts components: listening, speaking, reading, and writing. Most will applaud its efficacy on the grounds that such a program truly teaches reading as a communication skill grounded in the personal experience of the learner. Few will argue the motivational benefits that accrue at least in the beginning stages. The "crunch" generally comes on issues relevant to aspects such as balance of skills beyond those learned by simply recording a child's language output and having it read back to the teacher. One frequently hears comments such as, "After he has read his story, what more can you do with it without boring him to death?" or, "The group readily dictates story after story, but can't remember the words from one day to the next."

Part of the problem noted above relates to a general dichotomization so frequently perceived between language experience and basal reading (or programmed) systems. On the one hand, the view is held that learning to read is a holistic process, on the other, that the process involves a tightly sequentialized building of skill upon skill. It seems clear that neither system in its "pure" form can be effective for the greatest number of children. The answer seems to lie either in incorporating a number of language experience components into a basal system or in monitoring skill development within the language experience program. This chapter provides some ideas on how to approach the latter problem, especially in relation to the development of reading skills.

Frequently, balance in skill development suffers from a lack of planning beforehand what the total language arts program is supposed to accomplish for children. This means that teachers will bear in mind, in planning a program, specific areas (both cognitive and affective) to be developed. A close consideration of "readiness" to learn at all levels is also implied.

DIAGNOSTIC ASSESSMENT OF READING READINESS

At the beginning level, the child might well fail to remember *any* of the words from an experience chart. What are some of the prerequisites or "readiness" considerations to be borne in mind before too much attention is devoted to remembering words in print?

Listening: Auditory Processing (Sentence Level)

Before a child is ready to grapple with the formal reading task, it is essential that he possess a level of competence in the receptive skill areas. Foremost of these is competency in listening. Questions like the following should be considered:

1. Is the child able to listen with pleasure to picture books and stories read to him?
2. Is he able to respond to simple directions?
3. Is he able to recall a simple sequence of events from a story or an experience related by someone else?

Auditory Discrimination and Perception (Word Level)

Below are some questions to assess a student's auditory discrimination and perception development.

1. Is he able to hear differences in words? For example:
   a. Are these words the same or different: wet, pet? (beginning)
   b. Are these words the same or different: pet, pit? (middle)
   c. Are these words the same or different: tab, tap? (ending)
2. Is he able to recognize and identify rhyming words?
   a. Level One:
   Listen to these words: mad, bad, bid, sad
   Which word is different?
   b. Level Two
   Listen to this word and give a word that rhymes: fit
   c. Level Three:
   It falls from the sky and rhymes with *train*
   I am thinking of _____.

(Note the importance of integrating meaning and the rhyming aspect of words.)

Oral Language

It is impossible to separate the assessment of oral language from listening competencies because one is a natural outcome of the other. However, because one is receptive and the other expressive, pedagogically it makes sense to give each separate attention. There is no need to document the absolute necessity of a sound experiential-oral language as a prerequisite for successful reading. Some of the most crucial skills are presented here:

1. Is he interested in communicating ideas and feelings?
2. Is he able to use a variety of words to express ideas and feelings?
3. Is he able to recall and use new words related to new experiences?
4. Is he able to express ideas using complete sentences (for the most part)?
5. Is he able to organize his expression of ideas with respect to sequence?
6. Is he able to express simple interpretations (as opposed to isolated identifications of pictures)?
7. Is he able to supply endings to simple stories?
8. Is he able to recall from stories read to him:
   a. The general sequence of events?

  b. The main idea?
  c. The names of the main characters?
9. Does his speech reflect normal intonation patterns with regard to:
  a. Pitch: in relation to inflection signaling questions, etc.?
  b. Stress: in relation to key signal words in his language like
       "but," "because," etc. (as well as appropriate accent)?
  c. Juncture: in relation to appropriate chunking or phrasing of
       language as opposed to random chunking or isolated word
       calling?

Intonation patterns are frequently disregarded in considering readiness for reading. If one believes that reading is, at least in part, a process of anticipating what follows what in a sequence of words, intonation patterns play a significant role in this anticipation and predicting process.

Visual Discrimination and Perception

While it is true that the visual components of reading have often been over-played at the beginning reading stages, certain visual competencies of the child need to be taken into account. For example:

1. Is he able to get clues from pictures regarding action, relationships, mood, etc.?
2. Is he able to recognize differences in shape and size?
3. Is he able to distinguish differences in letter and word forms, e.g.:
  a. Level One (letters):
     To select the letter in the box that is the same as the one in the margin:

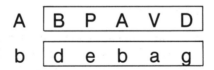

  b. Level Two (dissimilar words):
     To select the word in the box that is the same as the one in the margin:

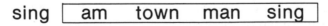

  c. Level Three (similar words):
     To select the word in the box that is the same as the one in the margin:

fall | fail   fain   fell   fall |

4. Is he able to hold in memory differences between letter and word forms? For example, Flash the letters and words in the margins above for 2 seconds (either on cards or overhead projector) and ask the child to circle the corresponding letter or word in the box.

Cognitive-Basic Literacy Concepts

Only the basic questions regarding literacy concepts as prerequisites to reading are posed here (more details are found in Chapter 10):

1. Is he aware of the purpose of reading as communication means expressing ideas, feelings, messages, stories, etc.?
2. Is he able to recognize and differentiate among the basic linguistic concepts:
   a. Letters?
   b. Words (and letters in relation to words)?
   c. Sentences (and words in relation to letters)?
   d. Numbers?
   e. Concept of sounds?
One way of determining the child's competence in this area is to administer items like the following:

Draw a line around each number in the box:[1]

| y   5   2   m |

Draw a line around each letter in the box:

| cheese   t   go   e |

Draw a line around each word in the box:

| the   boy   ran   down   the   hill |

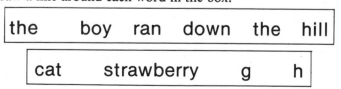

| cat   strawberry   g   h |

---

[1] Printed with permission from Downing, J., Ollila, L., Braun, C., and Evanechko, P. *The Canadian Readiness Test.* (unpublished manuscript).

Other means of determining the child's knowledge of word boundaries is to ask him to cut off all the words from a strip of paper with a sentence on it, or simply ask him to point to words in a book with fairly large print. The relationship of these types of measures to Piagetian psychology has been demonstrated by Froese (1976).

3. Does he automatically move his eyes in a left-to-right direction beginning on the left-hand side of the page?
4. Is the child able to make some association between the spatial arrangement of words and the temporal flow of oral language? For example:
   a. In the sentence, "The dog barks," point to the words "dog," "barks."
5. Is he curious about labels and signs to the point of recognizing some and asking about others?

Social-Emotional Aspects

Below are some questions to assess a student's social-emotional development in relation to reading readiness.

1. Is he able to share in some activities with other children?
2. Is he interested in listening to others as well as sharing his ideas?
3. Is he able to select some activities independently?
4. Is he able to sustain attention to these activities for 5 minutes or more:
   a. Without teacher attention?
   b. With teacher attention?
   It is important to take note of attentional factors both with respect to activity that involves a lot of action (gross motor) and activity that is more cognitive in nature (fine motor, such as looking at books and working with puzzles).
5. Is he able to listen to a story with sustained attention for at least 10 minutes?
6. Can he cope with minor stresses without more than momentary frustration?
7. Does he show other signs that he wants to read?

The teacher would do well to put items like the ones discussed above into a checklist (see Table 1), one for each child, noting specific areas of strengths as well as weaknesses.

Table 1. Sample checklist for beginning reading readiness

Name: _____ Date: _____			
Skill area	Seldom or never	Usually	Always
I. Listening			
1. Enjoys picture and story books	_____	_____	_____
2. Responds to simple directions	_____	_____	_____
II. Auditory discrimination and perception			
1. Hears differences in words			
a. Beginning	_____	_____	_____
b. Middle	_____	_____	_____
c. Ending	_____	_____	_____
2. Recognizes and identifies rhyming words			
a. Level One	_____	_____	_____
b. Level Two			
c. Level Three			
III. Oral language			
1. Interested in communicating ideas and feelings	_____	_____	_____
2. Uses a variety of words	_____	_____	_____
IV. Visual discrimination and perception			
1. Gets clues from pictures regarding action, etc.	_____	_____	_____
2. Recognizes differences in shape and size	_____	_____	_____
V. Cognitive-basic literacy concepts			
1. Recognizes the purposes of reading	_____	_____	_____
2. Recognizes the basic linguistic concepts			
a. Letters	_____	_____	_____
b. Words	_____	_____	_____
c. Sentences	_____	_____	_____
d. Numbers	_____	_____	_____
e. Sounds	_____	_____	_____
VI. Social-emotional			
1. Shares in activities	_____	_____	_____
2. Shows interest in listening to and sharing ideas	_____	_____	_____
3. Selects activities independently	_____	_____	_____

INSTRUCTIONAL PROGRAMMING
COMMENSURATE WITH NEEDS

A note of caution seems in order here. There is no suggestion here to delay transcription of the children's ideas into chart form until they have all the competencies suggested above. The contrary, in fact, is the case. The teacher can capitalize on a wide use of such experiences not only to determine readiness but also to teach many of the competencies requisite for formal reading. The only concern is that undue expectancies regarding independent reading and recall of words are not imposed on the child until he is ready. Such impositions are too prone to lead to frustration, wrong impressions of what reading is, and, generally, a sense of failure. This is not the place to expound on the difficulties involved in "unlearning" a negative self-image; however, that concern is paramount.

It has already been mentioned that the children's reading performance on an experience chart yields excellent feedback to the teacher about competencies that need to be developed with particular children. The following story is used to illustrate the point:

> On Monday we went to the ranch. It is Mr. Dale's ranch. Mr. Dale let us see the cows and bulls. He let us see his prize bull. Mr. Dale is very proud that he has a prize bull. It was a big scary thing. Like the bulls in the Calgary Stampede. Mr. Dale's ranch is real neat.

Using the "Sample Checklist for Beginning Reading Readiness" (Table 1), the teacher may note the children who have special difficulties with, say, auditory processing and then design instructional strategies accordingly.

Listening: Auditory Processing—Skill Development

Sequence   After the teacher has read the story with the children, she may probe them with questions related to sequence, e.g., "What time of day did we go to Mr. Dale's ranch?" "What happened as soon as we arrived?" "What was the first thing we saw?" "What happened after that?" etc.

For children from environments with limited structured activity (and thinking), or for slow learners, it is helpful to take snapshots of each event of a sequence (as in the excursion to the ranch) and to ask the children to arrange the snaps in the order of events while the teacher discusses the sequence, e.g., "Which picture shows what happened *first, second, after that, ...*" and so on.

Main Idea   The teacher gives children very brief experiences talking about the main idea, "What is the story about" or, "What is a good title for our story?" She encourages careful listening as children check, as she reads, whether each statement is about the title they have decided on.

Critical Interpretation   The teacher asks children (if they are living in the city or in a region where ranching is not possible) questions like, "Why couldn't your father do what Mr. Dale is doing?" "What do you think happens to the livestock when it leaves Mr. Dale's ranch?" and so on.

Auditory Discrimination and Perception—Skill Development

Beginning Consonants   The teacher might read a sentence from the chart, e.g., "Mr. Dale is very proud that he has a prize bull." She may then say, "There is another word that begins the same as 'proud.' Listen as I read the sentence and clap when I read the word. Let's listen to the words 'proud,' 'prize.' Say the words to yourself and feel your lips with your hand as you get ready to say the words and listen to the beginning of the words. What other words begin the same?"

It is a good idea to bring in meaning clues for the children who are ready. For example, "It begins the same as 'proud.' It is a farm animal with a curled-up tail. It is a _____."

Rhyming Elements Again, the teacher uses words from the experience chart as a basis for extending the concept of rhyming elements.

The bull belongs to Mr. Dale.
It is not for _____(sale)_____.

Oral Language—Skill Development

Vocabulary Extension   "What word did we use in the story to talk about Mr. Dale's bull?" "What other words can we use to show what kind of bull he was?" The teacher uses question probes related to size, e.g., huge, monstrous, etc. She also encourages use of simile, "As big as a _____." Other probes might relate to color, movement, etc.

Interpretation   "Why did Jack say that Mr. Dale was proud?" "Should he be proud? Why?" "Why is Mr. Dale's bull like the ones in the stampede?" "Why did Jack call it a prize bull?"

Syntactic Awareness For many children, there is little need to place much emphasis on this aspect of development in a formal sense, especially if their listening skills are well developed. For some, however, short interesting lessons are in order; e.g., some children tend to be more redundant than is necessary because they have not developed skill in even the simple co-joining transformations. The teacher might take two sentences like the following:

> Mr. Dale let us see the cows.
> Mr. Dale let us see the bulls.

"Susan told us these same ideas in one sentence. Let's listen to the sentence." Give further practice in this kind of co-joining. There is some experimental evidence that sentence-combining practice facilitates linguistic development (Mellon, 1969; Mulder, 1975; O'Hare, 1967).

Some children at this level experience difficulty with the use of the possessive form. Again, the teacher might ask questions like, "What does Jill mean when she says, 'It is Mr. Dale's ranch'?" The opportunities generated from a chart are endless.

Using Words to Denote Sequence Ability to follow sequence is, of course, first and foremost a listening skill. However, it is possible for a child to be able to follow sequence and yet not aware of key words that signal sequential organization when expressing ideas. It is useful for these children to get experience, using their dictated stories, to do a group project deciding on the kinds of words they might use to signal sequence, e.g., "*First* we ..., *then* we ..., *soon* we ..., *later we* ..., *before long* ...," and so on.

Visual Discrimination and Perception—Skill Development

Discrimination The teacher gives children their own copy of the story and asks them to perform tasks like the following:

"Find three words in the story that begin the same as 'story.' Draw a line under the beginning letter of each word."
"Find all the words that look like this. . .'the.' Underline them."
"Look at the words 'bull' and 'bulls.' Cross out the letter in 'bulls' that is extra."
"Draw a line under all the words that have one or two letters."
"Draw a line under the four longest words."

Memory The teacher puts some of the words from the chart on a large chart (especially some of the words she has used for discrimination exercises) and says, "In sentence one, find this word. . .

'went.' Underline it.'' (Flash the word for about 2 seconds.) Additionally, the teacher might make up memory exercises like this:

Give the children a series of words in boxes.

star	scary	school	scat

"Find this word . . . 'scary' in the box." (Flash the word for about 2 seconds.)

Cognitive-Basic Literacy Concepts—Skill Development

Purposes of Reading   Probably the most important developmental activity here is that the child pay close attention to the teacher's transcription of speech into print. Teachers can do much to dramatize what is happening by monologuing as they are transcribing and making sure that children both "hear and see" what she is doing. Furthermore, activities like sending a copy of an experience home with comments such as, "Now your parents can read about our trip to the ranch" go a long way in emphasizing the communicative purposes of print.

Basic Literacy Concepts (Language of Literacy)   A chart provides many opportunities for rich experience on the development of literacy concepts. Activities like the following are illustrative only:

"I will point to each *word* in the first *sentence* as we read together." Give the children a strip of paper containing the first sentence. Ask them to cut it up and put the pieces back together again, observing the chart model. Discussion of "How many words in the sentence," "Find the first word," "Find the last word in the sentence" are useful. "Put a line under each word in the last sentence." "Find another word that begins with the same letter as 'see.'" (Note that this is as much visual discrimination as it is development of cognitive aspects of literacy.)

Left-to-Right Sequence   Even if the children cannot read the words in the chart, it is wise for the teacher to read with them, sweeping her hand along the line using very decisive left-to-right motions. It may even be useful to color the left margin to emphasize it's starting function. The use of overheads in enabling children to follow left-to-right sequence as the teacher sweeps her hand under the print is valuable because overhead exposure tends to reduce a lot of extraneous stimulation. Thus closer attention is achieved.

Teachers should not forget the tremendous importance of exposing young children to many books. They should be encouraged not only to listen but also to follow along as the teacher reads. This is possible only with small groups unless the pages are projected on an opaque projector. Many schools, however, are also employing the services of parent volunteers and peers to perform this important function. Further suggestions related to aspects of literacy development are given in Chapter 10.

These examples for diagnostic-corrective teaching are by no means meant to be exhaustive. They are presented only to show how informal diagnosis and good teaching go hand in hand to ensure a balance in basic reading-readiness skill development.

DIAGNOSTIC ASSESSMENT
OF NEEDS OF BEGINNING READERS

There is no fixed day that one can say of a child, "He began reading today." The multiplicity of skills and the complex integration of visual-auditory-cognitive factors interplaying precludes such observation. Indeed, the child who is interpreting a picture or associating meaning with labels is reading in the truest sense. The key, of course, is association of *meaning* with pictures or symbols—no less.

Even if the child already is able to read charts like the one presented earlier with some degree of fluency, there is no guarantee that the needs of one child will be the same as that of another child. Indeed, the contrary is likely. This dictates the need for continuous alertness on the part of the teacher regarding cues that signal difficulties or potential difficulties that will keep the child from wanting to read. After all, this is the key to reading success because it is likely that only while the child is reading is he actually learning to read. The teacher's job is to make that task easier and more approachable for him.

Alertness denotes a teacher's awareness of what skills constitute the components of reading. In this way she can persistently check strengths and weaknesses of the reader. Whether this is done on the basis of a mental checklist or a more formalized record-keeping system will depend on the competence and confidence of the individual teacher. For purposes of clarifying the point, skill areas are discussed below with respect to scope and diagnosis.

Word Recognition Skills

Sight Vocabulary Most children develop beginning sight vocabularies as they are exposed to a rich environment of books, charts, interesting verses, and so on. Sometimes in the early stages they do well with some words but not with others. The teacher needs to assess specific aspects such as the following:

1. Is he able to recall:
   a. most words?
   b. only interesting content words (nouns)?
   c. polysyllabic words?
   d. function words (articles, conjunctions, etc.)?

   Is he able to recall each class of words above automatically? (Generally with less than a 2-second hesitation.)
2. Is he able to identify words in varying contexts?

Word Analysis (Phonic)

1. Is he applying and integrating auditory and visual discrimination skills? (Referred to under readiness assessment.)
   a. beginning consonants?
   b. consonants in final position?
   c. consonant clusters in initial positions (as in "block" and "clown")?

Word Analysis (Structural)

1. Is he able to make use of parts of words as an aid to recognition:
   a. in compound words (e.g., "into")?
   b. in inflectional endings ("s," "ed," "ing")?
   c. word part families (e.g., "all," "at," "ill," "ake," "or," etc.)?

Context Clues—Semantic and Syntactic

1. Is he able to use what he knows about oral language to make predictions about unknown words:
   a. Semantically? i.e., does meaning of part of a sentence signal possible words that could follow as in "up and _____","black and _____"; "a rainy _____"?
   b. Syntactically? i.e., does word order trigger clues to word identification as in "We saw the (a noun) ";"Karen called her (a noun) "; "The kittens were tired and (adjective) "?

These are but a few examples of the use of context clues in word identification. Certainly, normally semantic and syntactic cues work in combination to signal possible words that follow.

Integration of Phonic, Structural, and Context Skills

1. Is he able to integrage his oral language knowledge (semantic and syntactic and phonic and structural skills)?

In some of the foregoing examples, for instance, if he comes across the sequence "Karen called her m_____," does the reader's anticipated use of a noun and the "m" aid immediately in narrowing down the possible noun that it could be? The efficient reader makes use of syntactic, semantic, and visual cues in combination. Failure to achieve this results in problems later on.

Comprehension Skills

Literal Comprehension   If the young reader is using context clues for word identification, he has some level of comprehension.

1. Is he able to recognize:
   a. Details?
   b. Main ideas?
   c. Sequence?
   d. Characteristics of main characters?
2. Is he able to recall:
   a. Details?
   b. Main ideas?
   c. Sequence?
   d. Main characteristics of characters?

Inferential Comprehension

1. Is he able to make simple inferences? For example,
   "What do you think happened before?" "What do you think happened after?" (Given that some implied rather than explicit information has been given.)

Evaluative Comprehension

1. Is he able to make simple judgments? For example,
   "Could this story have happened in Timmins (assuming this is the child's home)? Why or why not?" "What sentence gives the best idea of what Tom is like?"
2. Is he able to respond emotionally to material he reads—fear, joy, sorrow, etc.?

The reader will find Barrett's *Taxonomy of Comprehension Skills* an excellent source as a check for levels of comprehension for all grade levels (see Smith and Barrett, 1974). Also, for the intermediate level, *Comprehension Strategies 1, 2, and 3* by Thorn, Braun, and Richmond (1973, 1974) provide excellent examples of comprehensive levels and appropriate questions and materials to develop comprehension at these levels. Some teachers may find it useful to construct a checklist of beginning reading skills (Table 2) like the one outlined for readiness skills (Table 1). The questions regarding word recognition and comprehension skills need merely to be put into condensed statement form.

Table 2. Sample checkist for early reading diagnosis

Name: _____	Date: _____		
Skill area	Seldom or never	Usually	Always
A. Word recognition			
I. Sight vocabulary			
1. Recognition			
a. Recalls most words	_____	_____	_____
b. Recalls interesting words	_____	_____	_____
B. Word analysis			
I. Phonic			
1. Integrates auditory and visual skills in identifying:			
a. Beginning consonants	_____	_____	_____
b. Consonants in final position	_____	_____	_____
II. Structural			
1. Uses word parts to aid recognition of:			
a. Compounds	_____	_____	_____
b. Inflectional endings	_____	_____	_____
III. Semantic-associational context clues			
1. Predicts unknown words from association of surrounding meaning clues			
a. Semantic clues	_____	_____	_____
b. Syntactic clues	_____	_____	_____
IV. Syntactic-graphic context clues			
1. Predicts unknown words from syntactic—graphic clues			
V. Integration of phonic, structural, and context skills			
1. Uses semantic, syntactic and phonic-structural clues in combination to unlock words	_____	_____	_____
C. Comprehension[a]			
I. Literal			
1. Recognizes			
a. Details	_____	_____	_____

Continued

Table 2. *continued*

Skill area	Seldom or never	Usually	Always
b. Main ideas	_____	_____	_____
2. Recalls			
a. Details	_____	_____	_____
b. Main ideas	_____	_____	_____
II. Inferential—uses implied information to			
1. Draw simple inferences	_____	_____	_____
III. Evaluative—uses information to			
1. Make simple judgments	_____	_____	_____
2. Respond emotionally to ideas in print	_____	_____	_____

^aIf the teacher finds that reading comprehension breaks down at any given level, she should determine the reason. The problem may be that the readability of the material used is too high or that the child has difficulty with the particular type of comprehension at a listening level. Immediate adjustments should be made.

CORRECTIVE TEACHING
COMMENSURATE WITH DIAGNOSTIC FINDINGS

We come back to the original problem: "What can I do with the chart story once we have read it together?" If the teacher is aware of what the normal skill expectations of the reader are (as outlined in the previous section), it is relatively easy to establish instructional priorities for individual children and groups of children. The aim here is to provide a few suggestions that may help in using the experience story to develop skills.

Word Recognition Skills

Sight Vocabulary   It is quite clear that the young reader will not become powerful unless he develops a ready sight vocabulary. This denotes not only that he can recall a word from one day to another but also that he can respond to it automatically. It is only this automatic response that makes it possible for him to use these sight words as a basis for predicting new words from context.

First this discussion deals with the child who is able to recall words but not with the automaticity that allows him to use them functionally. It is possible that the skills of visual discrimination and visual memory referred to in the readiness section are not quite as highly developed as necessary. The teacher should select words from the chart in which the student experienced the greatest amount of hesitation and prepare sets of word cards using highly similar words in each set. For example, if the difficult word is "ranch," the teacher would prepare a card like this:

```
1. rang
2. ranch
3. ran
4. reach
```

A good alternative is to prepare sets like this on transparencies and flash the words with the instruction before the flash, "Find the number of the word that is 'ranch.' " If the teacher is doing this with a group of children who need this practice, it is a good idea to use an "every pupil response" (EPR) technique. For example, she can provide each child with 3 x 5 cards each with a numeral from 1 to 4 on it (both sides). In this way all children can hold up, e.g., the card with "2" to show the teacher they know the correct response. An alternate EPR technique is to provide each child with a number fan (Figure 1.) The numerals again are written on both sides. The child simply points to the number of the response required, ensuring active participation on the part of all children.

Choral reading activities are most useful in developing facility and automaticity with words. This is so, especially if the teacher sweeps her hand underneath the line of print so that the children see the words as they "recite" together. Putting jingles, verses, or songs (even ones that children already know by heart) on the board or a transparency makes excellent material for this kind of learning activity.

Figure 1. A number fan. This technique is used by the Pyramid Title I School Project in Minneapolis, under the direction of John Manning.

Another technique useful for developing automaticity is to put words that require practice into various phase settings and use these in a fashion similar to the techniques described above. For example, four or five phrases from a recent chart story may be written on the board or transparency. The teacher can read them in turn and have the children show on their number fans which phrase has been read. Or, the teacher can flash phrases on the overhead projector and misread some and have the children indicate with "Yes" "No" EPR cards whether she was correct or not. For example, she might say, "I am going to flash a phrase. See if the phrase is 'on the reach.' " Flash the phrase "on the ranch" for a second or two and have children respond with their EPR cards.

Other means of developing automaticity include using difficult words in new but interesting contexts. Suppose that for three or four children the words that cause difficulty are: "scary," "prize," "went," and "the." The teacher might use these words and write short "stories" that include the children's names, e.g.,

> Jack, David, and Bill went to see the prize bull. David said, "The prize bull is scary, but it is not scary for me." Jack and Bill made a picture of the prize bull. The bull looked scary.

What some teachers do to help children read these "mini-stories" is to substitute pictures for some of the words that may cause difficulty. There are various games used to develop automaticity. Variations of "Bingo" are among the best because these require the children to look quickly for words.

So far the discourse has dealt only with the problems of automaticity. What about the child who has difficulty remembering words from one day to another? As mentioned earlier, the problem may be that he is not ready to read in the first place. In this case, the factors reviewed under "readiness" need to be re-assessed. Sometimes, however, the child recalls some words but not others. In this case, it is important to consider carefully the basic components or requisite competencies for good sight vocabulary development. Foremost is *meaning*. The child is more likely to acquire and to retain a word in print if it is "couched" in his experience and exists in his listening-speaking vocabulary. The greater the degree of meaning, the more likely he is to capture the word as his own in print (Brescia, 1975). This, of course, is the basis for enriching children's experiences with words and ideas. The more associations in terms of visual, auditory, tactile, taste, and smell a word holds for a child, the greater the retentive quality.

The North and South-Central Pyramid Title Project designed by John Manning in Minneapolis, Minnesota, employs various excellent procedures to aid children in the retention of sight vocabulary. Children are given a sheet of paper with target words which they number for use with EPR methods (Figure 2). After the teacher has given the children instruction with the words using EPR techniques (children responding both to graphic and meaning cues), the children fold the paper over the dotted line. They are then instructed to look at a word, pronounce it, and then to turn the paper to expose the blank lines and write the word by memory. Then they check back for accuracy. If there is an error, they re-write the total word rather than erase the error.

The foregoing, rather copious, treatment of sight vocabulary instruction is justified in that it demonstrates how the teacher can use diagnostic feedback from the day-to-day productions of thè children and plan instruction commensurate with this feedback. It is beyond the scope of this chapter to treat each of the areas detailed in the diagnostic assessment to the same extent. A few more examples follow.

Integration of Phonic, Structural, and Context Skills   It is only too common to find children who blunder along a sentence, picking in cafeteria-style one word by sight, sounding out the next two, another by sight, and so on. The child has not learned the first thing about reading, including the notion of what reading is: using grammatical, meaning, and graphic cues to discover the meaning communicated by the author. It is important for the teacher to have available a variety of teaching devices to help the child use these resources in an integrated fashion. A few examples follow.

Name: _____ Date: _____
2   proud
4   ranch
1   prize
3   stampede
5   neat

Figure 2. An aid for retaining sight vocabulary. This technique is used by the Pyramid Title I School Project in Minneapolis, under the direction of John Manning.

Exercises like the following help children to use a combination of sight vocabulary, grammatical, and meaning cues because only certain words fit grammatically into the slots.

Mark the word if it fits into this sentence,
"A fish can _____."

move	man	draw	splash
swim	doll	glide	blue
hit	talk	my	fall

An activity like the one above can often be used by readers who know only a few of the bottom words. A weak reader can be paired with a stronger reader, or the words can be tape-recorded.

Using the same cloze sentence, the teacher may find it necessary to aid a particular child in combining the use of context and initial consonants. He may present the sentence, "A fish can _____" with no letter cues for the cloze. The child predicts that it can be "swim," "dive," "splash," etc. The teacher then says, "A fish can s_____" (giving an audible as well as a visual cue). This can be extended to indicate that this eliminates "dive" but still leaves the possibility of either "swim" or "splash," which requires further cueing.

If the teacher sees the need for extended practice in the integration of word family (structure—auditory and visual) cues in relation to meaning cues, she might pick words from the chart story and follow a procedure like this: Prepare phonogram cards on strips about 3" × 16"[2]

neat/	beat	seat	heat
	1	2	3

The first word, "neat," is the key word. Using EPR fans, the teacher says to the children, "Look at the first word, 'neat.' Which word (pointing to the number 1, 2, or 3) rhymes with neat and means the opposite of 'cold'; which word rhymes with neat and means 'to win?' " If the aim is to give additional auditory (beginning consonant) practice, the question might be, "Point to the number of the word that rhymes

---

[2] Used in the Minneapolis Pyramid Title I Program.

with 'neat' and begins the same as 'same.' '' It is wise for the teacher to write the cue statements on the back of the strip beforehand.

Activites that involve integration of the structural (graphic) and syntactic elements include practice focusing on inflectional endings as both meaning and visual elements. For example, children might be given sets of words like "ranch" and "ranches" and instructed to note the difference in endings (visual). Then, they might underline the letters in the one word that tell that there is more than one. Or, given the set "look" and "looked," they might be instructed to compare the words visually and then to underline the part of "looked" that means that something happened before.

Comprehension Skills

While a detailed account of teaching procedures related to comprehension problems is not included here, the teacher needs to note which children are simply saying words and which children are comprehending them. Certainly, intonation patterns sometimes signal that a child is merely calling words. There is little value in asking literal comprehension questions related to the chart story because, hopefully, all children are involved in one way or another in the production. However, if a child makes nonsensical miscues in his reading such as substituting a verb for a noun or substituting words that do not fit semantically, he is obviously not comprehending. Probably, the best way of intervening in a situation like that is to allow the child to listen to his taped reading and to detect his own errors. Furthermore, he likely needs more of the integrated phonic-structure-context work outlined earlier. It is also useful to provide extensive practice involving reading for answers to specific questions, e.g., "Find the words that tell *where* we went." "Find the word that tells *how* Mr. Dale felt about his prize bull."

Skills such as main idea should be developed at this level, using the personal experience stories. The teacher should note which children are never able to volunteer titles for their stories. The kind of experience that might be provided for them initially would be for the teacher to suggest three alternative titles, two of which are totally obscure, and then to probe children as to *why* the one makes the most appropriate title. For some children, it is necessary to examine each statement in terms of "Does this go with (or talk about) the title?" For children who persist in having difficulty with this kind of "thinking" strategy, the teacher can provide corrective instruction in classification using pictures. For example, a series of cards with pictures of transportation modes (cars, trains, ships, etc.) can be used. The problem is, "All these pictures show someting that is *used* for _____." So, "travel" or "transportation" becomes a suitable title. A further extension may involve finding subclassifications, each with a separate title (or main idea), e.g., "land travel," "air travel," and so on.

The kinds of charts that evolve from field trips, science experiments, or classroom cooking and mixing projects provide excellent raw material for developing sequencing skills. Most children possess these skills but are not always clear about what is demanded when they are asked to "sequence" or "put in the right order." For this reason and for the sake of building strong awareness of key sequence signal words, it is well for the teacher to use questioning strategies that emphasize sequence vocabulary. For example, "What did we do *first?*" ... "*second?*" ... "*then?*" ... "*following this?*" ... "*last of all?*" and so on. When children encounter chronologically organized material, awareness of these sequence words provides the structure or organization for their reading. The importance of awareness of these words for organization in written expression is obvious. What can be done to aid in developing sequence is to cut the chart story into sentence strips and have the children find the sentence that tells what happened first ... second ... and so on.

It is certainly possible to use the chart story to develop inferential and evaluative skills. Asking children to infer feelings when these are not stated is one example. It is, however, at least as important that these skills are developed at this level through interesting stories that the teacher reads to the class. In other words, the important task is to focus on these skills more at a listening than a reading level for the young child. This will provide a basis for these skills at a reading level as the demands arise.

SUMMARY

The intent of this chapter has been to emphasize the need for a continuous interplay between diagnostic feedback that the teacher receives from a child's everyday performance and the sensitive programming for corrective and preventative purposes. In other words, the teacher designs instruction according to specific rather than general needs. Furthermore, the intent has been to emphasize the continuous interplay among the language arts skills—listening, speaking, reading, and writing—as a means of strengthening both word identification and comprehension skills.

LITERATURE CITED

Brescia, S. 1975. A study of the relationship between associative verbal encoding and sight vocabulary acquistion and retention. Unpublished master's thesis, The University of Calgary, Canada.

Froese, V. 1976. The interrelationship of conservation, reading readiness, and intellectual maturity measures in first graders. Read. Horizons 16(4):234–238.

Mellon, J. C. 1969. Transformational Sentence-Combining: A Method for Enhancing the Development of Syntactic Fluency in English Composition. Research Report No. 10. National Council of Teachers of English, Urbana, Ill.

Mulder, J. E. M. 1975. A study of the effects of sentence-combining practice on linguistic performance of adult learners. Unpublished master's thesis, The University of Calgary, Canada.

O'Hare, F. 1967. Sentence Combining: Improving Student Writing Without Formal Grammar Instruction. Research Report No. 15, National Council of Teachers of English, Urbana, Ill.

Smith, R. J., and Barrett, T. C. 1974. Teaching Reading in the Middle Grades, Addison-Wesley, Reading, Mass.

Thorn, E., Braun, C., and Richmond, I. 1973. Comprehension Strategies 2. Gage Educational Publications, Toronto.

Thorn, E., Braun, C., and Richmond, I. 1974. Comprehension Strategies 3. Gage Educational Publications, Toronto.

chapter 6

Language Experience for the Culturally and Linguistically Different Child

David Olshin

The culturally and linguistically different child often encounters a doubly difficult situation in school. Many of the published materials do not reflect either the experiences or the language of these students. Consequently, lack of interest and poor performance in language-related activities often set in. While the learning of Standard English is a worthwhile objective, it does provide additional problems. This chapter deals with these problems.

First, the terminology and rationale for using a language experience program with the culturally and linguistically different child is discussed. Then specific teaching suggestions are presented for the use of the children's own experiences, for oral-aural language development, for sequential teaching, for habituation and learning, and for sources of materials. Finally, a brief and selected outline of features of nonstandard English is presented for the teacher's information.

A NOTE ABOUT TERMINOLOGY

The terms "culturally deprived," "culturally disadvantaged," "culturally different," and "linguistically different" are used interchangeably in this article. For practical purposes they often have been treated synonymously in the literature, although this author believes that they are, in fact, not synonymous. This author prefers the latter two terms, which are more accurate and more current.

Characteristics of Culturally and Linguistically Different Children

It is not this author's intention to discuss characteristics that have been thoroughly described elsewhere (e.g., Black, 1965; Deutsch et al., 1967; Riessman, 1962). However, it is important to offset some unfortunate connotations about culturally and linguistically different children that have developed over the years.

As Bergeson and Miller (1971) have stated, these children are not nonverbal, do not lack experiences, and are not culturally disadvantaged. They do possess language, but it is not standard, middle-class English. They come to school with perhaps as many experiences as other children but not the experiences that appear to be critical in achieving academic success. While they may be deprived or disadvantaged in a number of ways, that is, socioeconomically and educationally, culturally different children do possess a rich cultural heritage in most cases. The major difficulty is learning how to handle the scholastic demands of the dominant culture that is significantly different in many aspects from their own.

Riessman (1962) has written that the culturally deprived child is relatively slow at cognitive tasks but is not stupid. To balance the impression the reader might get from the above statement, it is necessary to consider some points made by Anastasiow (1971) in discussing the reconstruction of sentences from white standard English to black and poverty English. He notes that the black child who changes sentences to conform to his language is demonstrating normal cognitive functioning but is presenting the language product in a different form. There is no reason to believe that the same does not hold for other linguistically different children, including the Canadian Indian and the Spanish American child. There is the danger that teachers may inaccurately perceive these reconstructions as errors rather than as the child's display of ability to maintain meaning while processing a different form of language. Anastasiow suggests that "the child's reconstructions are examples of an active intelligence'' (p. 34). Linguistically different children are capable of adequate cognitive performance, particularly in the use of their own nonstandard English.

Teachers who may not be aware of the background of experience and knowledge that culturally different children bring to school will probably not be familiar with the often complex cognitive structure represented by that knowledge and experience. Much of what they know and have experienced does not appear to be related to the academic tasks demanded of them. It is the responsibility of the teachers to discover what the children know and to relate that knowledge to the tasks deemed essential by the school, one of which is certainly learning how to read. If teachers do not carry out their responsibility, they run the risk of labeling these children stupid and then teaching in a manner that will ''prove'' that label (Seng, 1970).

Teachers must also learn to understand the language used by culturally different children in order to develop meaningful communication and to provide a starting point for building on that language (Ponder, 1971). Although teachers should be accepting of and respectful toward the language and cognitive functioning brought to school by culturally different children, they will need to help those children acquire, eventually, the language and thought processes of standard English. For, as Loban (1971) points out, society exacts severe economic and social penalties from those who do not speak it. Eventually, then, there has to be a transition made from the nonstandard to the standard form of English, at least in situations where the standard form is the appropriate one. It is not a case of replacing the dialect or language of the children, but of adding to it. For important emotional and social reasons children need to retain their nonstandard dialect or native language.

WHY THE LANGUAGE EXPERIENCE
APPROACH FOR LINGUISTICALLY DIFFERENT CHILDREN?

Although not new, the idea that the language experience approach can be an effective method of teaching reading to linguistically different children has become prominent in recent years. Because, in effect, the children develop their own reading materials through the use of their own experiences and language, the language experience approach avoids the difficulty culturally different students face when they are confronted by standard English upon entering school. In addition, the various facets of language development—listening, speaking, reading, and writing—become integrated into a natural language arts program rather than having an artificially separated program of reading instruction or "English" instruction. Oral and written language are equally important in an integrated language arts program. While this is an advantage for most children, it is magnified with culturally different children.

As Cramer (1971) has noted, the language experience approach to beginning reading instruction, when properly carried out in the classroom, provides an ideal bridge between the language of the child and the language he will need to read. If the teacher in recording the stories dictated by the children uses their language as given, there will be an accurate and complete match of oral and written language patterns.

GENERAL PRINCIPLES OF LANGUAGE EXPERIENCE INSTRUCTION FOR CULTURALLY AND LINGUISTICALLY DIFFERENT CHILDREN

Language experience instruction for linguistically different children involves differences of emphasis rather than differences of substance. The principles discussed will also be applicable, to varying degrees, for children who are not linguistically different.

Using the Language Children Bring to School

Stress should be placed upon the use of whatever dialect of the language children already speak when they enter school. That language is used for many purposes: as a means of thought and exploration, as a way of expressing feelings and emotions, and as a way of adjusting to other people (Loban, 1971). Language, in a sense, becomes the children's "Linus blanket" in the strange and sometimes hostile world of the school.

Halliday's Models of Language Use   Halliday's models of language use (1969) describe the range of uses that language serves for children. Four of the models are discussed from the standpoint of particular relevance for linguistically different children at the time they enter school. These models should be given careful attention.

Interactional Model   The interactional model of language use shows a sense of the person in relation to others. Conversation may involve small-talk or a serious exchange, and it may come from a close relationship or from a simple acquaintanceship. A greeting between acquaintances such as "Hi. How are you today?" "Fine" demonstrates the interactional aspects of language. Both parties implicitly understand that nothing more than a brief salutation is meant, even though the second person may be feeling terrible and would like to tell someone all about his troubles.

Personal Model   The personal model demonstrates the use of language as a means through which children learn much about themselves in relation to other people. Through language, children discover their own individuality and also make that individuality known to others. The statement "Bill and me are best friends" already indicates the position of the child in relation to others. Children often test their place in relation to others through language, that is, oral-aural situations where they hear themselves talk and get feedback from others about their talk. Role-playing provides a natural setting for this kind of language use.

Heuristic Model   The heuristic model points out the use of language as a critical aid to children in their discoveries about the external world in terms of both time and space. Questions are devices children learn to use to confirm and to discover what they may not be entirely sure of: "Dad, did they have jet planes when you were a boy?" "They speak the same way in Canada and the United States, don't they?"

Representational Model   The representational model describes a vital function of language that children learn early. It can be used as a carrier of information, as a means by which children convey messages to others: "I don't feel so good." "What's wrong?" "My head hurts."

As Braun (1974) notes, Halliday's models have crucial implications for teachers. They provide a benchmark against which teachers can assess the range of language uses that children possess. Such information will enable teachers to make adequate decisions on the environmental stimulation needed to provide opportunities for the development of the full range of language use.

Culturally different children, as will all children, learn early in life Halliday's instrumental model of language use. They soon discover the utility of language for the satisfaction of their material needs. They may learn the regulatory model too well. Language can be used to manipulate the behavior of other people. By making demands they are asking that something be done for them by someone else. Of course, demands are also placed on them by adults and peers: "Stop that noise." "Give me the ball."

However, culturally different children may not learn Halliday's imaginative model. Very early in life children develop the rhythmic patterns of speech and song in environments rich in rhymes, songs, and stories. Culturally different children who lack that rich environment or who come from an environment that provides rhythmic patterns of speech and song at variance with the standard language will need help in acquiring these standard patterns. Teachers will have to act as a language model by reading many interesting books to the children so that they can pick up the intonations of standard English, as well as enriched vicarious experiences. Choral speaking or singing of nursery rhymes, jingles, etc., will aid in providing global musical aspects of standard English.

Dialect Differences and "Errors"   One of the major hazards facing children with a nonstandard dialect is that they are often penalized unjustly for their use of that nonstandard dialect. Perhaps the greatest source of penalty arises from what teachers frequently misconstrue as oral reading errors when, in fact, the difference in performance between linguistically different children and other children is dialectal. Consider this brief passage, first in standard English and then in nonstandard English:

> Robert is good in class when he feels like it.
> He likes to play with the boy that sits next to him in school.
> He asked the boy if he wanted to play.

> Robert be good in class when he feel like it.
> He like to play wif the boy what sit nex to him in school.
> He aks the boy did he wanna play.

To treat differences such as those illustrated above as errors is the quickest way to "turn off" linguistically different readers. However, before teaching can be effective, teachers must be aware of the differences between their standard English and the nonstandard English of their students. For this reason, an abbreviated description of features of nonstandard dialects is included in an Appendix to this chapter.

Emphasizing Oral-Aural Language Development

Hildreth (1964), in an article reviewing linguistic factors important in early reading instruction, stated that "reading is primarily a linguistic process, one which requires grasping sentence meanings primarily in an oral context" (p. 172). The more extensive children's oral language experiences are, the better their ability should be in understanding authors' meanings when they read. She suggests a total language arts approach by noting that experiences in reading and writing are extensions of experiences in understanding language from speaking and listening.

In discussing the reading difficulties of non-English-speaking youngsters, Hildreth declares that, without oral fluency, they will only be able to learn how to make associations between sounds and letters arbitrarily. As they learn to speak the syntactic units of standard English, they will learn to read.

To some extent, nonstandard oral language will need to be modified, even from the time children enter school. Loban (1971) makes the point that some of the phonemes in the English language will be difficult or almost impossible to pronounce unless children begin to practice them early. This refers particularly to the phonemes not in the dialects of linguistically different youngsters. Teachers will have to provide many listening experiences through short skits, riddles, and dialogues. Tape recorders should be used. Loban suggests taping the material twice, once in standard English and once in the nonstandard dialect with which the children are familiar. The purpose is to focus the children's attention upon differences; otherwise, they will not be heard. They must be helped to hear that the phonemes, morphemes, and usage are not the same.

Johnson (1971) advocates the teaching of standard English to black children who speak in a nonstandard dialect as a second or foreign language. The essence of second-language teaching is to identify the interference points between the native language and English and then to develop audio-lingual methods to handle those interference points. Interference is the tendency of linguistically different children to impose the phonological and grammatical system of their nonstandard dialect on standard English.

Standard English is taught as an alternate dialect. Johnson identifies five steps in the teaching process: 1) without any stigma being attached to their dialect, the children recognize the difference between nonstandard and standard English dialects; 2) the children need to hear the standard English sound or pattern being taught; 3) they must be able to distinguish between the standard English sound or pattern and the corresponding interfering sound or pattern in the nonstandard dialect; 4) they must be given drills, in totally nonthreatening situations, that help in the reproduction of the standard English sound or pattern; and 5) they must be given opportunities to use the standard English sound or pattern in their own speech.

Johnson also recommends extensive use of the tape recorder, especially with earphones, to focus the attention of the children on the standard English sound or pattern being taught. He feels that the students may be more attentive to the electronic device (tape recorder) than to the teacher. In addition, the tape recorder can present the standard sound or pattern being taught without variation once it is put on tape.

Philion and Galloway (1969) have studied the language of a group of Indian children living on Vancouver Island in British Columbia. From their observations, it appears that the social uses of language are well developed but the cognitive uses of language are significantly restricted. Language seems to be used primarily to control behavior, to express feelings and, to a degree, emotions, and to keep the social machinery of the home running smoothly. While these are all important uses of language, the crucial uses of language for education—to explain, to describe, to instruct, to inquire, to compare, to analyze, etc.—seem to be lacking. The teacher's instruction must emphaize that part of language that can only be acquired through verbal teaching—the knowledge, the meanings, the explanations, the ability to question in search of information. An effective language arts program for these Indian children will have to stress a continuing effort on concept development; that is, the expansion of meaning for limited and narrow concepts.

The Indian children studied learn effectively through a process of imitation. They imitate and rely on nonverbal cues to the exclusion of verbal exchanges necessary for language development. However, this highly developed ability to imitate can be used advantageously by the teacher through the provision of clear verbal models of desired responses. For example, the teacher encourages the children to speak in clear, complete sentences by providing a model of the sentence in clear intonation and diction. The models presented need to make use of connecting words and prepositions. Small words in sentences that are often not heard clearly must be stressed.

The highly developed ability to imitate can lead to the danger of merely parroting the names of words without understanding their meanings. As a consequence, the teacher needs to be sure that words always appear in a context meaningful for the children. This possible danger, along with possibly limited conceptual development, suggests that an important part of the language program should involve an emphasis on oral reading, the development of listening skills, and word games. The teacher should read many stories to the children and then discuss them with the children.

To sum up, the process is the same whether discussing early reading instruction for standard English speaking children or for linguistically different children. The teacher should help the student to develop a firm foundation of oral-aural language and, when appropriate, extend that language foundation by developing reading and writing experiences.

Concrete, Structured, and Sequential Teaching

Language is abstract and symbolic in nature. Language represents experience. It is not the experience itself, but language and cognitive development can be facilitated by the use of methods that capitalize on direct experiences. These can be experiences that children bring to school or they can be experiences provided by the school. The point is that language does not flourish in a vacuum.

In discussing Montessori and Piaget, Gardner (1968) points out that these two giants of education agree that children are capable of manipulating transformations and other mental operations only when they manipulate objects concretely. Cognitive development occurs in preschool children when they utilize their senses more or less simultaneously: when they can feel, taste, smell, see, and hear in their learning activities. Children will more easily learn the concept that apples and oranges are fruits by feeling, seeing, smelling, and tasting them than by merely looking at pictures or being told.

Russell (1956) notes that concepts are based on generalization and discrimination. Children must be able to generalize the similarities between apples and oranges, for example, in order to classify both of them as fruits. They must be able to discriminate the differences between them as well in order to know that they are members of differing subcategories of fruits. In other words, generalization involves the determination of common characteristics, while discrimination involves the determination of different characteristics. Together, they produce a concept. The implication for teaching is that learning activities must be structured in such a way that children will be guided toward the development of concepts. Structured teaching necessitates careful planning in order to avoid the chance of incidental learning that, for linguistically different children, is more apt to be non-learning. Activities must also be in sequence in order to avoid the possibility of haphazard instruction. If students are to acquire concepts through generalization and discrimination, there has to be a continuous relationship among the activities provided by teachers.

Eventually, the learning process will shift more from the concrete to the abstract, from direct experiences to vicarious experiences. It is neither possible nor desirable that one learn completely from concrete and direct experiences. There are not many who would want to learn about the great, white shark concretely and directly. Ultimately, then, one depends upon his ability to use language to enhance learning. All children, including culturally different youngsters, can and do develop the ability to learn at abstract levels, under guidance, even though they lack the environmental experiences.

Providing Opportunities for the Habituation of Learning

A basic tenet of teaching English as a second language (TESL) is to provide many opportunities over a long enough period of time for children learning English to become accustomed to the necessary oral language skills so that they can function more nearly the way English-speaking children function. Zintz (1975) states that it may take a year or more to teach the commonest sentence patterns with dialogue practice, substitution drills, etc. In some cases it might take much longer than a year. Young, non-English-speaking children must learn listening and speaking habits before they are put into formal reading of standard English. Drill methods are critical, then, for instilling and reinforcing language habits. The same is true for children who speak a nonstandard dialect of English, but perhaps to a lesser degree.

Instruction Procedures

The following suggestions for instruction attempt to incorporate and to apply the principles stated. The classroom program must reflect: 1) a social environment that stimulates continuous practice in language usage; 2) a setting rich in the experiences, things, and ideas represented by words; and 3) an adult example and help in the maturing of language skills (Smith, 1969).

As precisely as possible teachers should assess the range and degree of language differences of the children in their classroom. Patterns of needs should be determined for each child so that a profile of individual needs emerges. A speaking-listening atmosphere should be created with the emphasis on experimenting with language. Tape recorders used individually and in groups on an extensive basis, dialogues with small and large groups, and informal oral language experiences are helpful in accomplishing the initial diagnosis of instructional needs (York and Ebert, 1970). Later, as children begin to read experience stories, teachers should maintain frequent anecdotal records of each child's reading performance. These anecdotal records should be compiled as the child reads and should not be left to imprecise memory. The recording of right and wrong responses (for the teacher's record only) will comprise the basis for diagnostic teaching techniques.

Developing Experiential Background and Language

There are many ways of successfully structuring language learning environments. One such program (in Tucson, Arizona) is described by Lavatelli (1971). On the door of this first-grade classroom was posted a large, printed chart with pictures of yellow and red apples. The chart, read to the class by the teacher, greeted them good morning and informed them that they would be tasting apples that day. However, they did not taste the apples until everyone looked at them, touched them, smelled them, and told about seeing apple blossoms. Some of the class had even climbed an apple tree. Then the children cut into their apples and discovered the texture, juiciness, and degree of tartness or sweetness. All of this incited the use of language. The verbal interaction was guided by an adult who acted as a model for more complex language and a more discriminating vocabulary while responding to the children's questions and statements.

The next day the youngsters discovered their pictures of the apples accompanied by speech balloons with their comments, in their language, making a large "talking" mural. Following a reading by the teacher, the children read their balloons and those of their friends. They seemed so closely identified with the experience that they hardly differentiated whether the teacher read it to them or whether they read it themselves. Shortly thereafter, a new mural emerged about going to the store to buy apples and sugar to make applesauce. The applesauce mural was later reorganized into a large book, which the children could read and reread in the school library.

The teacher, in summary, plans carefully so that the experiences involve multiple sensory stimulation, arouse intellectual involvement, and provoke verbalization. Experiences are used, therefore, to stimulate both intellectual and language functioning in a nonthreatening, absorbing atmosphere. Again, while these experiences are important for all children, they are perhaps even more crucial for culturally different children.

Field trips are a time-honored way to develop experiences. Lavatelli outlines how a walking trip or a bus trip can be planned to develop the goal of awareness of time.

Walking Trip

1. Record the starting time and compare with the return time
2. Decide the time the youngsters have to start back and let one or two be the "clock watcher." (This gives the children who can tell time the opportunity to use their skill and provides status to that skill.)
3. Look for calendars, clocks, etc., in public places along the walk
4. Record conversations that occurred during the walk; record the events that occurred by using the conversations
5. Place the events in a time sequence
6. Observe the timing of traffic lights or policemen directing traffic
7. Plan to visit the home of a child; an invitation could ask the children to come at a certain time; decide when the group must start to get there on time

Bus Trip

1. Plan to meet the bus at a specific time; record the time and make sure that everyone is ready to leave at that time; being on time becomes a group responsibility
2. Point out signs that give the opening and closing times of public places: stores, museums, etc.
3. Ask the people who work in places visited which jobs must be done daily, weekly, etc.
4. Note the schedules kept by buses, trains, and planes; discuss the need to maintain schedules
5. Keep a record of the time of departure and return and figure out the time of the trip
6. Plan for the trip; keep track of the days on the calendar; carry out the plans for the trip
7. Anticipate what should be seen and done
8. Develop a time orientation for the trip: "*Tomorrow* we *are going* on the trip." "The day for our trip is *today*." "*Yesterday* we *went* on a trip."
9. Reconstruct parts of the trip in various ways: discussing it, drawing pictures, dramatic play, etc.
10. Take pictures; have the youngsters put them in time sequence; have them write a story about each one
11. Observe the speed of the bus: fast or slow? Faster or slower than ____? "How can we tell?"
12. Make the children aware that prior arrangements have to be made before the trip

13. Use a trip to a museum or some other place with "old things" to help the children develop an awareness of past history (the "olden days")

Again, the emphasis is on structure, so that the trip is planned and carried out to meet specific objectives. Language and thought are stimulated but in a manner that focuses on the development of specific concepts and skills. The field trip is not simply a nebulous activity done to stimulate a language experience story somehow.

The Tucson program is described as a systematized and accelerated, but "natural," method of teaching language. Children learn language by interacting with adults who model many syntactic elements in their speech and who respond to the comments of the children in a manner that will extend their language. The children process what they hear and deduce generalizations that they then attempt to use. The youngsters hear many examples of well formed sentences that are directed to them so that they must interact with the ideas expressed and then, in turn, react to the speaker with their own comments. The conversation must be two-way so that the children cannot help but be involved. They are actively engaged in listening and processing what is said (Lavatelli, 1971). Furthermore, much informal reading is happening, thus giving the children an excellent opportunity to develop the basic concept of reading as a communication process.

In the Tucson program, the teacher supplies the children with examples of grammatical elements suited to their levels of sophistication. She then reinforces them for their attempts to practice new syntactic patterns and for increased language awareness. To stimulate language, the children participate in varied activities. In addition to trips, observing animals, cooking, and experimenting in physical science, all provide opportunities for language use. The youngsters' statements about these experiences are recorded by the teacher, an aide, or perhaps the children exactly as said. The language samples are analyzed, and subsequent steps are planned. When the stories are reread, the teacher, in conversation directed toward the children, includes statements designed to serve as a model of the next higher level of language use without "correcting" or imposing restrictions on the children's output. She asks questions to elicit the higher level of language and praises the children for their attempts (Lavatelli, 1971).

The Tucson program, in summary, is based on interesting activities, such as various trips and cooking food in class, that will stimulate the children to converse. Positive reinforcement is provided to increase the use of language (nonstandard form first and then standard form). Stories dictated to the teacher or to a tape recorder encourage the children to talk and provide them with feedback on how well they are doing. Fall and Spring comparisons of the dictated stories or tapes help the teacher and children to assess progress and therefore serve as reinforcement.

Developing Language Skills with the Camera

Language skills can be developed in a variety of ways, using a variety of techniques and materials. One interesting method is to photograph children's experiences and to use those pictures to aid in the development of specific language skills. Hoehn (1964), a second-grade teacher at Sandy Bay Indian Reservation in Manitoba, describes a planned experience involving the process of butter-making.

Pictures of various stages of the process are used to provide additional input to the limited amount available during the actual activity of butter-making. For example, a picture of one student shaking a jar is shown to the class. The teacher asks, "How is Janice shaking the jar?" Words such as "energetically" or "vigorously" are introduced or reviewed. Descriptive vocabulary can be elicited or introduced. For example, "The butter tastes like _____." "It is as smooth as _____." "It is as soft as _____." Vocabulary can be expanded beyond speaking and listening. Once the pictures are mounted, space is left so that the children can dictate descriptive sentences for the teacher to record beneath the photographs.

The pictures can be referred to in order to aid in the recall and clarification of sequence. The teacher can jumble the pictures and ask the children to arrange them in order on the chalkboard ledge or desk. This can provide an opportunity to elicit oral discussion: "Why must picture three come before picture four?" This also provides an opportunity to develop connectives that are important in thinking, speaking, and writing: "First we poured the cream..., then we..., after that..., soon..., before long...," etc.

After discussing the sequence of the pictures, the children talk about "what the pictures are all about." "Let's put them into the correct order and make a book out of them." "What's a good name for the book?" The teacher then discusses why the title is appropriate and why certain suggested titles are not appropriate because they relate only to specific pictures rather than to the total sequence. Children who can read the recorded statements below the pictures are encouraged to rely more on the words and less on the pictures for the main idea. Main idea skills are developed first through listening and speaking and then transferred to reading. The same essential thinking components are common and critical to all three facets of the language.

Once the children have identified the main idea or "what it's all about," the teacher takes subsets of pictures and probes for ideas suggested by the subsets. For example, the first four pictures might deal with "preparing for butter-making." This becomes the first main heading, and the content of each of the four pictures becomes the supporting details. Content of immediate interest, based on relevant experience, provides a realistic starting-point for teaching the difficult skill of outlining.

The pictures can also be used to develop left-to-right progression. The teacher arranges them in logical order and moves along from left to right as the pictures are discussed. Later, the dictated stories are used to extend the same skill by incorporating words rather than pictures.

As Hoehn notes, the suggestions provide a mere sampling and by no means exhaust the possibilities for developing language skills. Photographs can be used for developing sight vocabulary, context clues (listening and reading), visual and auditory discrimination, etc. Daily classroom activities and the children's experiences provide the content and scope for skill development that can be augmented through the use of a camera.

Developing Transformations and Related Cognitive Skills

Linguistic flexibility or free use of varied transformation is one of the marks of a fluent speaker. Transformations are statements of semantic and phonological, as well as grammatical, connections (Lenneberg, 1967). Sentence transformations can be developed in ways more meaningful than merely giving isolated practice exercises. For example, certain types of transformations, such as past tense, can be better learned through discussions about children's previous experiences. Such discussions provide practice in talking about events and objects not present at the time of the discussions. A variety of sentence transformations can be stimulated.

If there are systematic guidance and direction, the practice in remembering past experiences can involve skills such as making associations among events, arranging events in sequence, and categorizing the events. Children can be aided to recall details in chronological order and to record them in sequence. These are skills important to learning how to read, in which the ability to anticipate what will happen next can help students to figure out new words. These skills also help in the ability to make predictions. Lavatelli (1971) cites the example of a second-grade class that peeled an avocado, ate it, and then planted the seed. By rereading the books they wrote about the experiences, they were able to retrieve the experiences and, along with the recall, they discussed what was going to happen. The children discussed what changes might take place in the avocado. They recorded their predictions and played them back during the next few weeks to check their predictions.

To develop the skills of categorizing and associating, teachers can ask specific kinds of questions. These questions can cover: a) characteristics of objects observed dealing with size, shape, and color; for example, statements comparing size can be elicited: "It's smaller than my hand." "It's bigger than my fingernail"; b) origins of objects: "Where do they come from?" "Are they natural or man-made?" and c) relations of objects to each other: "What are they used for?" "How are they used?" "How do they taste or feel or smell" (sensory characteristics)? Responses to discussion-type questions are recorded and can become the basis for group stories (Lavatelli, 1971).

It is not only possible but also preferable to develop other important language-thinking skills while teaching students sentence transformations. Language acquisition, then, is an integrated process rather than a fragmented one.

Substitutions Substitutions and expansions are two basic types of transformations. Teachers can aid in the development of these transformations through the following types of exercises:

Substitutions for oral practice

1. The $\left\{ \begin{array}{l} \text{restaurant} \\ \text{store} \\ \text{bank} \\ \text{park} \\ \text{house} \end{array} \right\}$ is down the street

The teacher models, "The bank is down the street." The class repeats. Small groups and individual students repeat. Then the teacher says only the word "store" and the class repeats, "The store is down the street." The teacher says "restaurant" and the class repeats, "The restaurant is down the street," etc. (Zintz, 1975).

2. Please ask Bill to
- turn the lamp on.
- turn on the lamp.
- turn the lamp off.
- put the lamp on the desk.
- leave the lamp alone.

3. How many
- books
- pencils
- chairs
- tables
- people
are there in the classroom?

Expansions   Basic sentence patterns, by being expanded, are made to serve various purposes. Children who speak standard English get much practice in this, but children who speak nonstandard English will require much help with the following types of exercises (Zintz, 1975):

1. The flowers are beautiful.
   The yellow flowers are beautiful.
   The yellow flowers in the vase are beautiful.
   I gave the yellow flowers in the vase to the woman who lives upstairs.
2. People sing.
   People sing loudly.
   People sing loudly every Sunday.
   We could hear the people sing loudly every Sunday.
   We could hear the people sing loudly every Sunday when
     we were in Church.
3. We can go.
   We can go tonight.
   We can go tonight for a while.
   We can go until seven o'clock tonight.
   We can go to the park until seven o'clock tonight.
   We can go to the park until seven o'clock tonight when
     it gets dark.

Developing other Language Skills

In addition to finding out what help is needed to transform kernel sentences to other forms, teachers have to analyze how culturally different children put sentences together in order to become aware of other specific needs in language training. They should observe how various parts of speech are used. Do the children use auxiliary verbs? Do they use nouns alone (bird), or do they attach objective modifiers (small, brown bird)? Do they use prepositions properly to denote relations of time, space, and logical position (Lavatelli, 1971)?

York and Ebert (1970) cite the example of a first-grade teacher of Mexican-American children who typically have great difficulty with prepositions. She spent a few minutes every day playing the preposition game. She used some common classroom object and let the children check to see whether the child who is "it" can correctly put the pencil *behind* the record player, *under* the round table, *beside* the acquarium, *over* the sink, *between* two red books, etc.

The teacher can elicit yes/no questions with a "20 questions" game to develop auxiliary verbs and inverted subjects. The development of concepts by making generalizations and discriminations can be aided by this type of game. The children have a collection of objects in front of them. The teacher says: "I'm thinking of one object, and you have to find out which it is. Ask questions that I can answer by saying yes or no." The children must name the objects first. The teacher can be the questioner when a child has an object in mind. In order to discover the properties of objects, the teacher and children should not use the name of the object; therefore, "Is it round?" not "Is it a ball?"

A variation of this game would be to have the children answer the questions in reference to a particular collection of objects (Lavatelli, 1971). The child is thinking of one object:

Teacher:	Child:
Does the object have a sharp point?	No, it is not the knife or pencil.
Does the object have paper around it?	No, it is not the crayon.
Does the object have round edges?	No, it is not the button.
Does the object grow in the ground?	Yes, it is the bean.

To aid in the development of auxiliary verbs and concepts, teachers can use different interrogative words—how, which, who, what, where, when, why—a variety of auxiliary verb modals—be, do, have—and some negative questions, e.g., "Which objects are made of two or more materials? How can you guess which ones will float or sink?" These can be elicited as a game in which children play in pairs. The first child thinks of an object in a collection and has to answer questions. The second child must ask who, what, and where questions. Example: Second child, "Where can you find this object?" First child, "Out of doors." Second child, "How big is it?'' (Answer in comparison to the collection.) First child, "It is small." Second child, "What can you do with it?" First child, "You can eat it." Second child, "It has to be the bean" (Lavatelli, 1971).

Complex noun phrases, nouns with modifiers and determiners, require precise description and definition of properties of objects. Teachers can describe objects by properties without using the names of the objects, e.g., "Touch the short, yellow object." "Give me the long, wide object." These descriptions or variations can be elicited by having children work in pairs. They are separated by a screen, but each child has the same collection of objects. The first child must describe each object so that the second child can identify it. No names are used, only descriptions of the properties (Lavatelli, 1971).

MATERIALS

Almost all the materials that would be generally appropriate in early reading instruction could be applicable in a program for linguistically different youngsters. It is not the materials, per se, that are critical but rather how they are used. Various hardware items such as tape recorders, tapes, earphones, film projectors, film strips, record players, records, etc., would be valuable. Manipulatives of different kinds would be extremely important. Various games, puzzles, and kits would have a significant place in the instructional process. Of course, an interesting and comprehensive variety of books should be available to be read by the children when they are able or to be read to them.

The following sources provide information on materials. The materials cover a variety of categories. Books listed that children cannot read for themselves should not be discounted. They can still be used for listening and discussion. The sources are presented in chronological order.

1. Zintz, M. V. 1975. The Reading Process: The Teacher and the Learner. 2nd Ed. William C. Brown, Dubuque, Iowa.
   On pages 423-424 Zintz gives a brief list of textbook series available for teaching English as a second language. On page 434 he lists sources to contact for bilingual materials. They are:
   The Center for Applied Linguistics
      1611 N. Kent Street
      Arlington, Virginia 22209

The U.S. Commission on Civil Rights
  Washington, D.C. 20425
Materials Acquisition Project
  2950 National Avenue
  San Diego, California 92120
Dissemination Center for Bilingual Bicultural Education
  6504 Tracor Lane
  Austin, Texas 78721

2. Laffey, J. L., and Shuy, R. (eds.). 1973. Language Differences: Do They Interfere? International Reading Association, Newark, Del.

  There are several articles in this publication that contain suggestions on books, materials, and exercises relevant to children who speak nonstandard English. Refer to articles by Pilon and Seymour, for example.

3. Cooper, D. 1971. The black man's contribution to change. In: J. B. Bergeson and G. S. Miller (eds.), Learning Activities for Disadvantaged Children, pp. 232–248. Macmillan, New York.

  On pages 238–248 Cooper presents a variety of materials and sources under the title of Afro-American Bibliography. Her bibliography is divided as follows: Biographical Sources, Biographical AV, Books, Book Lists, Films, Filmstrips, Records and Tapes, Multimedia, and Addresses for Afro-American Bibliography. The original article was published in the Instructor, Volume 78, March 1969, pp. 95–105.

4. Smith, M. B. 1971. Curriculum innovations for disadvantaged children—What should they be? In: J. B. Bergeson and G. S. Miller (eds.), Learning Activities for Disadvantaged Children, pp. 84–97. Macmillan, New York.

  Smith lists a number of materials and books, under several sections, on pages 93–97. Her first section is titled Developmental Materials and includes the suggested level of the materials. Her second section is titled Books for Parents. The third section is titled Books, About Heroes, Today and Yesterday. Information includes title, author, and publisher. The fourth section is titled Library Books with Urban Settings and includes title, author, publisher, and level. The fifth and last section is titled Trade Books with Rural Settings. Information includes title, author, publisher, and level. The original article was published in Teacher's College Journal, Volume 37, October 1965, pp. 7, 32–39.

5. Ornstein, A. C. 1967. 101 books for teaching the disadvantaged. J. Reading 10:546–551.

Ornstein divides his list into several sections: The Past Re-examined; Current Literature which Reflects our National Challenge; Music and Art; Poetry, Theater, and Literature; The Sports World; and Fiction and Short Stories. Information provided covers author, title, publisher, price and recommended levels. The levels include junior high school, high school, and for all ages. The junior high school levels range from fifth to ninth grade reading level and the high school levels start from the eighth grade reading level. A brief synopsis of each book is also included. The books are meant for Black and Puerto Rican children.

APPENDIX:
FEATURES OF NONSTANDARD ENGLISH

This Appendix consists of information taken from the following sources: Gladney and Leaverton (1971), Johnson (1971), Labov (1970), and Zintz (1975). The samples cited have been modified and simplified to a degree.

FEATURES OF NONSTANDARD BLACK ENGLISH

Phonological

Substitution of *d* for voiced *th* in the initial position ("dat for "that," "dem" for "them," "dis" for "this")

Substitution of *f* for voiceless *th* in the final position ("paf" for "path," "wif" for "with," "mouf" for "mouth")

Substitution of *v* for voiced *th* in the final position ("breav" for "breathe")

Rs usually eliminated in the final position ("do" for "door," "saw" for "sore," "pa" for "par")

Ls often eliminated ("toe" for "toll," "hep" for "help," "too" for "tool")

Rs often eliminated in the middle position ("pass" for "Paris," "Cal" for "Carol," "cat" for "carrot")

Simplification of consonant clusters in the final position to single consonants, particularly *t, d, s,* or *z* ("pass" for "past," "men" for "mend," "bock" for "box")

Weakening or deletion of constants in the final position, particularly *d* and *t* ("ba" for "bat" or "bad," "row" for "road," "feet" for "feed," "boo" for "boot")

Grammatical

Verb Usage

Present tense, third person singular, lack of agreement ("he run" for "he runs," "she go" for "she goes")
Present participle form, omission of copula (linking verb) ("he talking" for "he is talking," "they playing" for "they are playing")
Reversal of present and past participle forms, irregular ("I taken it" for "I took it," "I have took it" for "I have taken it," "I done it" for "I did it," "I have did it" for "I have done it" or "I did it")

Future Tense

"I am do it" for "I will do it"
Substitution of "be" for "is", "am," and "are" and in sentences describing a recurring event ("he be doing it" for "he is (always, usually) doing it", "I be scared when it be dark" for "I am scared when it is dark", "they be playing in the alley" for "they are playing in the alley"

Past Habitual

"She been doing it" for "She (always) used to do it."

Negation

"She ain't walked" for "She hasn't walked." "We don't got none" for "We don't have any."

Direct Question

"How he fix it?" for "How did he fix it?"

Indirect Question

"I asked (aksed) did he fix it" for "I asked if he fixed it."

Noun Plural

"Them book" for "those books," "mens" for "men"

Pronouns

"Us, got to go" for "We have to go."

Possessive

"John hat" for "John's hat." "They paper" for "Their paper."

Features of Nonstandard English of Spanish-Speaking Children

The following structural contrasts between standard English and the nonstandard English of Spanish-speaking children are adapted from *Teaching English as a New Language to Adults* (cited in Zintz, 1975).

Use of "not" with verb forms: usually replaced by "no," e.g., "Tom is no here."

Use of "s" in simple present tense: tendency to drop inflections, e.g., "The girl eat."

Negatives with "do," "does," "did": no auxiliaries, e.g., "She no go/went to school" for "She did not go to school."

Adjectives usually precede the noun in English: adjectives usually follow the noun, e.g., "The dress blue."

Express future time by use of "going to": tendency to substitute the simple present tense, e.g., "I go to dance" for "I am going to dance."

Use of auxiliary "will" in future tense: tendency to carry over the inflection, e.g., "I see you later" for "I will see you later."

Use of "it" to start a sentence: tendency to omit "it," e.g., "Is Monday" for "It is Monday."

Use of "to be" to express age: "to have" is substituted, e.g., "I have ten years" for "I am ten years old."

Use of "to be" to express hunger, thirst, etc.: "to have" usually used, e.g., "I have hunger" for "I am hungry."

Use of negative imperative: replaced by "no," e.g., "No talk" for "Don't talk."

Questions with "do," "does," and "did": no auxiliaries, e.g., "This woman works?" or "Works this woman?" for "Does this woman work?"

Indefinite article in usual prenominal position with words identifying occupation: indefinite article not required, e.g., "He is doctor" for "He is a doctor."

KEY DIFFERENCES BETWEEN
ENGLISH AND SPANISH FOR TEACHERS

1. English uses voicing (voiced versus voiceless sounds) to distinguish *s* from *z* as the only contrasting item to separate meanings of words. This is never the only feature to separate meanings in Spanish. Examples: price—prize; seal—zeal; lacy—lazy.

2. English uses the sound difference between *n* and *ng* as a way to distinguish meanings. Spanish does not. Examples: sin—sing; fan—fang; ran—rang.

3. Many new consonant blend sounds of English must be learned by Spanish-speaking children. Example: *sh* in shape; *wh* in when.

4. English uses many vowel sounds to distinguish meanings, while Spanish uses only five. Practice is needed to develop auditory discrimination of vowel sounds. Examples: mit—meet; heat—hit; eat—it; met—mate; late—let; tap—tape; hat—hot; look—luck; fool—full; sheep—ship; bed—bad; caught—cut; coat—caught; pin—pine.

5. Practice needed in auditory discrimination of consonant sounds and clusters. Examples: dig—big; then—den; thank—sank; pig—pick; place—plays. Also, clusters like *k* in *walked*; *p* in *helped*; *ts* in *bats*.

6. Minimal pairs. The difference of only one phoneme between a a pair of words is a minimal pair, e.g., *dill—fill*. All of the vowel contrasts in number 4 above and the consonants sounds in the first part of number 5 are minimal pairs.

7. Modifiers do not follow the noun in English. Examples: "The small boy," not "the boy small." In addition, "the railroad station" is not the same as "the station railroad." "The pocket watch" is not the same as "the watch pocket."

8. Word order in English sentences is not as flexible as in Spanish sentences.

Examples:	Literal translation:
Ayer vine aqui	Yesterday I came here
Ayer aqui vine	Yesterday here I came
Vine ayer aqui	I came yesterday here
Aqui vine ayer	Here I came yesterday

All are grammatically acceptable in Spanish, but they are not all correct in English.

9. After learning to generalize from regular forms, children can have problems with some irregular words: Examples: "I teared the book." "I throwed the toy."

10. Stress and intonation are important in conveying meanings. Examples:"Which dress did *you* buy?" "Which dress *did* you buy?" "Which dress did you *buy*?"

FEATURES OF
NONSTANDARD ENGLISH OF NORTH AMERICAN INDIANS

There is so much linguistic diversity among North American Indians that it is not possible to present features of nonstandard English that would adequately represent all the various dialects of languages.

LITERATURE CITED

Anastasiow, N. 1971. Oral Language: Expression of Thought. International Reading Association, Newark, Del.

Bergeson, J. B., and Miller, G. S. (eds.). 1971. Learning Activities for Disadvantaged Children: Selected Readings. Macmillan, New York.

Black, M. H. 1965. Characteristics of the culturally disadvantaged child. Read. Teacher 18(b):465–470.

Braun, C. 1974. Language and thought. In: E. A. Thorn and C. Braun (eds.), Teaching the Language Arts: Speaking, Listening, Reading, Writing, pp. 27–45. Gage Educational Publications, Toronto.

Cramer, R. L. 1971. Dialectology—A case for language experience. Read. Teacher 25(1):33–39.

Deutsch, M. et al. 1967. The Disadvantaged Child: Studies of the Social Environment and the Learning Process. Basic Books, New York.

Gardner, R. W. 1968. A psychologist looks at montessori. In: J. L. Frost (ed.), Early Childhood Education Rediscovered, pp. 78–91. Holt, Rinehart and Winston, New York.

Gladney, M. R., and Leaverton, L. 1971. A model for teaching standard English to non-standard English speakers. In: J. B. Bergeson and G. S. Miller (eds.), Learning Activities for Disadvantaged Children: Selected Readings, pp. 108–115. Macmillan, New York.

Halliday, M. A. K. 1969. Relevant models of language. In: A. M. Wilkinson (ed.), The State of Language. University of Birmingham School of Education.

Hildreth, G. 1964. Linguistic factors in early reading instruction. Read. Teacher 18(3):172–178.

Hoehn, R. E. 1964. Using the camera to aid language arts skill development. Manitoba J. Educ. 9(2):32–33.

Johnson, K. R. 1971. Teaching standard English. In: W. W. Joyce and J. A. Banks (eds.), Teaching the Language Arts to Culturally Different Learners, pp. 121–129. Addison-Wesley, Don Mills, Ontario.

Labov, W. 1970. Language characteristics: Blacks. In: T. D. Horn (ed.), Reading for the Disadvantaged: Problems of Linguistically Different Learners, pp. 139–157. Harcourt, Brace and World, New York.

Lavatelli, C. S. 1971. A systematized approach to the Tucson method of language teaching. In: C. S. Lavatelli (ed.), Language Training in Early Childhood Education, pp. 101–118. University of Illinois Press, Urbana, Ill.

Lenneberg, E. H. 1967. Biological Foundations of Language. John Wiley & Sons, New York.

Loban, W. 1971. Teaching children who speak social class dialects. In: J. B. Bergeson and G. S. Miller (eds.), Learning Activities for Disadvantaged Children: Selected Readings, pp. 98–107. Macmillan, New York.

Philion, W. L. E., and Galloway, C. G. 1969. Indian children and the reading program. J. Reading 12(7):553–560; 598–602.

Ponder, E. G. 1971. Understanding the language of the culturally disadvantaged child. In: W. W. Joyce and J. A. Banks (eds.), Teaching the Language Arts to Culturally Different Children, pp. 59–67. Addison-Wesley, Don Mills, Ontario.

138   Olshin

Riessman, F. 1962. The Culturally Deprived Child. Harper & Row, New York.

Russell, D. H. 1956. Children's Thinking. Ginn, New York.

Seng, M. W. 1970. The linguistically different: Learning theories and intellectual development. In: T. D. Horn (ed.), Reading for the Disadvantaged: Problems of Linguistically Different Learners, pp. 99–114. Harcourt, Brace & World, New York.

Smith, D. V. 1969. Developmental language patterns of children. In: P. C. Burns and L. M. Schell (eds.), Elementary School Language Arts: Selected Readings, pp. 65–75. Rand McNally, Chicago.

York, L. S. and Ebert, S. 1970. Implications for teachers—Primary level: Grades 1–3. In: T. D. Horn (ed.), Reading for the Disadvantaged: Problems of Linguistically Different Learners, pp. 179–190. Harcourt, Brace & World, New York.

Zintz, M. V. 1975. The Reading Process: The Teacher and the Learner. 2nd Ed. William C. Brown, Dubuque, Iowa.

chapter 7

Language Experience: Basis for Development of Spelling Skills

Ves Thomas

In view of the recent emphasis upon integrating the language arts, teachers are sometimes left wondering about their responsibilities for skill development in areas such as spelling. Unfortunately there appear to be two dichotomous points of view with respect to the whole question of integrating instruction in the communication skills. On the one hand there are those teachers who are convinced about the merits of an integrated approach such as language experience, and they often take the position that a formal spelling program is, therefore, unnecessary and even undesirable. Then there is the other group of teachers which is understandably reluctant to forego totally a program that sets aside some specific time for spelling instruction. These more conservative individuals, therefore, tend to reject the entire language experience approach because of its apparent lack of concern for specific skill development.

The problem that appears to have arisen stems from a lack of understanding and flexibility on the part of both groups. The real question is not one of total acceptance or rejection; it is a matter of blending an integrated language arts approach with the more traditional separate subjects approach. In fact, the greatest danger may lie in the possibility that teachers may accept one approach to the total exclusion of the other. The only question worthy of discussion is how best to utilize both approaches most effectively in the process of assisting students to learn and to apply their spelling skills.

The major objective for teaching spelling is to help children spell those words that they are most likely to need in their present and future writing needs. As is the case in most skill-development areas, no single approach is superior to all others in achieving this goal. Research evidence and many years of experience have, however, identified certain specifics of the spelling curriculum and classroom instruction that are worthy of note. Those recommendations that appear to have the greatest relevance in terms of their applicability to integrated language arts approaches are examined here.

THE SPELLING CURRICULUM

Frequency of word use studies by Horn (1927), Rinsland (1945), Thomas (1972), and others have identified a basic core of 3,000 words that accounts for approximately 95 percent of children's writing needs. It is this core of words, supplemented by the addition of special words, that has formed the basis for most spelling curricula in Canada and the United States. Instruction relative to words that have this frequency of occurrence should not be left to chance. Nor should such word lists comprise a total skills program that concentrates on words in isolation.

The formal spelling period is not the best place for a student to be introduced to these core words. The very nature of these words and their place in the curriculum assume that children have experienced them in their listening, speaking, and reading. It is also highly probable and even desirable for the students to have been exposed to the need to write many of these core words within the context of their dictated or written charts, stories, and booklets. These various language experience activities allow the students to see how spoken language can be recorded in the form of writing. It is equally important for students to experience the further connection between their writing and their reading. In this way children can begin to see themselves as authors as well as readers. Spelling thus becomes one tool that the author must learn and apply if he is to safeguard his meaning. These are precisely the conditions under which children should become acquainted with core words and the need to spell them correctly. However, it would be folly to assume that this kind of limited exposure to spelling is sufficient to ensure adequate skill development. In fact, it is precisely at this stage that many integrated language arts approaches fail because they do not make specific provisions for further skill development. This is the stage at which language experience activities must be fused with a more formal approach to spelling instruction. It should be noted, however, that formal spelling, which often deals with words in isolation, must not be viewed as either the culmination or the end-product of the instructional program. Just as the need to spell must be developed within a meaningful context, application of the skill to a meaningful writing situation must be considered as the desired goal. In this regard, it is important for the students to view the instructional spelling program as an attempt to help them fulfill their obligations as writers. Good writers realize that the onus is upon them to make their writing readable, and mechanics such as correct spelling can be used to serve this purpose.

THE SPELLING PERIOD

Provisions for the specific development of spelling skills can be made by allocating 10 to 15 minutes per day from within the overall communications period. This period must be available in addition to the time spent during the integrated language arts activities that precede or follow the spelling lesson. The purpose of this designated instructional period is to provide the teacher with an opportunity to assess spelling skills already acquired, identify needs, and provide instruction for those who need it.

The first priority during this period is to assess spelling achievement relative to the high-frequency core words. Instruction must be provided for those who have not achieved mastery of the core vocabulary. For those who demonstrate the ability to spell core words correctly, there is a need to use this time to concentrate on supplementary words. The selection of certain additional words and not others must be based on the needs of the whole class as well as on an individual basis. Words that are liable to have frequent and continued use in connection with a particular project, topic, or interest should be added to the spelling curriculum once the core requirements have been mastered. Other words that are required in their writing but that tend to be used less frequently need not appear immediately in spelling lessons. Let exposure to such words in meaningful writing situations provide the readiness experience for their inclusion in a subsequent year of the spelling program. The child can profit from a series of exposures to the same word before meeting it in his formal spelling program. Initial exposure may result in a very general observation of a word such as "Mediterranean." The child's initial experience with this word may merely cause him to observe that it begins with a capital letter and that it looks like a very hard word to spell. Perhaps during a subsequent encounter with this same spelling demon, he may discover the actual meaning of "medi" or "terra." He may gradually blend these meaningful components into the correct spelling of the entire word. On the other hand, if this same child is faced with meeting and learning this word in a spelling list, he will likely rely heavily upon rote memorization and then find that he seldom uses the word except in spelling tests.

In the process of learning basic word lists, students should also be taught spelling skills that will help them to become independent writers. Not all words need to be learned separately on a memorization basis. Some spelling generalizations, linguistic cues, and phonological principles can be used effectively. Dictionary skills can be taught and encouraged. The use of proofreading techniques can help to eliminate many careless errors. The development of a desirable attitude to spelling is also of considerable merit. These are the skills that can help children to learn their required words, but they are also the skills that will eventually produce independent writers. Language experience programs continually place children in situations where this kind of independence is most desirable.

PRETEST BEFORE STUDY

Any teacher who plans to combine a language experience approach with a more formal spelling program must give very serious consideration to the use of the test-study-test technique. By using a simple pretest before the study of any word list, the teacher can give students full credit for those words that have already been learned in some other context. Equally important, the pretest identifies for each student those words that need to be studied and learned. By using this technique, teachers need not be concerned about the overlap of skills developed within the broader language arts program or anywhere else in the curriculum. If the pretest determines that a child knows all of his core words, he can then be freed to concentrate on a limited number of supplementary words. If further analysis indicates that the child has also mastered his supplementary words, he should proceed with other language experience activities whether or not such activities are closely related to spelling. The important point here is that a student should not waste his time studing words he already knows, nor should he spend time studying exotic words that have little relevance and utility in terms of their application to writing.

DIAGNOSIS AND PRESCRIPTION

Spelling is one curriculum area that is largely evaluated on absolute standards of right and wrong. All too often, little attention is paid to the type of spelling error being committed and the casual factors pertaining to such errors. This attitude is reflected in the fact that diagnostic tests in spelling are generally non-existent at a time when similar instruments are rather plentiful in areas such as reading. However, even with the limitation concerning the availability of diagnostic test instruments in the field of spelling, knowledgable teachers can informally do much more than they are now doing (Thomas, 1974).

Even in classrooms where spelling evaluation and diagnosis are carried out, they are usually restricted to an assessment of skills that result from a test situation. As a consequence, too little attention is given to an assessment of spelling problems exhibited in a meaningful applied context. Written language experience activities can provide a much more realistic source for evaluating skills that have been not only learned but also applied. Diagnosis of specific spelling problems related to letter and story writing can result in the prescription of a more meaningful program during the formal spelling period.

Using a pretest before study and then assigning only those words that a child spelled incorrectly is an obvious example of diagnosis and prescription that is confined to the formal spelling program. However, there are other techniques that can be applied not only to spelling test situations but also to children's writing in general. A spelling errors analysis is one technique that can be used in an effort to identify specific spelling problems and thus provide an indication of the most appropriate instruction to be prescribed.

In a study done by Thomas (1966), three types of errors were found to account for just over 50 percent of the 5,301 spelling errors made by 449 grade six students in Alberta. Further results indicated that instruction prescribed on the basis of such analysis produced significantly superior spelling achievement when compared with other experimental groups that followed more routine procedures. In view of these findings, it would seem that spelling errors should be examined periodically by teachers to determine the nature of the spelling problem and that such information should be used to plan a more meaningful instructional program. For most normal classes, it is probably sufficient to use rather broad categories such as those used in the Thomas study. In this regard, a detailed examination of those three error types that categorize the majority of spelling errors may be helpful.

Phonetic Substitutions

The category of phonetic substitutions is restricted to the application of regular phoneme-grapheme generalizations to syllables or words whose spelling is irregular. Misspellings such as "ruff" for "rough," "woch" for "watch," "clime" for "climb," and "moshun" for "motion" are all illustrations of this error type. The child who wrote the following sentence further illustrates this type of problem: "Thay lurnd to stay out of trubull." Phonetic substitutions represent the error type that is made most frequently by students in the elementary school.

Most frequently, phonetic substitutions result from an over reliance upon graphophonic cues and phonic generalizations. Instructional stress will obviously have to be placed upon the fact that many words in the English language do not have a direct correspondence between phoneme and grapheme. Much more emphasis will also have to be focused upon visual and kinesthetic memory for such words. The association of difficult words with others of a similar structure can also be helpful, e.g., "walk—talk—chalk." When rules and phonic generalizations are taught, they should be developed inductively in connection with the words to which they apply. Some emphasis must also be placed on the exceptions to the rules. Children should also be helped to see that phonic generalizations that are useful in reading may have considerably less utility when applied to spelling

Omissions

Errors of omission refer to any letter or any syllable omitted from its proper place in a word, except a failure to double. Misspellings such as "studing" for "studying," "everbody" for "everybody," "lovly" for "lovely," "lik" for "like," and "moning" for "morning" are all illustrations of errors of omission. Such errors are relatively common and are often the result of sheer carelessness at the time of writing. Teaching and encouraging the use of proofreading techniques can be effective in helping the student to overcome careless errors of this type. Proofreading one's own work is a difficult task, and children must be given considerable guidance, instruction, and practice if they are to develop these skills to a functional level.

Other causes for errors of omission are more serious because they may reflect a student's failure to obtain an accurate auditory image. When a student writes "studing" for "studying," his error may not be due to a careless omission but may actually be the result of faulty auditory discrimination and faulty auditory analysis. Graphophonic cues are of little value to the child whose pronunciation is faulty. Omission problems that relate to faulty auditory image can be dealt with in much the same manner as that which is discussed in the next section.

Confused Pronunciation

Confused pronunciation refers to those errors in spelling that result from careless, incorrect, or exaggerated pronunciation; e.g., "libary" for "library," "filum" for "film," "denist" for "dentist," or "handcups" for "handcuffs." Errors of this type illustrate the significance of a child's oral language development upon his success in writing.

In the first instance of language learning, the child comes in contact with words through listening. Later, as he learns to speak, the accuracy of his pronunciation is to some extent determined by his auditory discrimination capabilities and the correct pronunciation of the words spoken to him. Once an inaccurate listening vocabulary of certain words is thus established, very deliberate attempts may have to be undertaken in order to overcome the resulting problems in oral and written expression. The child who writes "denist" in all likelihood hears and says "denist" in spite of the teacher's best efforts at accurate pronunciation during the dictation test. The correct spelling of this word will likely not occur until the teacher can get that student to hear and to recognize his own basic problem in auditory discrimination. The student must then be helped to see how his auditory problem affects the manner in which he pronounces and eventually writes the word "dentist."

Teachers might bear in mind that the longer such habits of confused pronunciation are practised, the more difficult it will be to bring about the desired changes in auditory perception, oral expression, and spelling. The language experience approach offers teachers a unique opportunity to detect oral inaccuracies at an early stage. As children dictate their stories to the teacher, special attention can be focused upon the relationships that exist between oral and written words. In some instances it may be sufficient to focus upon the similarities between initial sounds and initial letters. Similarly, attention can be drawn to any part of the word, or the whole word, in terms of these phoneme-grapheme relationships which will be helpful in producing accurate pronunciation and correct spelling. At least tangentially related to confused pronunciation is the broader relationship of oral language development (and phonology particularly) to spelling. While little is known about *how* children organize the sounds they hear, the degree to which they organize or classify speech sounds bear a demonstrable relationship to spelling (Read, 1975). There are at least 25 properties used in describing speech sounds (frontness, tenseness, diphthonization, height, duration, etc.). Some of these properties are viewed by children to be more salient than others. It would appear that these groupings influence the spelling patterns of kindergarten and first-grade children even if at an unconscious level (Beers, 1974; Gerritz, 1974).

One might hypothesize that the development of these groupings is at least part of what Cazden (1975) refers to as the emerging notion of the child of the opaqueness of language. If this hypothesis is correct, then emphasis on "language play" (discussed in Chapter 2) to enchance spelling skills has merit.

Other Categories

In addition to an analysis of phonetic substitutions, omissions, and confused pronunciation, the following categories can be used to complete this type of diagnosis.

Doubling Doubling is the appearance of one letter where there ought correctly to have been two of these letters adjacent to each other; or, the appearance of a double letter for a single, e.g., "runing" for "running"; or, "writting" for "writing."

Insertions Insertions refers to any letter or any syllable that appears in a word where it should not appear, other than the erroneous doubling of a single letter, a phonetic substitution, or any form of transposition; e.g., "useing" for "using"; or "goodes" for "goods."

Transpositions   Transpositions refer to any two adjacent letters, each of which should be contained in the word, but which are in reverse order; e.g., "beleive" for "believe"; or, "heigth" for "height."

Homonyms   A homonyms is a wrong form of a word for which there are two forms, each having the same sound but a different meaning and spelling; e.g., "to" for "too"; or "maid" for "made."

Unclassified   Unclassified refers to any errors that do not appropriately fall within the above-mentioned classifications or errors which contain more than one type of error. This group usually contains words which are unreadable, words which are omitted and numerous careless errors; e.g., "cir" for "cheer"; "srath" for "scratch"; or "mlils" for "miles."

Perhaps the most important aspect of spelling-error analysis is to develop an awareness on the part of teachers that causes them to become more diagnostic in their instructional program. There is no need to administer formal tests to determine error types, nor is it crucial to apply very specific criteria. What is needed is an awareness that spelling errors often form a pattern of writing behavior that needs to be identified before it can be effectively changed. Identifying a particular category of errors and prescribing appropriate corrective measures can be effective in overcoming many spelling errors that would otherwise have to be dealt with on an individual word basis. Some words do not readily lead themselves to learning through generalizations, and these will have to be learned as separate words. On the other hand, many words can be spelled correctly as a result of more general knowledge about language and how it works.

Application

The application of this informal diagnostic approach may be illustrated with reference to specific samples of children's writing that were done outside of the spelling period. In the first instance, the composition was written by Joan, 7.5 years of age, who was completing grade two. Figure 1 is one page that was taken from her language experience booklet.

The first reaction to Joan's composition may be that in general she expresses herself quite well, her handwriting is readily legible, and her spelling is basically adequate. Upon closer scrutiny of her

My father is a carpender. Gregg
and me want a dog and my
father has to do about three
more jobs. Mom said " until daddy
is finish the jobs then you may
have a dog." Father will be finish
the jobs at the end of June.
Then we'll get the dog. But
we'll have troblee find one
because we want one thirdteen
inches and one that dosen't
cost very much. We got a cute,
playful and little dog last year.

Figure 1. A page taken from a second-grade student's language experience booklet.

spelling errors, however, one pattern or problem appears to dominate. The fact that Joan writes "carpender" for "carpenter," "finish" for "finished" (twice), "find" for "finding," and "thirdteen" for "thirteen" suggests that confused or incorrect pronunciation, especially as it relates to word endings, may be the major cause of her apparent spelling problems. In all likelihood, she writes "carpender" and "thirdteen" because that is the way these words have always sounded to her. It is also likely that she incorrectly pronounces these same words. Until a teacher can get Joan to hear the difference between "finish" and "finished" or between "thirdteen" and "thirteen," there is little purpose in merely treating these as spelling errors and have the child learn to write the correct form. In fact, it is not important at this stage for Joan to spend her time memorizing how to spell such words as "carpenter" and "thirteen," but it is vital for her to improve her aural-oral competence as a prerequisite for improving her writing skills. Such corrective and preventive measures may be initiated during the spelling period but they more properly belong within the context of the entire language arts program. Other spelling errors such as "troble" and "dosen't" are among the common demon words that need to be dealt with on an individual words basis. These particular demon words have a high frequency of usage and as such deserve some extra study time during the formal spelling period to ensure that they have been mastered.

The second writing sample was written by Brenda, who was 10 years of age and in grade four:

The big seekret

One day as Miss hen was walking down the road little pig came out of his caral skiping happaly and said I have a seekret and you downt know what it is. Miss hen knew that he said something but she pretended that she didn't hear him and you know how big beeked hens are. Miss hen or for short big beek witch all the animals on the farm call her went running down the road to the barn "oh oh" she was holaring little pig has a seekret and I don't know what it is well that fust to bad said black cow youl fust have to whate and see what it is Miss hen or big beek for short told all the animals on the farm but Mrs. pig all the farm anamails said the same thing youl just have to wate and see what it is Miss hen wated and wated and whated and wated untill it was time for the suprize and do you know what it was it was little pigs birthday and he was 3 years old. Well Miss hen was so mad that she ran away and was never seen again

the End

Obviously, Brenda has problem with her spelling. However, it is not enough just to identify these errors, count them, and have her correct each one. Nor is it sufficient to have Brenda study each of these words during the spelling period. A close examination of errors such as "seekret," "caral," "down't," "beek," "holaring," etc., reveals that these are basically phonetic substitutions in which the writer is applying regular phoneme-grapheme generalizations to words whose spelling is irregular. It may well be that Brenda will have to study many of these words on an individual basis, but first of all she should learn much more about the limitations and the application of spelling generalizations. Many of these phonic generalizations can also be focused upon within the context of the reading program, while others will need special attention during the spelling period. The main point here is for the teacher and Branda to become aware of the broader problem that is the cause of numerous individual spelling errors. Furthermore, it is important to note that errors of this type would probably not show up during the spelling period itself.

Another problem in Brenda's spelling is her apparent lack of knowledge concerning capitalization and punctuation. Once she learns the general rules in this regard, Brenda should readily eliminate many of her own composition errors. Just learning to capitalize the important words in a title and capitalizing proper nouns would considerably improve the appearance of the composition. Once again, it is a matter of identifying the underlying problem and applying the appropriate corrective and preventative measures.

One must not overlook the fact that although Brenda has made numerous spelling errors, she has also spelled many other equally difficult words correctly. This does suggest that she has the ability to learn, and it is likely that she will profit even more from individually prescribed instruction.

CASE STUDIES

To illustrate how an integrated language arts approach can be used as a basis for implementing many of the foregoing suggested instructional practices for teaching spelling, three case studies are presented. Individual case studies of teacher performance have been selected from grades one, two, and six to provide a cross-section of how spelling is introduced and taught at the elementary school level.

Marjorie M., a Grade-One Teacher

As a grade-one teacher, I use the language experience approach and I teach spelling within this context. Of course, I am aware of the fact that even the more traditional spelling programs do not require that first-grade students study word lists. Nevertheless, I am aware of the fact that this first year is vital to my students in terms of developing readiness for spelling. With respect to spelling instruction, readiness at this grade level includes the meaningful development of listening, speaking, and reading vocabularies. Readiness also includes the development of an appreciation of the function that spelling serves in the writing-reading process. I want my students to develop a proper attitude toward spelling; I want them to acquire a spelling conscience, but I don't want them to be fearful about trying to express themselves on paper.

The language experience approach provides me with an excellent base for developing this kind of spelling readiness. As people share their experiences, they are indeed increasing their vocabularies. These discussions also give me a chance to develop experience charts which enable the children to see the connections between oral language and written language. A further connection is then readily made between writing and reading. Furthermore, in the process of developing these charts, I am exposing my students to a core vocabulary of high-frequency words. This does not mean, however, that I hesitate to use highly technical and "big" words if they are a part of our oral language. These unique terms can provide a first exposure without carrying any implication that they must be learned and memorized for test purposes even during the students' second year at school.

Writing words and stories on the blackboard, on charts, or in the process of taking down a child's dictation allows me ample opportunity to point out certain characteristics of letter formation, spelling, and grammar. Reading these same compositions gives further opportunity for developing visual discrimination based on word forms as well as letter forms. My students initially meet spelling in an applied context; they view it as a tool to be used in producing comprehensible writing. They begin to recognize that a word needs to be spelled correctly if it is to be read easily at a later time. Even at this stage, my students begin to view themselves as authors and they accept the onus for the mechanics that they must use in order to safeguard their meaning.

I also feel that it is important for children to acquire the dictionary habit as one means of developing their independence as writers. Very early in the school year, we label various objects around the room and in our display corners. Children are then encouraged to begin their own picture cards and labels. Later in the school year, these cards can be arranged in alphaetical order relative to the initial letter. It is quite common for children to turn to these cards when they are writing their own stories, and then I help them only with those words that are not in their own picture dictionaries. There is little doubt that children learn how to spell many of the common words in the process of watching me write these words, when they write them, or when they are reading these same words. I help these children with the problems they have in trying to do their own writing, but I do not insolate spelling as a skill apart from what we do in their reading and their writing. We value the use of correct spelling as it relates to the communications process.

Janet R., a Grade-Two Teacher

For the past couple of years I have been teaching grade-two students, although I had taught at the grade-one level for 5 years. Basically I use a language experience approach, but I have learned to make many common-sense adaptations when these seem warranted. In addition to my integrated language program, I make special provisions for specific skill development in areas such as spelling.

With respect to the development of spelling skills, I am aware that beginning grade-two students have normally had no formal spelling instruction. However, I also know that some of them can spell many words correctly and all of them have acquired at least a minimal writing vocabulary. It is my task to determine just what skills and what words have already been learned and to ensure that further, more specific, instruction is provided for those who need it. In addition to this, my task is to continue to involve these children in a wide variety of language experiences that will serve as a readiness base for next year's spelling requirements. Thus my language arts program is really two-pronged. In one respect, I continue to follow an integrated sequence based on their grade-one language experiences. In this part of my language program, I concentrate the children's efforts on vocabulary extension, and I try to develop their communication skills. Gradually these children are becoming more independent in their ability to write and to read. I extend their use of picture dictionaries to include not only their own booklets but also several commercial varieties in our classroom activities. They also enjoy making their own special word lists based on their own interests and appeal. They usually try to list words that they would like to use in their own compositions. I examine their compositions very closely to see what kind of spelling errors occur most frequently. Even a quick analysis of the type tells me whether a particular student is relying too heavily upon phonic generalizations, whether he is having reversal problems, or whether his pronunciation is inaccurate.

The second part of my language program is to a large extent skill oriented. In the case of spelling, I set aside 10 to 15 minutes per day to focus specifically upon this aspect of skill development. By now I expect my students to be able to know how to spell those basic core words that most formal spelling lists provide. I am also aware that I must supplement these core requirements by judiciouly selecting a few additional words that we find particularly useful in other curriculum areas. Words can also be added on the basis of individual needs and interests. I realize that the spelling competence of my students varies considerably, and therefore I must in some way individualize at least a part of my instructional program. Bearing in mind that many of my students will already have learned how to spell some of the required words, I use the test-study-test approach with respect to every unit of new words. In this way, the pretest provides the child and me with an indication of which words have already been learned and which must be studied. Those who have few or no errors in the required list of words are free to study supplemental words, or at times they do other work that may or may not be directly related to spelling instruction. I try hard to keep students interested in spelling as a means of improving their writing. I do not want my students to see the spelling test as the end-product of their efforts. Much of what they study during the spelling period has come out of their writing, and that which they learn must go back to help them become better writers. The formal spelling period gives me a chance to concentrate on specifics and thus develop spelling skills that might otherwise be overlooked or never fully developed within the broader context of my language experience activities.

David R., a Grade-Six Teacher

I have taught sixth graders for many years, but it has only been during the past 5 years that I have used an integrated approach in my language arts program. Although I do not use the language experience program as such, I follow a thematic approach, which is really an eclectic version of several theories. As far as spelling instruction is concerned, it begins within the broad thematic program, then moves to a specific spelling period, and finally moves back again to the applied context.

My thematic program, at present, is focused upon a study of how people communicate. Within this context, we read, we talk and discuss, we listen, and we write. These activities are all necessary for us to learn about our topic, and they provide me with a meaningful context in which to assess and further develop their language skills. In addition to the readiness activities that all of these activities provide for future spelling requirements, their writing provides me with a realistic basis for diagnosing the spelling needs of each student. In the process of discussing a composition with a student, we will note certain spelling concerns that will be pursued during the spelling period. We will also discuss words that need to be added to our core lists. Examining such writing also gives us a chance to see how well previously learned skills are being applied. If spelling errors are identified, they are analyzed in an effort to help the student to see his own specific needs and to give him a reason for studying spelling.

Formal spelling instruction is scheduled for four 15-minute periods per week. These periods may not be entirely necessary for all of my students, but they are there to ensure that I do not overlook skill development in this part of my language program. Minimally, these periods could involve students in pretest situations and nothing more. Students who demonstrate mastery in their writing and in their pretests are free to do more productive activities. For others, demonstrated problem words and problem area become the focus of attention and study. The success of this formal study is assessed in terms of its application to our writing needs.

Together, the integrated thematic approach and the more formal spelling program provide me with the assurance that I have not left spelling to be developed through chance encounters; nor have I given the students an isolated program of spelling that emphasizes the acquisition of this skill for its own sake.

SUMMARY

In any language situation where communication is the desired objective, integration of the language arts is inevitable. In such instances, integration is not only assured, it is also meaningful. Similarly, skill development within the language arts must not only be integrated, it must also be meaningful to the learner. An integrated approach, however, neither precludes nor obviates the necessity for specific skill development. Once needs have been established within a communications framework and specific problems have been identified, there must be ample opportunity to assist the learner in developing the required skills. Language experience can create a means by which skills such as spelling can be introduced in the context of a need to communicate. Spelling is thus introduced as an aid to writing and reading and not as an end in itself. However, the introduction of spelling words in this manner should not be viewed as the total instructional program. Language experience can indeed provide the basis for the development of spelling skills, but further provisions must also be made for specific skill development. Beyond the spelling period and skills developed within that context, language experience once again can be used effectively as the basis for applying these skills within a meaningful setting. Thus, the spelling instructional program begins within a meaningful, integrated language arts setting, it moves to a specific skills development period, and finally moves back to all curriculum areas in which writing is the required means of communication.

LITERATURE CITED

Beers, T. W. 1974. First and second grade children's developing orthographic concepts of tense and lax vowels. Unpublished doctoral dissertation, University of Virginia, Charlottesville.

Cazden, C. B. 1975. Play with language and metalinguistic awareness: One dimension of language experience. In: C. Winsor (ed.), Dimensions of Language Experience, pp. 3–19. Agathon Press, New York.

Gerritz, K. E. 1974. First graders' spelling of vowels: An exploratory study. Unpublished doctoral dissertation, Harvard University, Cambridge.

Horn, E. 1927. The Basic Writing Vocabulary. University of Iowa, Iowa City.

Read, C. 1975. Children's Categorization of Speech Sounds in English. National Council of Teachers of English, Urbana, Ill.

Rinsland, H. D. 1945. A Basic Writing Vocabulary of Elementary School Education. Macmillan, New York.

Thomas, V. 1974. Teaching Spelling: Canadian Work Lists and Instructional Techniques. Gage Educational Publishing Limited, Agincourt, Ontario.

Thomas, V. 1972. The basic writing vocabulary of elementary school children. Alberta J. Educ. Res. XVIII(4):243–248.

Thomas, V. 1966. A spelling errors analysis and an appraisal of its usefulness in improving the spelling achievements of selected Alberta students. Unpublished doctoral dissertation, University of Oregon.

PART IV

INTEGRATION OF COMPONENTS

chapter 8

Incorporating Language Experiences into the Content Areas

Dianne Seim

To date, the majority of literature available regarding the use of an integrated language experience approach for teaching reading has dealt primarily with the use of this approach in teaching students the skills of "learning to read." Consequently, one of the principle criticisms of such an approach has been its failure to deal directly and effectively with the problems inherent in gaining meanings and ideas from the writing of others. Because "...reading is probably the major source of ideas, personal growth, vocational training, and participation in current events" (Spache and Spache, 1969, pp. 179–180), the language experience approach must concern itself with this ultimate goal of "reading to learn."

Because the communication arts serve as the medium of instruction for all subjects, the content areas would seem to hold vast potential for developing purpose and desire for "reading to learn." When reading is treated in an integrated manner with the other facets of language, and when the language arts are recognized as tools of learning rather than as subjects, the value of teaching the language arts within the content areas becomes quite apparent. By teaching reading, as well as other language arts within the content areas, the utility and importance of the language skills are demonstrated to the students.

The skills are taught and used within a meaningful context. Too, the difficulties arising from the student being required to transfer what he has learned in "reading" when it is treated as a separate subject to each of the content areas are overcome.

In the content areas experiences serve as the means for 1) providing the framework of basic concepts, 2) developing specific communication skills, 3) generating enthusiasm and purpose for reading to gain additional information and ideas, and 4) providing a catalyst for recreational reading. Initially, experiences provide the material for development of the specific mechanical aspects of reading. The learner must have experiences with "something" in order to have "something" about which to write, and that "something" may very reasonably come from within the content areas. This avoids the fragmentation of treating the language arts as a separate subject or subjects. The language arts are developed and perceived by the student from the beginning as the valuable tools that they are for learning.

Using experiences from within the content areas provides additional benefits for the learner by aiding him in the transition from reading materials he has written to reading materials written by others. If, through direct experiences while learning to read, the student has developed a core of basic concepts in the content areas, his transition to reading the writings of others to gain additional information will be greatly facilitated.

In addition to building a background for learning, the experience approach in the content areas creates opportunities for purposeful reading by the student. Through an experience approach that encourages further reading, the student establishes purpose for "reading to learn." Thus, the student develops within a meaningful context such skills as discriminating between fact and opinion, skimming to locate specific information, and critically analyzing information presented by the author. Meaningful vocabulary development also occurs as the student encounters unfamiliar words in reading and determines their meanings through context, conversation, or a dictionary.

However, reading is only one facet of communication, and it must not be isolated from the other language arts in speaking of the merits of a direct experience approach for providing motivation for additional, purposeful learning. As the student shares his learning with others, either formally or informally, in writing or in speaking, other communication skills develop, such as organizing information, listening to respond, and notetaking. Overall, the emphasis is upon meaningful application of communication skills. The learning experience has purpose.

PRACTICAL APPLICATIONS

The remainder of this chapter will deal with the specific examples for using direct experiences to assist the student in mastering the various communication skills while attaining the objectives of a given content area. The activities cited are intended only to be exemplary. Of major importance is the manner in which the skills are developed, rather than the specific content used to provide the examples.

Science

Regardless of the specific content through which they are developed, certain functional and cognitive skills can be identified for the teaching of science. In looking through a list provided by an author such as Victor (1970, pp. 24–25) many overlapping concerns between the "science" teacher and "language arts" teacher become readily apparent. For example, both are attempting to aid the student in developing the ability to:

1. Distinguish between pertinent and irrelevant observations, findings, information
2. Make comparisons
3. Organize effective reports
4. Analyze observations, ideas, readings
5. Formulate and understand operational definitions
6. Arrive at a decision by reasoning from known facts or evidence (infer)
7. Use tables of contents, indices, glossary of texts, and references

Through an experience approach, the language skills and the skills of the scientific process can be developed concomitantly. Activities stemming from two topics, "Snow" and "The Human Body," are used to exemplify this. These rather general topics have been chosen to demonstrate the worth of incorporating the language arts into the content area, science. It is hoped that the teacher will make the appropriate applications of these and other activities to his particular grade level and situation. *Note*: Specific science and/or language skills are provided in parentheses following the brief description of each activity. These skills are intended to be illustrative, not all inclusive, e.g., observing, classifying, etc.

Snow   Take the students out into the school yard. Be sure that they have materials for recording observations and data. Observe the snow from a standing position and describe it. This description may be either verbal or written or both. If written, the writing may be in narrative form, in phrases, or in single words (observing, describing, communicating).

Move closer to the snow in order to observe it in more detail. Some ways the detailed observation may be accomplished are by measuring the snow to determine its depth, taking the temperature of the snow in several places for comparative purposes (e.g., in a sunny area, in a shaded spot, near a building), comparing the snow temperature with the air temperature, and using a magnifying glass to examine snow crystals. The snow crystals may be drawn as an important way of recording information of this type. If it is snowing, the student may compare new, falling snow with snow that has previously fallen. They may also incorporate other senses by tasting clean snow to see whether they can determine any flavor to the snow, by listening carefully while walking on snow in various areas, and by feeling snow by running their hands through it, rolling in it, or rubbing it against their faces (analyzing, observing, communicating, describing, inferring, interpreting, keeping records, comparing, manipulating science equipment, noting similarities and differences, measuring, working together).

Gather snow samples to take back into the classroom. Melt the snow to see what the water content is and to determine how long it takes the snow to melt. Do this at different temperatures, and plot the results. Have the students filter the water that remains to see what impurities are in the snow. Have the students set up hypotheses to test to determine whether the impurities get into the snow before or after it reaches the ground. This can be done by collecting some snow as it falls to the ground and by gathering some that has been on the ground for a period of time. This experiment should take place on several days (analyzing, applying previously learned knowledge, conducting experiments, determining pertinent and irrelevant information, formulating and testing hypotheses, induction, inferring, interpreting, making comparisons, manipulating science equipment, noting similarities and differences, observing, predicting, using number relations).

Record weather conditions over a given period of time. Determine when it snows. Observe the conditions. Record and graph the snowfall. Go outside a number of times during the period in which the recording occurs. Observe the snow closely, using some of the techniques described for the intial outdoor session, e.g., taking the temperature of the snow (applying previously learned knowledge,

classifying, communicating, constructing graphs, induction, interpreting, keeping records, manipulating science equipment, comparing,
noting similarities and differences, observing, measuring, using
space/time relations).

Investigate the effects of drifting snow. Compare drifting in a
variety of areas of the schoolyard. If possible, set up a snow fence;
predict, observe, and record what happens over a period of time
(analyzing, experimenting, constructing graphs, describing, observing, hypothesizing, induction, making inferences, interpreting, record
keeping, comparing, measuring, predicting).

As can be noted, a vast number of science skills are developed
through activities such as these. A number of language skills that
developed throughout the activities can also be identified. While the
students are outdoors, they are continuously involved in oral language
development; they are continuously talking with the teacher, and
with one another. An activity in the snow always generates much
spontaneity of expression. Participating in the snow experiences
requires the students to listen, to follow directions, as well as to
respond to one another. In addition skills in gathering data and
recording it for purposes of reporting it when they return to the
classroom are developed.

Upon returning to the classroom, the students continue their
science learnings and language development. For students who are
just beginning to learn to read, the obvious activity is to write stories
describing their experiences with the snow. Other writing activities
for students of various ages include listing descriptive words for
snow or words that indicate what they did with the snow (verbs) or
experimenting with various styles of writing such as free verse—or
possibly haiku. One student's effort is recorded here:

> Daintily floating
> White, fragile, lacy crystals,
> Snowflakes falling down.

From the results and information gathered, the students may
share their findings with others through pictures (which can be titled
to develop the skill of determining main ideas and/or to provide
additional words for reading), plays, reports (oral and written), and
group discussions. Reporting requires the student to develop skills
such as organizing and condensing information. Of course, reporting
activities also involve the development of listening skills on the part
of the persons receiving the information. The use of different tech-

niques for sharing their findings, such as through free verse and also through scientific reporting of facts, demonstrates the importance of developing various skills. Group discussions, when used purposefully, provide for the development of skills such as making concise and worthwhile contributions, staying on the topic, and supporting statements with facts.

As a result of their direct experiences with snow, students should be motivated to learn more about snow. Interest may be aroused for reading poems and library books such as Keat's "The Snowy Day." Motivation may be aroused for additional experimentation with snow and for "reading to learn" to gather scientific information about snow, such as physical properties of snow, how snow is formed in the atmosphere, insulation properties, and crystallization. Additional reading may be done to verify the students' own findings from experimentation with information presented by other authors. All of these activities will involve the use of a wide variety of reference materials and the development of study skills such as various library skills and using the index and table of contents of books. In addition, students may develop a desire for reading in such interest areas as how different groups of people use snow for housing or for recreational activities in the snow.

The Human Body Form pairs in the classroom. Examine the heartbeat of each partner by feeling the pulse at a pressure point such as the wrist or neck. Record this information. Predict, observe, and plot on a graph how this changes through exercise and body movement. Various movements of the body may be studied and compared at the same time, e.g., movements of joints, the tongue, and the eyelids (observing, analyzing, communicating, experimenting, constructing graphs, describing, hypothesizing, induction, interpreting, comparing, using space/time relations, predicting, working with others).

Study the various taste areas of the tongue through direct investigation such as by blindfolding one student and having the partner feed him various foods ranging in taste from sweet to sour to bitter. Before the students taste any food, they may predict how the tongue will react. One student can record in writing the descriptive word(s) given for the taste by his partner. The foods may be classified according to their "tastes." The results of this experimentation may be recorded in charts, graphs, or diagrams. The students' findings can be verified with other resource materials. Other body systems can be studied in similar fashion (observing, analyzing, applying previously learned knowledge, classifying, communicating, experimenting, constructing charts, describing, hypothesizing, induction, inference, interpreting, predicting, using a number of experiments to obtain valid information).

In addition to studying the various systems of the body, the students may study aspects such as general growth and development, proper diet and food intake, and birth. Guest speakers may be invited to visit the classroom. Thus, the students receive knowledge through vicarious experiences by listening to others. To be most beneficial, this requires that the students have sufficient background (which involves the purposeful application of language skills used in preparation for the guest) and that attention is given to the development of specific skills of attentive listening to obtain facts and general concepts, skills for questioning, skills for processing and organizing information received, and skill in the courtesies of listening. Videotapes and films are additional sources of vicarious learning that develop information-gathering skills such as listening for facts and notetaking. Further vicarious learnings occur through readings in various types of resource materials such as textbooks, library books, encyclopedias, and magazine and newspaper articles. The student learns the skills of altering reading style and pace to glean information presented in different forms. Also, he develops skills of critically analyzing what authors have said, particularly when he reads about a topic that has materials available presenting more than one view, such as the affect of diet on hyperactivity. Too, the student learns to update information through, for example, using articles that have recently appeared in the newspaper and periodicals to update information that appears in an encyclopedia.

Writing and speaking skills are developed through preparation of various types of reports and participation in group discussions. For example, the student must use research skills involving the use of various reference materials, must gather and organize information, must learn to support his information or position with facts (and must learn to verify the facts presented by writers), must learn to be concise, and must learn the proper manner for crediting other authors. If the report is to be given orally, the student develops a host of skills for presenting an effective "speech," including those involved with how to organize the report and how to present it effectively to maintain audience interest and attention. In preparing written reports, the student applies skills such as those involving proper sentence structure, capitalization, and punctuation. Furthermore writing in science develops the writer's skills in a style of writing that is precise and concise.

Not to be overlooked are the values of using these types of science experiences for teaching students basic reading and writing skills. Vocabulary development occurs as the students use words that refer to the human body. In addition to providing material for concept development necessary for reading what other authors have written and for writing experience stories, this topic provides many opportunities for labeling charts and diagrams. For example, in the activity involving the taste areas of the tongue, a diagram of the tongue may be drawn and labeled to present words for vocabulary development and for developing word recognition skills in reading.

Social Studies

As with the other subjects, skill development is an essential part of social studies. In pointing out the need for developing social studies skills, Kenworthy indicates that "facts can be forgotten or become out-of-date, but skills ... will usually be of service throughout life" (Kenworthy, 1969, p. 124). He stresses the fact that skills must be continually reinforced in a variety of situations. Though there are many specific skills that must be developed in social studies, Kenworthy (1969, p.124) offers the following groupings and presents in his text a discussion of these, to which the teacher might wish to refer:

1. Locating, gathering and evaluating information and ideas
2. Organizing information
3. Communicating ideas and information (including listening, reading and presenting ideas in oral and in written form)
4. Interpreting graphic materials
5. Critical thinking
6. Living with others
7. Globe and map skills

As was witnessed in the discussion of the relationship between science and language arts skills, social studies and language arts share many common concerns with regard to skill development. Two general topics, "Community Services" and "Land Use," have been chosen to exemplify this and to demonstrate the logic of developing language skills within the social studies content area. Again, the topics selected are general enough to allow teachers at various grade levels to adapt them to their particular classroom situations and/or to gain some specific suggestions about how the language arts skills might be developed through an experience approach in social studies. Also, the social studies skills listed in parentheses following the activity suggestions are intended to be illustrative, rather than inclusive.

Community Services   Determine and list the types of services available within your neighborhood or a larger area. Make a chart recording the persons responsible for providing each service. Discuss with others, both in and out of the classroom, what a service is, who provides services, and why we need services. Identify and create your own examples of services in the classroom. Role-play the services provided by other people (locating and gathering information and ideas, organizing information, communicating ideas and information, using graphic materials).

Organize and prepare for visits to a variety of establishments that provide the services in your neighborhood. This may be done as a class, or if your situation permits, in small groups. If the activity occurs with small groups visiting various establishments, the students should keep notes and report to the total class. In instances for which it is not possible to arrange visits, invite speakers into the classroom. The students should be involved in making the arrangements for visits and classroom guests (locating and gathering information, organizing information, communicating information).

Prepare in advance simple questionnaires for use in discussions with persons in service occupations, and interview them. Discuss ways in which the students and other persons within the neighborhood can assist the people providing the services. Work on these courtesies and/or skills in the classroom. For example, students can learn to address an envelope properly to be of the greatest benefit to the postal worker. Record the information obtained from interviews, and disseminate it to others in the community through a newsletter or another suitable format (locating, gathering and evaluating information and ideas, organizing information, communicating ideas and information, living with others).

Evaluate the services that are available in your neighborhood or larger community, and determine which services should be provided but are missing and which ones are unnecessary. This could be done by comparing lists of services provided in your neighborhood with those in other neighborhoods either through direct study or through research. Investigate the possibilities for new services such as recycling centers, recreation programs for senior citizens, and family planning centers. The investigation/analysis should be done from a variety of perspectives, for example, environmental impact or needs of special populations within your neighborhood. Make a map of the neighborhood. Indicate the location of existing services and recommendations for additional services (locating, gathering and evaluating information and ideas, organizing information, critical thinking, living with others, map skills).

Study the interactions of people in service occupations with the people whom they service. This may be done through direct observation and/or through discussions both with the people in service occupations and the people who receive services. Plan the most effective way for recording and presenting this information to other members of the class (locating, gathering and evaluating information and ideas, organizing information, communicating information, living with others).

Interview people who are involved in various services. Discuss with them why they entered that particular service, what they find interesting about working in the service, etc. The students might design a questionnaire that they will use in interviewing people in all of the services. With the results obtained through this interview method, the student could create a chart indicating how the people within each service responded to each question. This would allow students to analyze the information they gathered (locating, gathering, and evaluating information, organizing information, communicating ideas and information, using graphic materials).

Attention is now turned to specific language skills that are developed in activities such as the above. With regard to reading, younger students in particular may write stories reporting their observations and experiences in identifying services and visiting various establishments; from these stories specific word-recognition skills may be developed, as well as such comprehension skills as sequencing ("What I Did When I Visited X") and determining main ideas (in simplest terms, the "most important thing" a certain person does for others). Students of all ages may, and should, become involved in reading materials to gain additional information. This will range in complexity from reading simple library books about "community helpers" to reading requirements for service careers. The latter will involve various types of reading materials, including library books, reference books, and magazines. Interest may be aroused in recreational reading about people in various service occupations.

The teacher may encourage students to learn to read materials such as contracts that the students will encounter as adults and that they will be expected to sign in order to receive various services. An activity such as this is extremely beneficial in developing critical-thinking skills.

Another activity given meaning and stemming from experiences with people in service occupations might be learning to read applications for jobs and applications to receive various services provided by the government. This promotes skills in following directions and filling in forms correctly, thus developing writing skills as well.

A number of suggestions within this "Community Services" topic recommend notetaking and reporting. Reporting enables the student to develop language skills of gathering, condensing, and organizing information as well as to develop specific skills in the mechanics of writing a report or preparing and delivering an oral report. Listening to the reports of other students also becomes an important aspect of language development, as does participating in group discussions.

Interviewing is another important activity to be used in promoting language skills. The student must develop interviewing skills, including preplanning, opening the interview, sticking to the topic of the interview, and closing the interview, as well as listening and reacting to what is said during the interview. Preparation of a questionaire before an interview promotes other vital language skills ranging from organizing materials to spelling words correctly.

Several field trips and invitations to guest speakers have been recommended in studying this topic. Planning for, preparing, and following up with trips and classroom visitors provide excellent opportunities to develop letter-writing skills within a meaningful context. Students become involved in writing invitations and thank-you letters, which promotes a variety of skills from using the proper form to spelling words correctly to addressing envelopes. In addition, some contacts might be made via telephone, stimulating interest in proper use of the telephone and in telephone courtesies. A telephone activity might even be extended to include use of the telephone book, which entails the use of such skills as alphabetizing and using guide words.

Land Use Take a walk around the neighborhood to look at how land is being used; for example, look at the land being used for single-family dwellings, parks, and hard-surfaced areas such as sidewalks, streets, and parking lots. Write about this. Make a sketch map of your findings (locating and gathering information, communicating information, using map skills).

Look at new construction within the area. Find out what building materials are being used. Make wall charts showing where the materials came from. Study and map transportation networks for getting materials to your community. Analyze whether the buildings under construction are being built on the land best suited for them or whether the land would be better suited for farming, park land, or some other use (locating, gathering, and evaluating information and ideas, organizing information, using graphic materials, critical thinking, map skill).

In the classroom, fill a large flat box with soil. Contour the soil inside the box in any manner so that it is no longer a flat surface. Then make a flat map of the area inside the box. This will facilitate the understanding of three-dimensional objects applied to a two-dimensional surface. Study the land formations within the community. Map them. Make the formations within the box. Study the land usage as it relates to the various land formations (locating and gathering information, critical thinking, map skills).

Go to the city government office responsible for zoning. Study the various zones and zoning regulations. Record this information. Attend a city council meeting to determine how zoning laws are established. Analyze these laws to see if they take into account needs of the community for a long period of time or whether they only meet the immediate needs of vested interests. Report the findings (locating, gathering, and evaluating information, communicating information, critical thinking, living with others).

While developing important skills and concepts in social studies, the students are building their language skills in numerous ways. As has been noted previously, a number of stories and charts containing phrases or single words from which specific reading skills can be developed arise from experiences of this nature. Students also develop new vocabulary when looking at building materials and information regarding such topics as land formations and zoning. Information such as that dealing with new construction can be used to promote skills in classifying and categorizing. Also, building materials can be labeled to provide experience in reading new words. Labeling to develop word-recognition skills also can be incorporated into the mapping activities.

Listening skills are sharpened when students have experiences such as going to a city council meeting where opposing views are likely to be presented. These include listening for specific facts, listening to distinguish between fact and opinion, listening for main ideas, and listening for supporting evidence. Current issues such as those discussed at the city council meeting are reported in the newspaper, which gives the student an opportunity (and perhaps because of their experience the motivation) to read the newspaper article(s) and to study the accuracy of reporting. The students may enjoy writing their own newspaper articles first and then comparing their articles to those they read. Obviously, writing the articles would develop a host of writing skills. If there were more than one newspaper reporting on the city council meeting or on an issue such as zoning, the students would have the opportunity to develop skills of critical reading by noting the "slant" taken by each newspaper.

Research skills such as using the library card catalog, using an index, and using various types of references may be promoted as students read to learn about how land formations develop, how weather affects land formations, and how land formations influence the weather. As students read about how different people around the world live on different land formations and how these people use the formations, the students may be encouraged to become engaged in recreational reading about people and their customs in those areas. Perhaps a writing activity will develop in the form of students obtaining penpals to learn more about the people in the various countries. Additional information regarding how people live on and with different land formations may come to the students through vicarious experiences provided by various media including videotapes, films, filmstrips, and slides. When the students have a variety of materials available on a given topic, they have a good opportunity to look at the material critically to determine its accuracy, another very important communication skill.

Mathematics

In looking at the possibilities and merits for incorporating language experience into mathematics, it is essential first to identify the major goals of a mathematics program. Major aims of a mathematics program have been identified by such authors as Marks, Purdy, and Kinney (1970). A condensed version of their list (pp. 20–22) follows:

1. development of concepts
2. development of mathematical understanding
3. development of skills of computation, measurement, and construction

4. ability to solve problems
5. development of appreciation and favorable attitudes

It would seem that an experience approach that provides activities requiring students to apply mathematical concepts and functions would be highly effective and desirable. To illustrate how such an approach might be used, activities are suggested revolving around two general topics, "Clothing" and "Life Expectancy." As was mentioned in the preceding examples for science and social studies, these suggestions are intended only to be illustrative, from which the teacher will select and/or alter activities for his particular classroom situation. Again, the emphasis is upon the manner in which experiences and language arts skills might be incorporated in the mathematics content area, rather than the specific content used to exemplify this. *Note*: The major mathematical aims, as provided in the above list, are identified in parentheses following each activity.

Clothing   Count the number of shirts of each color within the classroom. Perform a similar activity with any other articles of clothing. Count the number of buttons on each shirt. Record this information on a group-experience chart. Do this on a number of days. Compare the results (development of concepts).

Bring a large number of buttons from home. Each student should contribute to the button collection. Classify the buttons in various ways. The students can create sets by color, number of holes, shape, etc. Record the information. This may be recorded according to each item or as a class in pictures or on a chart or graph. Label the picture(s) or chart (development of concepts, development of mathematical understanding).

Perform various mathematical operations with the buttons, and write out the experiences as a beginning for story problems. As an example, one student wrote the following:

> I had four buttons.
> Mrs. Boot took three buttons.
> I have one button.

This information may then be transferred to mathematical symbols; for this student it was: $4 - 3 = 1$. A more advanced example involves placing the buttons in sets and recording the information, e.g., two sets of 2. The degree of sophistication depends solely on the ability of each student (development of mathematical understanding, development of skills).

Compare the labels on clothing to note fabric content and to determine information about percentages. After examining the information presented on the labels, students can create word problems using unknowns such as, "A blouse had three types of fabric in it. They were rayon, nylon, and dacron. If the rayon made up two parts, the nylon made up five parts, and the dacron made up three parts of the fabric, what percent of the fabric was dacron?" (development of skills, ability to solve problems).

Look through a catalog to determine prices of items. Determine what it would cost to clothe the students in the classroom in various sets of clothing. This requires the skills of multiplying unit prices times number of articles required and adding the total. An order blank could be filled out, requiring the student to read to follow directions as well as to perform the mathematical operations. Figuring the tax would involve working with percentage (development of skills, ability to solve prolems).

Select a set of clothing and figure the cost. As a group activity, the students can total the class cost and determine the average cost per pupil, using skills such as addition and division. Carrying this further, some students may figure the difference between the average cost and the actual cost for each student. These differences may be plotted on a chart or graph (development of skills, ability to solve problems).

Allot each student a given amount of money. Determine how each would spend it to outfit themselves. Extend this to include how this money (or additional amount) would be spent to outfit the student's family (development of skills, ability to solve problems).

Perhaps the most obvious incorporation of language arts skills in mathematics is developing the vocabulary unique to mathematics. This occurs initially through oral communication. In addition to developing vocabulary, through oral communication students form basic mathematical concepts that are necessary for reading word problems and other mathematics material in the future.

Charts that list words and accompanying symbols may be prepared by the entire class or by the individual. Labeling items and pictures of items provide another way of developing vocabulary and engaging students in reading numbers as well as other words, such as, "Here are 3 buttons." "Here are *three* buttons." To learn more about counting and numerals, students may read picture books and other easy-to-read books from the library.

As was indicated in the activities, students may develop their own word problems from activities in which they participate. This provides excellent opportunities to incorporate thinking and writing skills. As students gain experience and pleasure in preparing mathematics problems, they become interested in reading those prepared by other authors. In addition, more advanced students begin to use mathematics texts and other reference books to determine how to perform certain operations. Students also engage in conversation with other students and adults to gain information about performing operations, which is another language skill.

Activities such as these involving clothing may lead students to read additional materials. For example, the students may find an interest in reading stories about how clothes are made or about properties of elements that make up certain fabrics, and they may become interested in studying about the durability, washability, or insulation properties of one or more of the elements. They may be motivated to research a topic such as the history of buttons, or they may become interested in recreational reading about clothing that other people wear. As they read these materials, students are required to use such number skills as finding the page in a book from the number given in the table of contents or index and reading charts and graphs.

Through activities such as filling out an order form, students develop concomitantly skills in language arts involving reading and following directions and skills in computations with numbers. This type of activity may be carried a step further by having students fill out and read the "fine" print for charge accounts and credit cards. This develops the students' understanding of interest rates, as well as their skills in reading critically and reading to gain specific factual information. Gaming situations may be created whereby students go into debt and feel the pressures and frustrations of attempting to get out of dept, while they are faced with the advertising campaigns and temptations of additional purchases.

Life Expectancy   Take the students to a nearby cemetery. Use the dates of birth and dates of death to determine the life spans (ages) of persons buried there. Determine the average life span. Do this for both men and women (development of skills, ability to solve problems).

Study the geometric shapes of the headstones plus any shapes found in the designs on the headstones. This may lead to the reading and study of geometric shapes in art, on signs, and in the construction industry. Study of the latter may lead to the study of topics such as which shapes are stronger than others and what volume various shapes hold. This leads the students to establishing and testing hypotheses as well as to a variety of mathematical computations (development of concepts, development of skills, ability to solve problems).

Read the local newspaper. Do a comparative study between the current average age of death as compared to that found at the cemetery. It probably will be necessary to use the average age of those who died before a definite year, such as 1945. This study may lead the students, depending on their ages, to the actuary calculations done by insurance companies. A worthwhile activity might be to invite someone from an insurance company to the classroom to speak to students about current statistics and how they are computed (development of skills, ability to solve problems).

Specific language skills to be considered again include development and formation of basic concepts through oral communication (refer to the previous discussion in the "Clothing" section). Throughout the activities, the students develop oral communication skills as they interact with their classmates and teacher.

The reading of headstones can lead to development of basic word-recognition skills. Knowledge of abbreviations also may be developed. An interesting activity stemming from these readings of headstones is the creation of crayon rubbings to take back to the classroom. This allows the students to compare and to identify information that appears on several, or all, headstones. Some students may wish to do some creative writing of epitaphs.

Students may become interested in finding and reporting on additional information regarding life expectancy through magazine articles and various other resource materials. This requires them to use library skills as well as skills involving notetaking, organizing information, and effectively presenting information either orally or in writing. In addition, when doing research, students will need to read graphs and charts that present numerical information.

A study of insurance rates and how they are calculated could be an offspring of this topic. Students could learn to read insurance policies and to calculate premiums and dividends, as well as to learn to fill out forms properly. An activity of this nature provides an excellent opportunity to develop vocabulary. In addition to developing reading and writing skills while working with policies and other forms, students can learn to ask questions to obtain the specific information they need to clarify a particular point.

This topic may also be used to stimulate interest in the study of birth. Students may read birth announcements in the newspaper. This may promote not only additional reading regarding various aspects of birth, but may also motivate the study of such topics as measurement (weight and linear). Additional readings by students might include reading about various measurement devices or about the meanings and sources of names. From the life-expectancy theme, a new topic relating to various aspects of birth could readily be designed that would incorporate language arts in mathematics.

SUMMARY

This chapter has presented the rationale and demonstrated some of the merits of incorporating language experience in the content areas. Specific suggestions for activities were made which considered the aims and skills identified for particular content areas plus specific language arts skills that can be developed concomitantly. Obviously, the limitations of time and space allow the suggestions to be only exemplary. Hopefully, however, they will serve as pragmatic illustrations of the theory and will lead the teacher to his own skill-development activities within the content areas.

While it is not difficult to recognize the benefits of an experience approach that incorporates the language arts in the content areas, we must not assume that if experiences are provided, the skills will "just develop." The onus is on the teacher. The teacher must be knowledgable of and identify the language arts skills, as well as the skills and concepts to be developed within each of the content areas. He must create guides and checklists to ensure that the skills are being developed. He must be prepared to teach them and not leave their development to happenstance.

LITERATURE CITED

Kenworthy, L. S. 1969. Social Studies for the Seventies. Ginn and Company, Toronto.
Marks, J. L., Purdy, C. R., and Kinney, L. B. 1970. Teaching Elementary School Mathematics for Understanding. McGraw-Hill, Toronto.
Spache, G. D., and Spache, E. B. 1969. Reading in the Elementary School. Allyn and Bacon, Boston.
Victor, E. 1970. Science for the Elementary School. Collier-Macmillan, Toronto.

chapter 9

Children's Language Expression through Poetry

Victor Froese

This chapter presents a number of ways (15 in all) with which a teacher may prompt students to write their own poetry. With preparation, persistence, enthusiasm, and luck, the quality of the poetry produced can be surprisingly high: an outcome encouraging to students and teacher alike. In fact, experiences in language are the very essence of poetry.

Teachers can promote the best efforts of students by keeping in mind several basic points. First, stress the expression of *meaning* as a primary skill. Forms are secondary in most instances (except when they help to generate ideas). Second, poetic forms are useful insofar as they assist in expression, rhythm, or appearance. They should be generally an out-growth of the idea or meaning—form and meaning should be complementary. Third, much input, stimulation, and sensitization are necessary before writing begins. Teacher and children together can explore and learn to appreciate the unique aspects of children's poetry. Reeves (1971) states, "Adult poetry is an exploration of the interior world of the mature mind—poetry for children, an exploration of the outer world, the world as reported by the senses." Finally, first impressions, however good they are, are rarely what we read. Most good poems have gone through revisions. There is a place for "polishing" poetry. The teacher's attitude toward a poem as something that emerges through rearranging the lines, playing around with possible choices of words, rhythm, imagery, etc., will help students produce more satisfying and more effective poems.

For each of the 15 approaches discussed here, an explanation is first given; then, when possible, children's examples follow. A number of suggestions for beginning work on each form are given, but the teacher should use her imagination freely to come up with other possibilities. Finally, a number of references are given both for those who wish further examples and for those who would like more in-depth treatments of the suggested forms. Many of the children's examples are taken from the present author's collection, *Century of City* (1974).

1. CATALOGUE VERSE
Explanation

Usually catalogue verse is a listing of things, ideas, feeling, etc., that have something in common. The length of line as well as the length of the poem may vary. It is the rhythm of the arrangement of words that gives catalogue verse its distinctiveness. Naturally, imagery adds to it as well.

Examples

The Sound of Rain
The sound of rain
is
pitter
patter
drip
splatter
drop
crash
thunder
thrash
bolts
lightning
splash
frightening!
Rainbarrel
bang
hail
rang
ring
zoom
ping
boom!
    Anita Bolbecher
    Gr. 5

Hockey
slapshot
wristshot
backhand
penalties
puck
stick
skates
equipment
losing
fighting
shooting
missing
scoring
winning the Stanley Cup
fans
teams
    Jim Newman
    Gr. 5

Beginning Work

In keeping with the name "catalogue verse," have students examine catalogues and make lists of words that interest them. Alternately, think about a topic and make a list of free-association ideas.

Next, experiment with re-arranging the words to get some rhythm. It is most helpful to read them out loud. In fact, have the whole class read a list that they have composed; the rhythm or lack of it will become very apparent.

2. SHAPE POEMS

Explanation

Various names describe this kind of poetry, depending on its exact format. Its origin goes back hundreds of years. For elementary school children it probably is not important to dwell on the differences (where they exist) among pop poems, visual poetry, concrete poetry, and shape poems. The essential ingredient is that the print or format helps to enhance the visual imagery for the reader—the "medium is the message," in a sense.

Examples

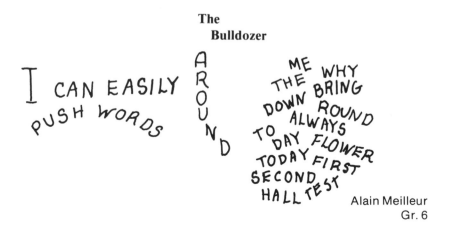

The
Bulldozer

Alain Meilleur
Gr. 6

the wonderful mouse
from
the tip
of his
nose a
mouse is
cute, he
is so small
and furry. and
wherever he goes it always
seems, he is in such a hurry.
he's always scampering
here and there, in and out of
holes always running
away from the
cat, who follows
him, wherever he goes, most people hate mice
but i think they're cute, even though they
may make nests, in the toe of some old boot.
some mice are gray
and blackish, some are
very white. some are
brown and grayish.
some are black as night,
a mouse is quite a clever chap
who'll do anything for cheese,
and into the smallest tiniest
hole, a mouse could probably squeeze.
a lovable pet, a mouse pest, a mouse is both
of these, always taking people's food,
never saying, "please", sharp, bright teeth, and as hungry as a whale, from the tip of his nose to the end of his tail.

Karen Crossley
Gr. 6

Beginning Work

Get students interested in manipulating words and word shapes by
cutting out words, titles, etc., from newspapers and magazines. Talk
about how the size, style of letters, and arrangement help to convey
a message. Another approach is to begin with a shape such as a cone,
square, or triangle. List things that come to mind about the shape.
Next, revise the words or statements to get rhythm (e.g., rearrange it
until it *sounds* good). Finally, arrange the words in the form of the

original shape. Remember to begin with ideas or meaning; end up with the shape or format.

References

Finlay, I. H. 1971. Poems to Hear and See. Macmillan, New York.
Gross, R. 1967. Pop Poems. Simon and Schuster, New York.

3. EXTEMPORANEOUS EXPRESSION

Explanation

This type of verse relies on the spontaneous expression of students. The teacher helps the student to bring out the poetic nuances of his verbalizations; it is somewhat akin to creative dramatics, role playing, or impressionistic painting. Careful listening to children's talk will reveal natural rhythms and occasionally even rhyme. Because of their rather uninhibited expression, imagery is often unique and quite unorthodox. Extemporaneous expression is not an experimental form; in fact, much of Old Testament writing is of this type. Note: catalogue verse is essentially a type of extemporaneous expression.

Examples

My Feather Pillow

SADNESS is having to part with your favorite feather pillow
    that over the years gains sentimental value.
    is finding out you're allergic to your night time pal, your
    pillow, with your own initials on it!
ANXIETY is knowing he has to go and time just drags on. You
    can never find a replacement for such a treasure, you know.
DESPAIR is looking at pillow after pillow and not one will fill
    that gap in your heart and make your head happy by sur-
    rounding it in soft cuddly fluff.
AGGRAVATION is finding out your new pillow is as hard as
    a rock and having to sleep with your head at a ninety degree
    angle. Boy! What an ache you have the next day.

My new guy tries but he just isn't right. But I guess I will have
to make do, because you can't have everything you want.

Arden Alexander
Gr. 6

Clay

Shaping clay, shaping clay,
Pinching, squeezing, shaping clay.
Oh now
More water, more water!
There, made it!
For a minute there, thought it would ruin.
Oh, now wheel stopped!
Pump! Pump! Pump!
There, now it's going.
Oh dear, it's slanted.
Now the wheel is going to fast.
Darn it all!
More water, more water.
There, now it's fixed.
Stop, stop, stop wheel!!
There, all done.

Shelley McIvor
Gr. 6

Beginning Work

Have children observe the movement of clouds, trees, flags, or
clothes on a line. Describe and arrange their observations in an
interesting format. Other techniques for motivating extemporaneous
expression are: 1) associations (e.g., school, church, home); 2) comparison or contrast; 3) litanies (e.g., "I can hear Christmas..."
"We love our country..."); 4) rearrange prose in poetic form if
suitable; 5) epigrammatical sayings (e.g., "It all depends on how
you look at things"); 6) chronological happenings; and 7) riddles
(e.g., eliminate what something is *not*).

References

Wolsch, R. A. 1970. Poetic Composition. Teachers' College Press, New York.

4. SENRYU

Explanation

Senryu (pronounced sen´ru) is an old Japanese poetic form which is
closely related to the Haiku. Because Haiku has rather strict criteria,
much of children's verse labeled Haiku is in fact Senryu. It does not
require the capturing of a "moment," or giving a "hint" of the
season, or the exact number of syllables (i.e., 17). Senryu has basically the Haiku format (five syllables, seven syllables, five syllables)
but usually deals with common or humorous incidents.

Examples

Dreams

Every string of dreams,
Has several tears to be shed,
Most of which are lost.

Colleen Penner
Gr. 5

Beginning Work

Review the matter of syllables and make a Senryu frame to use at first. This makes the form visible.

e.g. ___ ___ ___ ___ ___   (5)
     ___ ___ ___ ___ ___ ___ ___   (7)
     ___ ___ ___ ___ ___   (5)

It is best to try to capture an idea—a sunset, winning a game, eating a special meal—then revise and experiment with condensing the ideas into the Senryu form (see also the suggestions for Haiku).

References

Wolsch, R. A. 1970. Poetic Composition. Teachers' College Press, New York.
Hopkins, L. B. 1972. Pass the Poetry, Please! Citation Press, New York.

5.   HAIKU

Explanation

The classical Japanese Haiku follows these general rules: it 1) consists of 17 Japanese syllables: line one has five syllables, line two has seven syllables, and line three has five syllables; rhyme is avoided; 2) contains some reference to nature or the seasons; 3) refers to a particular event or a precise moment; and 4) presents an event as happening now—not in the past. Because this form is based on the Japanese syllable—which is really a unit of duration—translation is difficult.

Examples

Snow

The snow on the trees
Fell down on me like feathers
Glistening on my coat.

Kim Isleifson
Gr. 7

Sunlight

The sunlight beams down
Upon the sparkling landscape.
Dancing spotlights blink.

Maria De
Gr. 2

Beginning Work

Simple objects from nature may be used to stimulate writing: leaves budding out, a thunderstorm, the first snowflakes. A bumblebee, a cricket, etc., may be caught in a jar and released to capture the "moment" idea.

Films such as "Haiku: An Introduction to Poetry" (Coronet Films) or "In a Spring Garden" (Weston Woods) can be used effectively to motivate writing.

It is best to begin with descriptive or pictorial types of Haiku and then to progress to using suggestion and more subtle techniques.

References

Caudill, R. 1969. Come Along. Holt, Rinehart, and Winston, New York.
Issa, et al. 1969. Don't Tell the Scarecrow. Four Winds Press, New York. (Available from Scholastic.)
Lewis, R. (ed.). 1965. In a Spring Garden. Dial Press, New York. (Available from Dell.)
Henderson, H. G. 1967. Haiku in English. C. E. Tuttle, Rutland, Vermont.

6. CINQUAIN

Explanation

As the word cinquain (pronounced sing-kan') suggests, this is a five-line verse form. It consists of 22 syllables broken into a two, four, six, eight, two pattern and is sometimes referred to as a syllable cinquain. This form was originated by Miss Adelaide Crapsey, an American, in the early 1900s.

For elementary school students the word cinquain is perhaps more appropriate. It also consists of five lines. Line one, the title, consists of one word; line two consists of two words *descriptive* of the title; line three gives some *action* relevant to the title (three words); line four consists of four words indicating *feelings* about the title; and line five consists of a one-word synonym for the title. Cinquains generally do not contain rhymes, and punctuation is optional as well.

Examples

Black

Sometimes sad
Dark, shadows, harsh
Ashes after a fire,
Night.

Gloria Foster
Gr. 9

Nothing

Void, soundless
Sad nor happy
Boring and never filling
Emptiness.

Darell Lough
Gr. 7

Beginning Work

Two structures (one in parentheses) that simplify the writing of cinquain are:

Line 1:	The title or subject	(1 word)
Line 2:	Two adjectives describing the title or subject	(2 words)
Line 3:	Three adjectives (or action words about the title)	(3 words)
Line 4:	Four words forming a phrase or clause (or feeling about the title)	(4 words)
Line 5:	Repeat title or subject (or use a synonym for title)	(1 word)

Pictures or slides may be shown to trigger ideas for students' writing. You may try spraying a scent in the air while students have their eyes closed—capitalize on spontaneous remarks.

References

Hopkins, L. B. 1970. City Talk. Knopf, New York.
Powell, B. S. 1972. Making Poetry. Collier-Macmillan, Don Mills.

7. DIAMANTE

Explanation

The diamante (pronounced dee-ah-mahn-tay) is a relatively new form developed by Dr. Iris M. Tiedt. It has been widely disseminated through the May 1965 *Elementary English* journal where her article "A New Poetic Form: The Diamante" appeared.

It is a good form for expressing and contrasting opposites such as friend-enemy, love-hate, school-vacation, summer-winter. Because of its format, this form captures rhythm very easily; rhyme is not needed. Precise language and imagery may be practiced through the writing of diamantes. The diamante form looks like this:

Line 1:	Noun
Line 2:	Two adjectives
Line 3:	Three participles (*-ed or -ing words*)
Line 4:	Four words (*nouns related to the subject*)
Line 5:	Three participles (*-ed, -ing*)
Line 6:	Two adjectives
Line 7:	Noun
	(*opposite to the first noun*)

Examples

Fire

Flamboyant, destructive
Crackling, hissing, burning
Flame, death --- tragedy, scar
Frightening, destroying, chasing
Disastrous, ruinous
Char

Elaine Hughes
Gr. 9

Man

Kind, gentle
Playing, laughing, loving
Worker on the world
Killing, yelling, hating
Ignorant, rough
ape
Pam Penney
Gr. 6

Beginning Work

Interesting words to begin diamantes may spring from social studies (peace-war), science (micro-macro), health (sickness-health), reading (compare-contrast), etc., courses. Building lists of various parts of speech can be a rewarding activity for subsequent writing. For younger children it may be advisable to omit the word "participle" and simply talk about -ed words or -ing words. It should also be pointed out that -ed and -ing words should not normally be mixed. The *fourth* line of a diamante often contains the transition from the original subject to the final and contrasting noun.

References

Tiedt, I. M. 1965. A new Poetic form: The diamante. Elem. English 46(May): 588–589.

Hopkins, L. B. 1972. Pass the Poetry, Please! Citation Press, New York. (Available from Scholastic.)

8. COUPLETS

Explanation

A couplet consists of two lines that rhyme at the end, both lines having even rhythm (i.e., same meter). The lines may be any metrical pattern or length. Iambic pentameter ($-/-/-/-/-/$) is a particularly well known pattern.

Couplets may be used independently or as stanzas in a longer poem. They are effective in summarizing ideas such as proverbs or as epigrammatic comments (terse and/or witty statements).

Examples

The Streak

Streakers bare,
Peekers stare,
Everywhere on the square.
If you're there, beware!

Alfred Lamoureux,
Gr. 7

Beginning Work

For younger students rhyming games can be effectively used to teach and practise rhyming. Nursery rhymes, chants, etc., may be used. Examples:

1. One, two   2. Here We Go Round the Mulberry Bush

_____   _____

(fill in some possible lines)
3. Hickory, Dickory, Dock

_____

Dr. Seuss books are also a good source of clever and often witty rhymes. Have students read them out loud or clap their hands to feel the rhythm. For older students, couplets may be question-and-answer, statement-and-restatement, or a series of couplets (or stanzas). Other possibilities include variations in length or meter that could serve as an introduction to the clerihew.

References

The Selected Verse of Ogden Nash. 1945. The Modern Library (Random House), New York.

Boyd, G. A. 1973. Teaching Poetry in the Elementary School. C. E. Merrill, Columbus, Ohio.

9. TRIPLETS

Explanation

A three-line stanza with some rhyme is known as a triplet, or tercet. Triplets may carry the rhyme in the first and third lines, the first and second, the second and third, or in all three lines. Some triplets are complete in themselves, others are stanzas for longer poems. Occasionally, the unrhymed line in one stanza may rhyme with another line in a following stanza.

Example

I'll Never Forget the Day

I'll never forget the day
I learned that Christ was born
One glorious Christmas morn.

I'll never forget the day
I really understood
The meaning of Christmas and brother hood.

I'll never forget the day
I saw a picture of Him,
He who is our kin.

Cheryl Pawling,
Gr. 7

Beginning Work

It is generally easy to begin the writing of triplets by using repetition such as:

Halloween is pumpkins,
Halloween is scare,
On Halloween almost anything is fair.

Try beginning with Christmas, happiness, flowers, etc. In the intermediate grades, several stanzas of triplets may form a longer poem.

References

Wolsch, R. A. 1970. Poetic Composition. Teachers' College Press, New York.

10. QUATRAINS

Explanation

Four-line poems or stanzas, known as quatrains, may be written in a variety of rhyme schemes or lengths. Writing quatrains is also good practise leading up to the writing of ballads, which often use a particular quatrain form. The common rhyme schemes are aabb, abcb, and abab, but others may easily be found.

Example

The Beach

The sea is my teacher,
She pounds when she's mad.
The beach is my pencil,
My book and my pad.

The gulls are the pupils,
White with down.
This is my school,
My home all year round.

Lori Dobson,
Gr. 5

Beginning Work

Begin by reading many poems—humorous and serious, old and new—from any sources at hand. Next, observe. Observe things in motion; observe colorful things; observe new places or things; observe how others write quatrains. Experiment. For the lower grades think about things with four parts—the seasons, for example. List related associations, making certain that the last words form a rhyme scheme.

Mother:	____,	____,	____.
Father:	____,	____,	____.
Son:	____,	____,	____.
Daughter:	____,	____,	____.

References

Opie, I., and Opie, P. (eds.). 1973. The Oxford Book of Children's Verse. Clarendon Press, Oxford.

The Selected Verse of Ogden Nash. 1945. Modern Library (Random House), New York.

Hopkins, L. B. 1972. Pass the Poetry, Please! Citation, New York.

11. BALLADS AND BLUES

Explanation

Traditional ballads were passed on by word of mouth; they were story poems and were often sung. For this reason many ballads have refrains. The traditional ballads, in fact, were more likely to be tragic than humorous. Often they lack "poetic justice," that is, things do not necessarily end happily or fairly. More recently, the folk-type of singing has revived the ballad form that may be heard on radio and television. Because ballads use plain language and describe common situations, they are all about us just waiting to be recorded. Ballads deal with heroes and villains; they may be sad or funny; they are repetitive and full of action. Ballads are usually made of couplets, triplets, or quatrains. When quatrains are used they *may* have an abcb rhyme scheme and a rhythm pattern like the following example:

$$-/-/-/-/ \text{ (a)}$$
$$-/-/-/ \quad \text{(b)}$$
$$-/$$
$$-/-/-/-/ \text{ (c)}$$
$$-/-/-/ \quad \text{(b)}$$

A refrain may be added where desirable. Strict adherence to these conventions is not recommended for elementary school children.

Blues are a special kind of ballad usually dealing with fear, failure, or lonesomeness. Often the first line is repeated twice, and the third line rhymes with the first two.

The Ballad of the Haunted House

The wind blew hard and the storm clouds grew,
The sky turned gray instead of blue.
I was all alone in this big haunted house.
No one was with me, not even a mouse.

My friends had dared me to stay here all night,
And I had this feeling I was in for a fright.
There was this sound in the attic that bothered me so;
What it was, I really didn't know.

It was a thumping, a bumping, a weird sort of sound,
As if dozens of people were dancing around.
I had to find out, I could stand it no more,
So I crept up the stairs that led to the door.

I cautiously opened the door very wide
And now I could see just what was inside.
A table stood in the half lit room,
Six chairs were seen in the cobwebby gloom.

The chairs were empty but the table was laid,
With dishes and glasses full of pink lemonade.
The ballroom nearby had a dim yellow light,
But though quite dark, I saw a blood-chilling sight.

Six dancing couples were out on the floor,
They floated about, They all seemed to soar
About in the air. They were ghosts, without doubt!
I could see right through them as they danced about.

And each couple danced to a haunting refrain
Played by a headless figure, I maintain,
Seated at an organ that puffed and wheezed
While white, bony fingers flew over the keys.

The sight that I saw, I could stand it no more;
So quickly I turned and fled out the door.
I couldn't believe the adventure I had.
I was out of that house and I truly was glad.

I'll never go back there. Never again!
But visions of ghosts in my mind will remain.

Jackie Robson,
Gr. 6

Beginning Work

Because many recordings of ballads are relatively popular, it is a good idea to use them to create interest in this type of poetry. Songs such as "Blowin' in the Wind," "Where Have all the Flowers Gone," "When Day Is Done," or "Desert Pete" may be suitable for some elementary classes. Write out some of the verses on the board after listening to the records. This will aid in associating poetry and song. Consider the rhyming patterns and the rhythm (clap hands if necessary). Initially students can pattern their own ballads after the samples or even fill in the nonrepetitive lines with their own versions.

Another approach is to read the prose versions of ballads such as "Robin Hood" (see references below). Then try to write one episode in ballad form. Other well known suggested titles are: "The Pied Piper," "Frankie and Johnny," and "Waltzing Matilda."

References

Wosch, R. A. 1970. Poetic Composition. Teachers' College Press, New York.
Mannig-Sanders, R. 1968. Stories from the English and Scottish Ballads. Heineman, London.
Ledhas, S. N. 1969. By Loch and By Lin. Holt, Rinehart, and Winston, New York. (Tales from Scottish Ballads.)
Grigson, G. 1959. The Cherry-Tree. Phoenix House, London.

12. JINGLES

Explanation

Jingles consist of a series of sounds or repeated phrases and are basically a carefree play with language. The "jingle" of the lines is the most important; sense is somewhat secondary. Some are nursery rhymes, some are counting rhymes, some are games:

Little Miss Muffet
One, Two, Buckle Your Shoe
Eeny, meeny, miny, mo
Here We Go Round the Mulberry Bush

Jingles should be written for enjoyment; otherwise, little time need be spent on them. Most children know many common jingles but may benefit from writing their own.

Examples

> Hickory, Dickory, Dee
> My cat ran up the tree.
> I worried and frowned
> Until he came down,
> Hickory, Dickory, Dee.
>
> A   is for an Apple,
> B   is for a Bat,
> C   is for a Cuckoo-Clock,
>   some Custard, and a Cat.

Beginning Work

Make a list of beginning lines; then see who can complete the jingle. Here are some starters:

Hey! Diddle, Diddle...
Hot cross buns...
There was a Crooked Man...
Baa, Baa, Black Sheep...
Pease Porridge Hot...
Humpty Dumpty...

Any book of nursery rhymes will contain numerous jingles if you need more. A catchy technique is to use the "Jane Small Ate It All" format, and have the students supply names.

Jane Brooke was the cook
But Jane Small ate it all.

Jane Dwyer lighted the fire
And Jane Brooke was the cook
But Jane Small ate it all.

Other starters would be to make up advertising jingles such as those heard on TV or such as the ice cream man might use when driving down the street.

Older students might be able to write modern parodies of nursery rhymes such as those found in Eve Merriam's *The Inner City Mother Goose.*

References

Opie, I., and Opie, P. 1964. A Family Book of Nursery Rhymes. Oxford University Press, London.
Merriam, E. 1969. The Inner City Mother Goose. Simon & Schuster, New York.

13. WORK SONGS

Explanation

Children have endless rhymes for skipping, bouncing a ball, sweeping, or washing. Work songs are common to most cultures in adult life as well. Today most children and adults are familiar with Belafonte's "Bananaboat Song" and other popular work songs, i.e., "John Henry," "Pick a Bale of Cotton," etc.

Examples

Weed-Pulling Song
Tug! Tug! Yank 'em out,
    Drag them from the ground,
If the garden is to grow
    There can't be weeds around.

Two Songs for Pumping up Air-Mattresses
#1 Down-up, Down-up, Down-up, Down—
    UP!
    Down-up, Down-up, Down-up-down-up-down—
    UP!
    Pinch, Plug, Stop.

> #2   Step on it, Step on it,
>   A hundred times or more.
>   Step on it, Step on it,
>   Until you can no more—
>   (and it still won't be filled!)
> Roland Froese
Gr. 5

Beginning Work

Discuss skipping, pantomiming, and action songs familiar to your students, or play some recorded work songs for them. Compose work songs related to social studies, chores or duties (e.g., erasing the chalkboard, polishing silverware, or waxing the car). The key is to capture the rhythm of the activity through repetition, onomatopoeia, or alliteration.

References

Langstaff, M., and Langstaff, J. 1970. Jim Along, Josie. Harcourt Brace, Jovanovich, New York. (A collection of folk songs, singing games, and action songs for children.)

Wolsch, R. A. 1970. Poetic Composition. Teachers' College Press, New York.

14.   LIMERICKS

Explanation

Few people need an introduction to limericks or to Edward Lear who wrote them to amuse children. Limericks can be used to help overcome a dislike for poetry and to discover the fun of rhythm and rhyme. Essentially limericks consist of five lines with a rhyme scheme of aabba and a metrical scheme of three beats in the first, second, and fifth lines, and two beats in the third and fourth lines. In most of Lear's limericks, the last line is a variation of the first, but modern limericks generally contain a different (although rhyming with the first two lines) last line—a sort of punch line that is often witty. Limericks most frequently begin with a subject, a name, or a locality. Often they are playing with language and require oral reading or the decoding of symbols. Generally, limericks deal with imaginary situations or people.

Example

> There was a young girl named Heather
> Who claimed to enjoy the weather,
>   But when it got hot
>   She said, "I do not!
> I'm right at the end of my tether."
>
>   Brenda Froese
>   Gr. 7

Beginning Work

Write a line on the chalkboard, for example: There was an old man named Yahoo. Make up a list of words which rhyme with the last word, then use them to end the second line. Make up a third line. Again build a list of rhyming words to be used as endings for line four. Line five can end with a word from the first list.

Another approach is to get a book of limericks and make a list of first lines only. These may then be used as starters.

References

Brewton, S., and Brewton, J. 1965. Laughable Limericks. Crowell, New York.
Hopkins, L. B. 1972. Pass the Poetry, Please! Citation, New York.

15. CLERIHEWS

Explanation

A clerihew consists of two couplets of unequal length, the first usually being shorter. Often clerihews are satirical or humorous and most are biographical. Usually the first line contains the name of a person—one's own name, a historical character, a movie star, or a sports personality. Generally, the shorter the lines, the more effective the clerihew. The first line is normally followed by an accomplishment in the second line and a personal reaction to that accomplishment in the third and fourth lines. This form was named after Edmund Clerihew Bentley, the English originator of this type of quatrain.

Example

> Bobby Hull
> Ain't dull.
> He signed a paper
> For a one million caper.

Beginning Work

Treat clerihews lightly—as a way of poking fun at ourselves and others. Begin by building a list of popular names such as movie stars, television personalities, superstars in sports, etc. Next match rhyming words with each name. Then build a clerihew frame like this:

Line 1:	a name
Line 2:	some accomplishment or "boo-boo" (rhyming with the name)
Lines 3 and 4:	a reaction to line 2, usually humorous; lines 3 and 4 rhyme.

The rest comes easily. Try one yourself, it's enjoyable and easy.

References

Jones, R. 1969. Explorations: A Practical Study of Children Writing Poetry. McGraw-Hill, London.
Wolsh, R. A. 1970. Poetic Composition. Teachers' College Press, New York.

chapter 10

Developing Basic Literacy Skills

Carl Braun

It is possible, if not highly probable, that the high degree of formalization of the educational process often results in price tags that escape our awareness. There is evidence, for instance, to suggest that the highly structured nature of reading programs can negate the central purpose for which they were designed—to teach reading as an active communication process. That is, the central purpose gets lost in the effort to sequentialize and program the isolated skill components that presumably constitute the total reading act. The position taken here is that conscious effort should be expended at all levels of reading instruction to: 1) develop the notion of reading as communication in the early stages of reading, and 2) build in informal components to ensure that this central objective is maintained through the grades.

Stauffer (1971) has stated that "sound instruction from the very beginning must operate on the premise that reading speaks to the reader in a communication act similar to oral communication" (p. 17). The reader should, from the very beginning, get inspiration, pleasure, and satisfaction that exert a "conscious integrative effect upon him" (Stauffer, 1971, p. 17). As indicated in Chapter 1, capitalizing on the reader's experience is a first step in this direction.

Recent research points to a number of reasons why such "integrative effect" is out of reach for many beginning readers. As early as 1957, Vernon concluded that one of the major causes of reading disability was that the reader remains in a state of "cognitive confusion" over the process of reading:

> The child...may indeed have learnt that printed words have some relation to spoken words; and, with a few simple words, he has memorized the spoken word that corresponds to a particular shape. But he does not seem to understand why .... He appears hopelessly uncertain and confused as to why certain successions of printed letters should correspond to certain phonetic sounds in words (Vernon, 1957, p. 48).

Vygotsky (1962) lent further support to the abstract nature of the literacy task as a stumbling block for young children learning the written form of the language. He held that as a result the child has only a vague idea of its usefulness. Clearly, one's perception of the usefulness of language, whatever the medium, is intimately related to its function as a communicator.

Reids's (1966) and more recently Downing's (1971) research have confirmed the inability to cope with the abstractness of language as equivalent to Vernon's notion of cognitive confusion. Both researchers have established empirically that young children lack specific expectancies of what reading is going to be like, of what the activity consists of and the relationship between reading and writing. Furthermore, children lack the linguistic equipment to deal with new experiences, calling letters "numbers" and words "names," interchanging words and sentences. Downing (1975) emphatically points out the implications of this level of confusion at the beginning reading stage:

> Many children today are being confused by ill-conceived phonic methods and materials. These often overemphasize the coding method to the neglect of the communicative purpose of writing. This type of instruction misleads the beginner into believing that reading is decoding one set of meaningless visual symbols (letters) into another set of meaningless auditory symbols (phonemes). The way to avoid this type of cognitive confusion is to make sure that the majority of the child's first experiences of the written code stress its communicative function. The language experience approach seems ideally suited to this instructional goal since it gives the child first-hand experiences with the purposes of writing.... teaching of these letter-sound relationships should always be in the genuine context of encoding or decoding thoughts and feelings (p. 144).

To this point the discussion has focused only on the danger of cognitive confusion at beginning reading levels. It is entirely possible that part of this confusion (i.e., failure to be in tune with the purpose of the written code) may persist long after the beginning reading stages. In fact, it is not unthinkable that extreme rigidity in a program and sterile materials may contribute to the development of such confusion even for the child who has at one time been in a state of cognitive clarity. For this reason, the suggestions for informal activities that follow include ideas that extend beyond the beginning reading level. There is no intention that the types of activities outlined will constitute "the reading program." The activities, experiential in nature, are the type that make the transition from speech to print as smooth and as natural as possible, leaving little doubt as to the purpose of print—communication.

ACTIVITIES

Sign and Billboard Reading

Sign and billboard reading can be used to develop the communication functions of symbols. Ask children in the early stages of reading to make a rough copy of a sign on a billboard they pass on the way to or from school. Have the child read the copy to the class. As part of their early reading experience, give children wide exposure to street signs and labels: "Walk," "Don't Walk," "Keep off the Grass," "Poison," and "Danger."

Classroom Labeling

Labels are an efficient way of motivating children to read and to associate oral and written language. Labels may be placed on desks, coat hangers, doors, and various other objects in the classroom long before the child is introduced to a formal reading program. At first, labels may be simple naming labels. Gradually they may extend to labels that give the children simple directions. Labels can be placed on interest centers, on articles in a simulated classroom grocery or toy store, or a simulated classroom post office.

Directions

Labeling of furniture and other objects in the classroom is closely associated with labeling directions—north, south, east, west—in the room. Apart from providing reading experience, labeling directions provide good background for map-reading skills.

Time-related Reading

Have children relate the day of the month and the week to number symbols. This is an excellent way of establishing an association between sound, symbol, and referent. Have children make their own cumulative calendar, adding the new date each morning. This provides a further means of communication development. Ask children to check the date on their personal calendar with the date in the daily paper and the television guide. Construct a large classroom calendar to note important class events that are coming up.

Teach children to tell time on the clock. Relate the lessons to interesting events: recess, meal time, or a favorite television program. The activity links sound, symbol, and experience and proves to the child that decoding symbols is meaningful.

Map-reading and Construction

Very young children can profit from constructing, either individually or in groups, crude maps on large sheets of paper. Have the children make maps of the classroom, their room at home, and the playground. For a young child, construction of a map may be little more than a mechanical exercise. Have the children label, on the maps, features of special importance. To add interest to the project, use the maps for treasure hunts.

Introduce many variations of interesting map-reading activities before confronting the child with an atlas. Children enjoy following a crude mimeographed map of the route they are taking on a field trip whether they are walking or riding. Predicting left and right turns adds considerable interest.

Recipe Reading

Encourage children to read and to follow directions on how to mix paste and finger paints. These activities provide a natural way for associating symbol, sound, and action. They lay the foundation for establishing reading as a communicative act.

Riddles and Jokes

Bring in books of riddles and riddle cards. Write a "riddle of the week" on the chalkboard. Riddles provide incentives for the reluctant reader and afford the slow reader opportunities to re-read material of interest to him. The child may be motivated to copy the riddle so that he can read it to his family. Thus, his newly acquired skill has added social relevance.

Provide the child with short anecdotes and jokes that he is able to read with little difficulty. The experience can enhance his image. The response of the listener, apart from providing social reinforcement, will certainly substantiate the notion that reading is, indeed, a communicative skill.

Classroom Plans

Plans for interesting projects, field trips, puppet shows, or athletic functions can be recorded on charts. The charts can be made by the children or by the teacher after children have suggested what should be included. Charts can list simple rules for safety standards to be observed by the class. For children whose reading skills are more advanced, brochures about field trips can be used to extend reading skills.

Weather Charts

Stimulate children to note temperature, humidity, and precipitation. When this information is recorded on a chart, many opportunities for related activities can ensue. Each week, day-by-day comparisons of temperature can be made. The range of temperature can be noted: lows and highs. The children can learn to work out the average temperature for the week. When these charts are compiled in loose-leaf books, many interesting comparisons can be made. The weather for a specific week in November can be compared with the weather for a week in March. Whatever reading and writing skills are required are related to the child's world.

Television Guides

The average child watches television for hours. The school can capitalize on the many opportunities television opens for activities related to reading. Give each child in the classroom a modified television schedule listing interesting children's programs. The schedule will provide a situational reading opportunity that few children will pass up. Depending on the age of the child, the schedule can easily be integrated with reading and writing activities.

Hobby Centers

Most children are highly motivated to read about their hobbies. The domain is unlimited. Encourage children to read up on how to feed tropical fish, how to assemble a model airplane, or how to discover a new world with a microscope. This kind of activity can be adapted for use at almost any reading level. Vary the number of pictures that accompany verbal descriptions. Vary the difficulty of the material and the amount to be read. It is also important to consider the different degrees of structure and aid necessary for children in the class. For example, for the reluctant reader, the teacher or another pupil might state specifically that in a particular paragraph the reader will find information on how to determine whether his hamster is male or female. The key is to find material that the child needs to know at the moment.

Classroom Diary

A resourceful teacher can devise many interesting variations of classroom diaries. The class may decide at the end of the week which activities or incidents are of sufficient interest to be included in the diary. The entries for the week can be made by an individual pupil or a group. For a younger class, the children can dictate to the teacher what should be included for the week. Encourage the inclusion of specific names of children who were involved in activities, and make sure that all children are included at one time or another. The use of names will encourage even the reluctant reader to read at least some of the entries at a later date.

Classroom Newspaper

Many opportunities for writing can be stimulated by providing an audience for the writing. The classroom newspaper that is circulated among classmates, teachers, and parents offers such an opportunity. De-emphasize "correctness" particularly for young children. Freedom from fear of making errors can encourage even the reluctant writer to submit a contribution, be it a report on an interclass soccer game, a letter to the editor on his ideas about changes he would like to see in school, a story, a cinquain, a Haiku, or a review of a book that "turned him on." This is not to suggest that children should not be encouraged as early as possible to edit, either individually or in pairs. Certainly, one could argue that constant exposure to poor models might impede clarity and conciseness in communication.

Bulletin Board Displays

Attractive bulletin boards with a frequently changing format can do much to focus children's attention on news articles, social and athletic events, and other items of general interest. Encourage children to contribute to bulletin board displays. Their contributions will help make the displays a center of interest. Adapt these displays to varying levels of difficulty. For the reluctant, disabled reader, a newpaper headline and a picture may be all that will capture his interest until he gains in motivation and skill.

Reference Reading

Provide opportunities early for simple reference reading. The newspaper can be used for this purpose. The children can get information on local events, check sports news, and get facts about the latest space flight. These are only a few ways in which reading can be done in a situation that has relevance for the young learner. The obvious reference sources—dictionaries, atlases, encyclopedias—should be introduced gradually. In early assignments, have children look up a limited amount of specific, interesting information. The activity can teach the learner that "this is a source where I can find what I need to know," rather than "this is where I'm forced to flounder in boredom."

Photographic Stimulus

Many children find it difficult to discuss an event such as a field trip even a short time after the experience. While any interesting event is good grist for the language chart mill, the language chart frequently uses more teacher-language than child-language and so negates many of the benefits that can accrue from the experience. When children have difficulty in recalling highlights and sequence, a series of four or five photographs may help stimulate recall. It may be useful to initiate discussion with the group by placing the photographs in logical sequence. Labeling the picture is one way of incorporating reading with the exercise.

Record what the children say about the pictures. With older children, the labels on the pictures can be used as main ideas of an outline after they have decided on a topic that encompasses the whole sequence of pictures. These experiences should help children develop links between experience, oral language, and written communication. Specific application of the use of photographic stimuli was discussed in chapter 2.

DEVELOPING THE CONCEPT OF LITERACY—AUDITORY-VISUAL INPUT

Closely related to the whole concept of cognitive confusion, as has been mentioned earlier, is the child's conception of the relationship between the *spatial* flow of symbols and the *temporal* flow of sounds. Recognition of this fact has a number of very basic implications.

Knowledge of this relationship is prerequisite to the child's understanding of the commonality that exists between speech and print: communication. At the prereading and beginning reading levels, this suggests that the child can conceptualize the fact that his name tag "John" can be substituted for the oral stimulus "John." Then, too, this suggests that knowledge of the fact that white spaces between words in a written sentence in some way relate to segmentations or boundaries between words in a spoken sentence. Many of the foregoing activities should facilitate development of this aspect. However, at a more advanced level, and more analytically, the child will recogize the relationship between syllables as discrete segments of a word in relation to spoken segments of the same word. It would appear that a lot of wasted motion occurs at the readiness and beginning reading levels to develop auditory and visual perception skills as isolated entities. While, superfically this may seem logical, the act of reading goes beyond the perceptual and certainly beyond isolated perceptual entities. Some have reacted with surprise to findings that show some reading disability cases to be superior in discrimination abilities to normal readers (Robinson, 1953; Serafica and Sigel, 1970). Reading involves an integration of these entities and that implies cognition. Downing (1973) states:

> It is not the ability to hear different phonemes or see different characters that is the difficulty in learning to read. The heart of the problem lies in the cognitive processes that enable the child to conceptualize these linguistic units and understand how the phonological code is related to the written or printed code (p. 74).

Rodenborn (1971) supports this position in his interpretation of research data on auditory-visual integration abilities of good and poor readers. Such research studies postulate perceptual rather than cognitive abilities as requisite for the decoding aspects of reading. Authors like Raab, Deutsch, and Freedman (1960) have concluded that good and poor readers can be differentiated on the basis of their ability to shift from one sensory modality to another. Similarly, Birch and Belmont (1965, p. 303) suggested that "the acquisition of auditory-visual integration. . . may well represent a primary competence requisite to the acquisition of literacy." Rodenborn argues that these measures of perception and integration are often influenced by many other factors, including the child's skill at problem-solving (a cognitive task). What these tests may actually be measuring, he feels, is not the child's auditory-visual integration per se, but his degree of understanding of such concepts as the symbolic function of the visual stimulus and the relationship between the spatial flow of symbols and the temporal flow of sounds.

While evidence is limited, a few researchers have suggested that the familiarity with music symbolization may enhance the reading skills of the young learner. Movsesian (1967), for example, found gains in reading proficiency as a result of a program introducing music and reading concurrently. While Movsesian attributed gains to the children's improved auditory and visual percepton, there is reason to believe that the gains may have been accounted for, at least in part, by a reduction in cognitive confusion through the highly regularized musical code system. The suggestions that follow are aimed at developing and reinforcing visual-auditory integration in a more specific sense than the suggestions noted earlier.

Double Auditory Stimulus

Probably the easiest introduction to the idea of emphasizing the segmentations *between* and *within* words is to introduce a simple two-or-four-line verse:

> See the little monkeys
> Playing in the zoo
> Teasing mother monkey
> What a thing to do.

Simply teach by rote the words to the verse and have children repeat it chorally. Then, have them clap once for each word or word part (or for each time their jaw moves as they are saying the verse). There is no need, in the early stages, to mention the fact that the jaw makes two movements for the word "monkeys" (two syllables) and only one for a word like "see" (one syllable). This can be done when the words are introduced visually along with the auditory.

Double Auditory-Single Visual Stimulus

Depending on the age and interest of the children, present verses and rhymes of varying types orally. Then, introduce some of the same material in print (overhead, chalkboard, or chart paper). Have the children repeat a verse while they are seeing the print (point to words), and have them clap the words and word parts. At this stage, point out (and perhaps underline) the words that require more than one clap. Again, it is well to relate this to the number of times the jaw moves in saying the word (e.g., saying "monkeys" requires two movements of the jaw and two claps so the word has two parts).

Children enjoy the variety brought in by having rhythm instruments introduced as a substitute for clapping. This may simply mean that two or three children accompany the choral speaking by beating on a tin can, triangle, or whatever.

Double Auditory-Double Visual Stimulus

For teachers so inclined, it is an excellent idea to introduce children to notation on the staff, showing the relatively simplified consistent symbolization of music in relation in the highly complex and irregular system of orthography. For example, the verse from the earlier choral speaking example might be introduced as shown in Figure 1. When the children have worked with a number of examples like the one in Figure 1, repeat some of the "songs" and instruct them to clap every time you point to a note (while they are singing, of course). This should lead to the generalization that one clap corresponds to one movement of the jaw, to one word (or word part), and to one note. For teachers who feel unable to work with music notation, making strokes on the board corresponding to words and word parts is equally valuable.

Substitution of Auditory-Visual Stimulus

At this time, it is useful to use some of the songs and verses introduced and to substitute new words, e.g., you may want to supply another set of words to the "monkey song":

See the little monkeys
Climbing here and there
Teasing other monkeys
Tails up in the air.

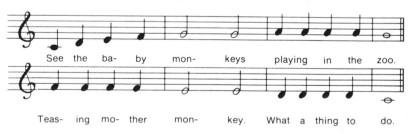

Figure 1.   The verse from a choral speaking example written as notation on the staff.

It is a good idea to substitute words of class interest. Incorporating names of children into the songs and verses is always of high interest, for example:

> Here is Sherry Whitfield
> Happy as can be
> Hear her now she's singing
> One, two, three

Point out that you need only three notes for the last line rather than five as in the "monkey song." This substitution exercise will certainly help focus on the meaning aspect of the activity.

A number of suggestions are in order with respect to these substitution activities. First, it is a good idea for the teacher to work out many of the substitutions with the children, e.g., "We needed two claps, and two notes for 'playing'; let's try 'climbing' and see if it fits in with the two notes. 'In the zoo' needed three notes, one for each word; let's see if 'here and there' fits in the same way." Encourage children to clap as they try different words and combinations of words for "fit." The second suggestion here is that the visual component be kept strong throughout; for each new phrase or line, have them check the "fit" both auditorally against the number of claps and visually against the number of notes (or strokes).

The creative teacher will think of many extensions of the foregoing activities. For example, a musical roll call might go like this: "When I call your name, sing and clap it back to me. How many notes (or strokes) will I need to write the music for your name?"

A variation making use of children's names might be to select children who have polysyllabic names and have them sing something like the notation shown in Figure 2. Show them the reduction of the number of notes needed to put to music the abbreviated versions of their names. Again, stress both the visual and the auditory components.

Encourage children to place strokes or notes above the lines of simple nursery rhymes they know. Emphasize the need to check with the number of movements of the jaw or the number of claps required to ensure the correct number of notes.

Figure 2.   Notation making use of a child's polysyllabic name.

SUMMARY

Activities designed to clarify and at the same time pull together the auditory and visual features of words and strings of words, thus introducing multi-discriminating features, should aid in the development of cognitive clarity and ultimately, the communicative function of written language.

LITERATURE CITED

Birch, H. G., and Belmont, L. 1965. Auditory-visual integration, intelligence, and reading ability in school children. Percept. Mot. Skills 20:295-305.
Downing, J. 1971. How children develop concepts of language. In: C. Braun (ed.), Language, Reading and the Communication Process, pp. 113-119. International Reading Association Monograph. International Reading Association, Newark, Del.
Downing, J. 1973. Comparative Reading. Macmillan, New York.
Downing, J. 1975. What is decoding? Read. Teacher 29(2):142-144.
Movsesian, E. A. 1967. The influence of teaching music reading skills on the development of basic reading skills in the primary grades. Unpublished doctoral disseration, University of Southern California.
Raab, S., Deutsch, M., and Freedman, A. M. 1960. Perceptual shifting and set in normal school children of different reading achievement. Percept. Motor Skills 10:187-192.
Reid, J. 1966. Learning to think about reading. Educat. Res. 9:56-62.
Robinson, H. M. 1953. Supplementary Educational Monographs No. 77. University of Chicago, Chicago.
Rodenborn, L. V., Jr. 1970-1971. The importance of memory and integration factors to oral reading ability. 3:51-59.
Serafica, F. C., and Sigel, I. E. 1970. Styles of categorization and reading disability. J. Read. Behav. 2:105-115.
Stauffer, R. G. 1971. The quest for maturity in reading. In: C. Braun (ed.), Language, Reading and the Communication Process, pp. 9-19. International Reading Association Monograph. International Reading Association, Newark, Del.
Vernon, M. D. 1957. Backwardness in Reading. Cambridge University Press, London.
Vygotsky, L. 1962. Thought and Language. MIT Press, Cambridge, Mass.

PART V
EVALUATION

chapter 11

To Talk of
Many Things...

Victor Froese

> "The time has come," the Walrus said,
>   "To talk of many things: . . .
> Of shoes—and ships—and sealing wax—
>   Of cabbages—and kings—
> And why the sea is boiling hot—
>   And whether pigs have wings."
>
> Lewis Carroll (1946, p. 197)

This chapter provides some responses to commonly made charges against the language experience approach. Charges such as stereotyped use of charts, needless repetition, and teacher inflexibility are not addressed here because such charges are not criticisms of the language experience approach (in fact, similar charges may be directed toward any method or approach); these are essentially criticisms against poor teaching. More specifically, this chapter argues that showing any one method to be the best is not a useful approach. Following that, the most common charges against the language experience approach will be addressed, and procedures for coping with these criticisms will be suggested. At this point the reader may wish to review the general definition of "language experience" in the initial sections of this volume.

OVERVIEW

The chapters in this book present a rational approach to using language experiences rather than the often "evangelistic" attitude. These authors believe that there are sound psychological and pedagogic explanations for such an approach, and faith in the dictates of one or the other proponents of it is not required. When possible we prefer to base our judgments on empirically supported practises and experiences shown to be successful in the classroom. At present, considerable evidence has accrued so that what once was "teacher intuition" has now been evaluated in some way and it is such results that the informed teacher should be aware of.

While it is not difficult to cite reputable studies that support the language experience approach (Harris and Serwer, 1966; Kendrick and Bennett, 1967; Stauffer and Hammond, 1965; Vilscek, Morgan, and Cleland, 1967), these simply substantiate the fact that language experience was superior in a particular experiment. These studies do not prove that language experience is a superior method because similar claims (i.e., better experimental results) can be made for other methods. The contention here is that unquestionable methodological superiority cannot be established and need not be. What is important is that teacher preference and the most philosophically suitable method be matched. This type of reasoning can be substantiated to some extent by examining Dykstra's (1970) observations regarding the second-grade phase of the Cooperative Research Program (i.e., extension of the First-Grade Reading Studies).

Dykstra presents comparisons for basal, Initial Teaching Alphabet (i.t.a.), language experience, linguistic, and phonic/linguistic programs. From examining his data, it quickly becomes evident that there is considerably more variation within any one program type than there is between projects (that may contain any combination of the programs listed above). As a result, Dykstra (1970, p. 492) suggests:

> In four of the ten projects, for example, each of the experimental treatments resulted in the same mean reading comprehension score. In another four projects, the grade score differences between the highest achieving program and the lowest achieving program was two months or less.
>
> Findings of this nature emphasize the importance of the total learning situation in influencing pupil progress in beginning reading instruction and suggest that future research in beginning reading should focus on trying to determine what elements of the total learning situation differentiate two school systems which use the same published materials, which enroll children who look very similar in readiness characteristics, but which produce second-grade readers who differ markedly in average reading achievement.

A second reason for not using methodological comparison studies as evidence of superiority of a particular method is that progress in reading should not be thought of as a gradual and even progression—it might have plateaus, periods of very rapid learning, and periods of slow growth. An indication of sporadic or cummulative growth can be seen in longitudinal studies only. For example, Kendrick and Bennett (1967, p. 38) found that at the end of first grade 10 out of 15 comparisons favored the traditional method (basal), while at the end of second grade, of the significant findings 12 favored the experience approach (language-experience) and 11 the traditional method.

A third reason why the superiority of one method over the other is not crucial is that other factors such as socioeconomic status are probably more important (i.e., in predicting success in reading). In one of the most ambitious studies of reading comprehension in our time—spanning 15 countries—Thorndike (1973, p. 177) concluded that: "A second main finding is that in the developed countries an appreciable prediction of the reading achievement of individual students—and an even more substantial prediction of the average reading achievement of children in a school—is provided by information about their home and family background."

COMMON CRITICISMS OF LANGUAGE EXPERIENCE

Some aspects of the language experience approach are commonly criticized (Spache and Spache, 1973) and consequently require careful examination. It must, however, be reiterated that the position taken here is not one of blanketly endorsing the language experience approach; rather the point of view is that it is one of several sound approaches and that teachers philosophically suited to it should use it. Even more important is the decision as to whether the approach is most suitable for the student(s) being taught by it.

When making the above argument the writer is reminded of a passage in Lee's (1960) *To Kill a Mockingbird.* Lee's narrator, Scout (Jean Louise Finch), tells of her school experience (1930s) with her new teacher from northern Alabama. She recounts to her brother: "Miss Caroline told me to tell my father not to teach me any more. 'It's best,' she said, 'to begin reading with a fresh mind. I'll take over from here and try to undo the damage.' I retired, meditating upon my crime. I never deliberately learned to read, but for all the evenings in my memory I had been wallowing illicitly in the daily papers, or anything else Atticus happened to be reading when I crawled into his lap every night" (p. 23).

As in this incident, real language experience is most often criticized because it does not follow a predetermined skills sequence. Consequently, that is the criticism discussed first.

Criticism 1—The Language Experience Approach Does Not Ensure a Balance or Sequence of Skills

This is an interesting criticism because it probably rests on a confusion between teaching and learning in the first place. Does the fact that a teacher "teaches" or "covers" all skills in a scope and sequence chart ensure that children have *learned* those skills? Do the supposed "skills" actually exist and are they truly different? The answer to both questions is probably "No."

There is, in fact, no reason why a language experience program cannot have a skills list; in fact, such guides are encouraged (see individual chapters and Part VI, Appendices A and B regarding skills). What differentiates the experience approach is that the skills are not taught in a predetermined order but, instead, according to diagnosed needs. This will, of course, dictate individual or small- or large-group teaching at times.

As a rule, the less predetermined structure in the classroom is visible, the more structure is necessary in the teacher's head. Most basic language skills are teachable from any kind of written or spoken material. Children's spontaneous language contains all basic language structures (Hatch, 1969, p. 32; Riling, 1965, p. 182) and shows more diversity than most "controlled" textbooks (Packer, 1970). In fact, Riling (1965, p. 183) concludes that "even as early as Grade 4, in narration, children use the chief structures of the English language proportionately in a way that approaches the use of them by adults who write nonfiction for books, magazines, and newspapers." There is very little evidence that the children's own language is restrictive in any sense. What is necessary is an ability to identify and to capitalize on the skill, structure, or usage being exhibited by the student. That brings us to a second common criticism of the language experience approach.

The second question posed at the beginning of this section deals with the actual existence and discreteness of the multitude of skills commonly listed. Even a cursory examination of most skills lists will make it obvious that some of the skills require similar mental processes. Williams (1959) listed the critical reading skills in 10 basal reading series and found skills such as "anticipating outcomes," "drawing conclusions," "establishing sequence," "forming an opinion." Obviously, these require similar cognitive operations. In fact, Spache and Spache (1973, p. 546) go one step further to conclude that "all the separate skills identified by various authors or test makers may simply be labels given by them to the kinds of *questions* they ask, rather than distinct, trainable reading behaviors." While that is a reasonable conjecture, some empirical evidence exists as well and it points to a much shorter list of comprehension skills or factors—perhaps two to nine (Davis, 1968; Lennon, 1962; Sochor, 1959).

The other language arts—composition, listening, and speaking—are not nearly as well researched as reading, and, consequently, even less is known about the skills involved. Most skills in these areas are logical listings and have yet to be empirically determined.

The discussion is not intended to discount skills lists and sequences as useless or irrelevant but rather to put them into a reasonable perspective. The teacher or student-teacher is advised to consult local, district, or state/provincial curriculum guides for suggested skills lists for the language arts. From these guides, the teacher may wish to construct simplified lists which serve as checklists for individual students' evaluation or teaching (see other chapters for specific examples).

Criticism 2—Teacher Skill in Diagnosis is Essential to Teaching by the Language Experience Method

This comment is naturally related to the previous discussion (Criticism 1). If diagnostic teaching is to occur, the teacher must know what to look for. One way to accomplish that is to begin with a list of skills and compare students' competencies to the list. If the skills lists are graded, the procedure is somewhat simplified, and even informal, teacher-made tests or exercises can pinpoint areas in need of direct instruction.

It is this author's contention and experience that teachers and student-teachers can learn to diagnose adequately under supervised practise conditions; it may even be a legal responsibility (Dunn, Dunn, and Price, 1977, pp. 418–420). In fact, it seems somewhat foolhardy simply to "cover" skills because they are listed somewhere rather than to base one's teaching on recognized needs (although the former is not an uncommon practise).

Figure 1 suggests a simplified procedure for diagnostic teaching. Many useful materials are available to assist the teacher in such diagnostic sequences. In fact, it is essential that a great deal of in-

Classroom Activity   **Teacher Preparation**

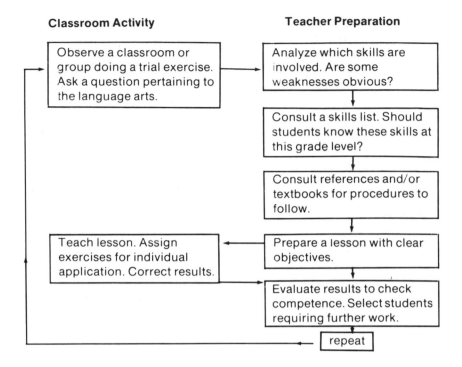

Figure 1. Flow chart showing a simplified procedure for diagnostic teaching.

dependent work be done under such conditions because the teacher is involved with individuals or small groups a majority of the time. The reader may consult individual chapters in this volume for specific references to materials and activities. The reader interested in detailed skills lists should consult Guszak (1972) for reading skills and Lamb (1972) for language skills. Both sources have skills arranged by grade levels.

Criticism 3—Evaluation of Progress
Relies too Heavily on Teacher Observation and Opinion

Implicit in this statement is the assumption that teachers are not competent observers and that their judgments are not as accurate as some other (usually unspecified) forms of evaluation. There is evidence to suggest that teachers' observations are affected by numerous factors (Braun, 1976, p. 187), such as name connotations, quality of handwriting, appearance, the sex of the student, and amount of training.

Because teachers' observations and judgments are broader based than a specific subtest on a standardized test, generalized student ratings correspond well with total readiness or achievement test scores. For example, Kermonian (1962) found that teacher ratings and Metropolitan Readiness scores correlated 0.73, and Hitchcock and Alfred (1955) found that eighth-grade English teacher ratings correlated 0.83 with the Stanford Achievement Test: Reading (total). These are reasonably high relationships, and they indicate good agreement between teacher judgment and general test results.

Naturally, the teacher's observational skills can be improved through practise and guided observation (by means of checklists, skills sheets, and published observation guides). This volume includes many specific suggestions to help make teachers' observations more complete and accurate.

Criticism 4—There is a Lack of Structure and Direction for Teachers of the Language Experience Approach

This criticism is generally found in conjunction with arguments for a more formally structured language arts program (e.g., textbook-oriented, basal reader, or kit). The somewhat fallacious corresponding assumption is that individualization results from variable pacing through the same materials (or the skills in different materials).

In fact, a good effort has been made in packaging language experience materials (Allen, 1975) in the form of detailed teachers' manuals. However, most other attempts tend to result in what the writer classifies as language-second-hand-experience approaches. Using the students' experiences as a basis in the language experience approach almost automatically results in varied materials and different sequences of skills. Individualization involves more than differential pacing; it involves capitalizing on interests, current needs, learning styles, degree of structuring needed, and pacing.

One need only consult the contents and references of the various chapters to see that structure and direction *are* possible in a language experience approach. The structure and direction may not be as easily detected by the casual observer in the classroom because they reside more in the teacher's capacity to identify and to use the "teachable moment" and because the teacher modifies structure and direction according to identified needs. Naturally, the teacher in the language experience method must do more than read the directions from a teachers' manual to her students—little skill is required to do that.

Criticism 5—The Language Experience
Approach is an Introductory System Only

This argument is often expressed—and with some justification. Mostly, however, it is used as an excuse for considering the language experience approach in a very limited way. In fact, the word "introductory" here has two distinct meanings: it refers to primary-grade language arts instruction, or it refers to beginning-English language instruction for speakers of foreign languages or of English dialects (Ching, 1976, pp. 33–35).

Language experience as presented in this volume is not restricted to children writing and reading their own work (although that is not nearly as restrictive as critics contend). The reader should review Hatch's and Riling's studies documenting the sophistication of school children's language. All resources in and around the school become the basis of experience on which language and general knowledge are built. The authors of this volume have worked with teachers in very isolated communities (no electricity, telephone, or running water), in inner-city situations, and in wealthy suburbs, in several provinces and states, and have never found a situation lacking important experiences suitable for language and concept development.

When using all the resources mentioned above and the type of language experience advocated here, it need not be an introductory system only. Spache and Spache (1973) briefly mention a junior high school language experience program in which they were involved, and they concluded: "Tests at the end of the first year of the project showed significantly greater gains in reading, language usage, study skills, and social science than these pupils had shown in previous years" (p. 252).

Many secondary school teachers use teaching procedures that the present author would classify as "language experiences" but that they label as integrated projects, consumer research, or communications courses. In each case the focus is somewhat different, but the total effect is one of combining experiences with language use and development (reading, note-taking, oral reporting, interviewing, writing, propaganda analysis, etc.). Chapter 8 contains many suggestions for capitalizing on language experiences.

Criticism 6—Record-keeping and Reporting is a
Problem when Using the Language Experience Approach

Implied in this comment is the notion that we don't have a score on the same tests for every student and hence we cannot compare achievement within the class or to previous classes. The above criticism may also refer to the difficulty of keeping good anecdotal records. Because of the importance of this topic, Chapter 12 deals with reporting in more detail.

Many schools in the United States and Canada, especially elementary schools, report entirely by the anecdotal method and probably do not keep records in terms of letter grades or percentages. This situation has its advantages because more effort may be put into diagnostic teaching and formative evaluation than into summative evaluation (measurement of final outcomes). But these more informal assessment procedures also invite careless, incomplete, and inaccurate record-keeping.

Some record-keeping can be and should be done by the students themselves. Each student should have a folder in which to keep samples of work for each reporting period; these also serve as the basis for teacher and parent-teacher conferences. Other areas of student record keeping would include: lists of books and magazines read, units of completed work, skill cards done, schedules of individual conferences, personal vocabulary file, examples of handwriting, poetry forms tried, and individualized spelling units completed. Record-keeping encourages self-evaluation, awareness of progress, and self-responsibility.

The teachers' record-keeping should emphasize those areas not easily done by the student. Checklists may consist of specific language skills (such as suggested in other chapters of this volume) along with comments about the students' emotional, motivational, and personality factors. Any symptoms of physiological disorders should be noted as well. Areas of particular strengths and weakness should be noted to assist in grouping for further instruction. Often groups of teachers can collaborate on constructing guide sheets for teacher observation and the collection of data to suit local needs. Occasionally the records for each child should be reviewed to ensure that enough information has been recorded for evaluation and conference purposes.

The emphasis and further development of *competency-based* (or criterion-referenced) instruction and evaluation in the last decade is of special importance to the teacher using the language experience approach. While not a new concept, and overlapping somewhat with "informal" testing, it has been elaborated more recently. Essentially it is a form of evaluation using a predetermined standard or objective rather than a standard determined by the group taking the test (as in most standardized achievement tests). Commercial tests of this variety are becoming available, and the teacher should consider them as alternatives to other norm-referenced tests.

Many schools prefer to give an annual achievement test to supplement their observations and to give some indication of the students' growth in particular achievement areas such as reading, English usage, listening, arithmetic, science, and social studies. While achievement tests are often selected by committees on a district-wide basis, their contents, reliability, and validity should be carefully checked by examining the test manual and reading the reviews in Buros (1972, 1975).

If the teacher using a language experience approach uses some of the suggested record-keeping procedures, reporting to parents and school officials should be simplified. If more detailed assistance is required in diagnosing learning needs, the reader may wish to consult Potter and Rae (1973) for informal measures or Burns (1974) for more formal tests.

Criticism 7—Common Tenets of the Language Experience Approach Imply that Print is "Talk Written Down"

There is little doubt that oral and written language are different in form, although the difference is probably more exaggerated in mature language. At any rate this is not a serious problem (in fact it may be helpful), at least not for the elementary grades, because the evidence is that speech is more advanced than written expression (O'Donnell, Griffin, and Norris, 1969). The effect of "talk written down" is a positive one as a result. That is, if writing is modeled after speech (which is better developed), it should have the effect of producing more mature writing. In the junior high school grades, however, the trend reverses: writing maturity surpasses speech, and reading ability surpasses listening ability (Sticht et al., 1974, p. 82). At any rate, the teacher should take advantage of these differences rather than treating them as disadvantages of some sort. It is reasonably easy to design language "experiments" to emphasize the differences between oral and written language (Froese, 1975).

SUMMARY

This chapter's purpose was to provide some responses to seven common charges leveled against the language experience approach. It is this author's contention that teachers wishing to use the language experience procedure outlined in this volume should be well acquainted both with its rationale (as outlined in Chapter 1) and strengths, as well as with its criticisms and sources of "weaknesses."

In most cases practical suggestions have been made to overcome the criticisms stated, and the reader has been referred back to examples of useful activities within this volume or to other sources of useful information.

Most charges against the language experience approach are not based on a careful examination of empirical evidence but are more akin to Carroll's "shoes—and ships—and sealing wax"—a potpourri of arguments that tend to disappear when examined closely.

LITERATURE CITED

Allen, R. Van, and Allen, C. 1975. Language Experiences in Reading. Encyclopedia Britannica Press, Chicago.

Braun, C. 1976. Teacher expectation: Sociopsychological dynamics. Rev. Educat. Res. 46(Spring):185–213.

Burns, P. C. 1974. Diagnostic Teaching of the Language Arts. Peacock Publishers, Itasca, Ill.

Buros, O. K. (ed.). 1972. Seventh Mental Measurements Yearbook. Gryphon Press, Highland Park, N.J.

Buros, O. K. (ed.). 1975. Reading Tests and Reviews II. Gryphon Press, Highland Park, N.J.

Carroll, L. 1946. Alice in Wonderland and Through the Looking Glass, p. 197. Grossett & Dunlap, New York.

Ching, D. C. 1976. Reading and the Bilingual Child. International Reading Association, Newark, Del.

Davis, F. B. 1968. Research in comprehension in reading. Read. Res. Q. 3(Summer):499–545.

Dunn, R., Dunn, K., and Price, G. E. 1977. Diagnosing learning styles: A prescription for avoiding malpractise suits. Phi Delta Kappan 58(January): 418–420.

Dykstra, R. 1970. A reply to Robert Emans' reaction to the summary of the second-grade phase of the Cooperative Research Program in Primary Reading Instruction. Read. Res. Q. 5(Spring):492.

Froese, V. 1975. Exploration with language. In: O. H. Clapp (ed.), On Righting Writing, pp. 68–74. NCTE, Urbana, Ill.

Guszak, F. J. 1972. Diagnostic Reading Instruction in the Elementary School. Harper & Row, New York.

Harris, A. J., and Serwer, B. L. 1966. Comparison of Reading Approaches in First-Grade Teaching with Disadvantaged Children. (The CRAFT Project). Cooperative Research Project No. 3677. The City University of New York, New York.

Hatch, E. 1969. The Syntax of Four Reading Programs Compared with Language Development of Children, p. 32. Southwest Regional Laboratories, Los Alamitos.

Hitchcock, A. A., and Alfred, C. 1955. Can teachers make accurate estimates of reading ability? Clearinghouse 54:422–424.

Kendrick, W. M., and Bennett, C. L. 1967. Effectiveness of a Second Grade Language Arts Program. Cooperative Research Project No. 3235. Department of Educ., San Diego County, San Diego, Cal.

Kermonian, S. B. 1962. Teacher appraisal of first grade readiness. Elem. English 39:196–201.

Lamb, P. 1972. Guiding Children's Language Learning. Brown, Dubuque, Iowa.

Lee, H. 1960. To Kill a Mockingbird. Lippincott, Philadelphia.

Lennon, R. T. 1962. What can be measured? Read. Teacher 15(March): 326–337.

O'Donnell, R. C., Griffin, W. J., and Norris, R. C. 1969. Syntax of Kindergarten and Elementary School Children: A Transformational Analysis. National Council of Teachers of English, Champaign, Ill.

Packer, A. B. 1970. Ashton-Warner's key vocabulary for the disadvantaged. Read. Teacher 23(March):559–564.

Potter, T. C., and Rae, G. 1973. Informal Reading Diagnosis: A Practical Guide for the Classroom Teacher. Prentice-Hall, Englewood Cliffs, N.J.

Riling, M. E. 1965. Oral and Written Language of Children in Grades 4 and 6 Compared with Language of Their Textbooks. Cooperative Research Project No. 2410. Southern State College, Durant, Oklahoma.

Sochor, E. F. 1959. The nature of critical reading. Elem. English 36(January):47–48.

Spache, G. D., and Spache, E. B. 1973. Reading in the Elementary School, pp. 252–255. Allyn & Bacon, Boston.

Stauffer, R. G., and Hammond, W. D. 1965. Effectiveness of a Language Arts and Basic Reader Approach to First Grade Reading Instruction. Cooperative Research Project No. 2679. University of Delaware, Newark, Del.

Sticht, T. G., Beck, L. J., Hauke, R. N., Kleiman, G. M., and James, J. H. 1974. Auding and Reading. Human Resources Research Organization, Alexandria, Va.

Thorndike, R. L. 1973. Reading Comprehension Education in Fifteen Countries: An Empirical Study. John Wiley and Sons, New York.

Vilscek, E., Morgan, L., and Cleland, D. 1967. Coordinating and integrating language arts instruction in first grade. In: R. G. Stauffer (ed.), The First Grade Reading Studies, pp. 147–153. IRA, Newark, Del.

Williams, G. 1959. Provisions for critical reading in basal readers. Elem. English 41(May):323–330.

chapter 12

Record-keeping

Carl Braun

The more loosely structured the learning program, the more prone it is to attacks on the basis of accountability. The question of accountability is heard not infrequently regarding language experience programs. There are at least two reasons for this. First, these programs are frequently implemented without any concern for a "mapping" of skills and competencies on the assumption that "we'll simply let learning happen." Such a total disregard for planning and structure is hardly in tune with the loud cries for "accountability" and "back to basics." Second, in the absence of such "mapping" or structure, records are often poorly managed or not kept at all.

Whatever, the point on the continuum between a highly structured and a highly flexible system in which the teacher finds herself, some systematic form of record-keeping is essential whether one is concerned about accountability to parents, to the larger public, or to the learner.

A logical outgrowth, then, of any pupil evaluation is a well organized attempt on the part of the school to maintain records of each pupil's progress. This record-keeping may take many forms: anecdotal, checklist, or matrix. Whatever the format, such records should meet the following criteria:

1. Reflect the objectives of instruction
2. Be efficient and practical (i.e., adaptable to the individual teacher's needs)
3. Be designed for effective transmission of information
   a. For the learner's feedback
   b. For the immediate and intermediate modification of instructional procedures

c. For short-range feedback to parents
d. For long-term records in the school files (Braun and Giles, 1976, p. 177)

   The first step toward effective classroom accounting, then, is to systematically collect information about what is happening in relation to specific objectives. With the use of systematic procedures, the teacher can become increasingly efficient in controlling factors related to the learning process. When information is recorded on a regular basis, there is constant feedback as to the effectiveness of various instructional procedures so that these procedures can be maintained or altered to meet the specific needs of the learners.

CHARTING INDIVIDUAL STUDENT DATA

The position taken here is that effective accounting proceeds from the charting of individual student data to the transcription of these data to group or classroom records. From this standpoint the checklist has considerable advantages over anecdotal procedures. For this reason, the checklist format is discussed here.

   In Chapters 2, 4, 5, and Part VI, Appendices B and C, checklists for individual observations have been outlined. For example, the "Sample Checklist for Beginning Reading Readiness" (Chapter 5, Table 1) and the "Sample Checklist for Early Reading Diagnosis" (Chapter 5, Table 2) are illustrations of a recording format that reflects specific instructional objectives. In this sense that kind of format can be highly sensitive to instructional adjustments of individuals as well as groups of students. Diagnostically, it allows for more than inspection of isolated skill areas; it is sufficiently comprehensive to give a profile of relative strengths and weaknesses.

   Some teachers find it efficient to use a looseleaf book of checklists. The number of copies of the checklist for each child depends on the number of times the teacher wishes to make entries. The looseleaf is tabbed with children's names so that the teacher can readily locate information for each child. When constructing these checklists it is an excellent idea to leave space at the bottom of each page for notes that relate to observations not accounted for in the checklist.

   Individual data charts like the ones referred to are valuable in spotting individual children who need specific help or a changed emphasis in instruction. Often, however, it is necessary (or even desirable) to instruct larger groups who share similar instructional needs. The following data summary sheets show one way of developing such summaries.

GROUP SUMMARY RECORDS

The summary sheet in Table 1 shows how data from the "Sample Checklist for Beginning Reading Readiness" (Chapter 5, Table 1) might be used as a basis for a group summary. This form summarizes data taken only from the section "Auditory Discrimination and Perception."

Table 1 provides one way of summarizing data. Admittedly, the format involves a lot of paper work. However, it does provide a wealth of specific information for instructional grouping. For example, the teacher can see at a glance that David, Janice, Stan, and Gordie need to receive assistance in most basic elements of auditory discrimination. This might consist of game activity in the listening center, song activity, nursery rhymes, etc. On the contrary, Jack, Sally, Roma (and possibly George, Lee, and Sam) require very little or no further specific attention in this area.

To illustrate a further method of compiling or summarizing data, the "Oral Language" section is abstracted from the "Checklist for Beginning Reading Readiness" (Table 2). Table 2 illustrates an efficient format. Again, the data provides quick reference for immediate instructional grouping. For example, if the teacher wants to work with the children on picture interpretation (6), she will find that Dana, Fran, and Rae are the only children requiring extensive work in this area. Further examples of this format are found in Chapter 4 regarding skills in writing.

As children progress in reading, it is useful to know not only skill weaknesses and strengths but also the general level at which they are able to read material. In this way the teacher can select corrective material suited to the particular level of the child. Tables 3 and 4 illustrate one format that provides for both identification of the skill weakness and the general reading level of the child. The skills are abstracted from sections of the "Diagnostic Reading Checklist" in Part VI, Appendix B.

In Tables 3 and 4, only children who have weaknesses in specified areas are noted. Again, these can be identified readily as the teacher organizes for corrective instruction.

Table 1. Data summary—Auditory Discrimination and Perception

Skill area	Seldom or never	Usually	Always
1. Hears differences in words			
a. All parts	David, Janice, Stan, Gordie	George, Lee, Dora, Tim	Jack, Sally, Roma, Sam, Tara
b. Beginning		Lorna	Tom, Lori, James, Les, Todd
c. Middle		Tom, Lorna, Mary, Jackie	Les, James, Todd
d. Ending	Tom, Lou, Don, Jane	Les, James, Todd	
2. Recognizes and identifies rhyming words			
a. All levels	David, Janice, Stan, Gordie	George, Lee, Sam	Jack, Sally, Roma
b. Level One	Dora	Dora, Tim, Sam, Tara	Les, Todd
c. Level Two	Dora, Tim, Don, Jane, Peter, Tom, Les	Tim, Les, Todd	Les, Todd
d. Level Three		Todd	

Table 2. Data summary—Oral Language

Skill	Name																		
	Ada	Allen	Amy	Bert	Brent	Connie	Dana	Ellen	Frank	Fran	Henry	Kate	Lee	Nora	Rae	Stan	Tara	Vera	Vern
1. Interested in communicating ideas and feelings	U	A	A	S	U	U	U	A	U	U	U	A	S	A	U	A	A	U	A
2. Uses a variety of words	U	A	U	S	U	A	S	U	A	S	A	A	S	U	S	U	A	U	U
3. Recalls and uses new words	U	A	U	S	U	A	S	A	A	U	A	A	U	U	S	U	A	U	A
4. Expresses ideas in sentences	S	U	A	S	U	U	S	U	U	U	A	A	S	U	S	U	A	S	A
5. Organizes ideas in sequence	S	U	A	S	U	A	S	A	A	U	A	A	S	U	S	U	A	U	U
6. Expresses simple picture interpretations	U	A	U	U	A	A	S	A	A	S	U	A	A	A	S	U	A	U	A
7. Supplies endings to simple stories	A	A	A	U	A	U	U	U	S	S	A	A	U	A	U	A	A	U	U
8. Recalls ideas from stories	U	A	S	U	A	U	S	U	U	U	A	A	A	A	S	U	A	U	A
9. Uses normal intonation in speech	U	A	S	U	U	U	S	A	A	S	S	A	S	A	U	U	A	U	A

S, seldom; U, usually; A, always.

Table 3. Word analysis

Structural	Instructional reading level					
	1	2	3	4	5	6
Recognition						
Number of word elements in a word (compounds)						
Base words/inflect endings		Bill				
Base words/affixes		Jack, Susan, Jim	Joe, Vern			
Compared words						
Contractions						
Possessives						
Identification						
Number of word elements in a word						
Base words/inflect endings	Ann, Jim	Jack, Susan, Jim				
Base words/affixes		Jack, Susan, Jim, Warren				
Compared words			Joe			
Contractions						
Possessives				Frank, Sue		

Table 4. Word recognition

Semantic-associational	Instructional reading level					
	1	2	3	4	5	6
Identifies words from clues:						
1. Comparison or contrast						
2. Synonym						
3. Summary						
4. Mood		Jack, Sally				
5. Familiar expression			John, Ted			
6. Classification			Winnie, Karen		Jack	
7. Familiar experience						
8. Appositive				Gordon, Tara, Jill		
9. Simile						

There is no limit to the variations in format that can be used, as long as the teacher is clear regarding the objectives of instruction. For instance, Chapter 8 points to specific diagnostic areas in spelling. These areas become ready categories for data or record-keeping checklists.

SUMMARY

This chapter has focused heavily on very specific skills. This is for illustrative purposes only and should not be misconstrued to mean that these are the only concerns in record-keeping. Certainly not! Documentation of books read, interests, progress in reporting, and organizing written work is a mere sampling of areas that are at least as important as the areas illustrated. It should be noted further that record-keeping is a highly individual concern and will vary widely from one teacher to another. The important concern is that records *are* kept to obviate the concern noted at the beginning of this chapter: that programs at any level be accountable.

LITERATURE CITED

Braun, C., and Giles, T. E. 1976. Strategies for Instruction and Organization. Detselig Enterprises Limited, Calgary, Alberta.

chapter 13

Guidelines to Evaluate the English Component in the Elementary School Program

NCTE Committee

In 1972 the Committee on Guidelines to Evaluate the English Component in Elementary School Program was established by NCTE. The committee, representing elementary school people from all areas (teaching, curriculum planning, administration and teacher education), was to develop guidelines which elementary and middle schools could use to assess their programs.

The committee members were in agreement that a list of broad questions derived from basic educational principles could be generated which would provide pre-service or in-service teachers, school or district curriculum committees with appropriate guidelines to stimulate discussion about and critical examination of language arts programs.

Reprinted by permission from Language Arts 53 (October 1976), 828–838.

Much has been learned about child language in the last ten years. The fields of linguistics, psychology, psycholinguistics, and sociolinguistics are involved in ongoing research in child language learning, resulting in knowledge and principles about language and thinking. These principles must be taken into consideration in the organization and evaluation of any language arts curriculum. Additionally, the great diversity in America, reflected in any school system through differing values, attitudes, and concerns of parents, teachers and the community, must also be recognized during the process of curriculum evaluation, expansion, or change.

The questions and statements in these guidelines should stimulate thinking and discussion on the part of school personnel which considers both the latest principles suggested by scientists interested in all facets of child language and the diversity found within their own school system. The guidelines should lead local school committees to thorough evaluation of their language arts curriculum so that it builds on the language strengths which children have when they come to school. Building on these strengths will help children expand their learning in all areas of language arts.

The horizontal divisions of the guidelines are concerned with the various areas of the language arts curriculum. The first is concerned with the *general* aspects of the language arts which must be considered in an integrated fashion. Following the general concerns are sections which deal with specifics for each of the major areas of the language arts: listening, speaking, reading, and writing. Each area has been considered separately because we believe each deserves consideration for appropriate time in the curriculum. Sometimes, because of various pressures or because of the emphasis in commercial materials, too much time is spent in one area of the language arts curriculum to the neglect of another.

The guidelines are also categorized vertically, with columns of concerns for: 1) individual and group differences, 2) principles of language learning, and 3) objectives and evaluation.

In each section the guidelines are presented as a statement of concern, followed by questions. This format allows for flexibility in the use of the guidelines. We have circulated these questions among language arts supervisors, teacher educators in language arts and elementary school teachers. They represent the thinking of many people. In answering the questions relating to the overall statement, a committee may generate objectives which are best for their local needs.

As these guidelines were disseminated it became obvious that the whole area of viewing experiences—the child's active involvement with perceiving a variety of stimuli in the environment—enhances language development and learning. We have attempted to integrate viewing experiences as part of many of the considerations in developing a language arts curriculum. However, greater consideration needs to be given to viewing and its implications for curriculum. Language arts is an umbrella to all aspects of the elementary school curriculum. Languaging is integrally involved in art, music, physical education, science, math, social studies, and human relations. This must be kept in mind in developing an exciting, integrated curriculum which will make learning a whole, real-life experience for children.

General Aspects of the Language Arts

Concern for individual and group difference	Concern for principles of language learning	Concern for objectives and evaluation
The language arts program must be interesting to attract and involve students. 1. What experiences which involve children's senses and physical activity are the major focus of the program? 2. How are students involved in understanding the purposes for activities? 3. How are students involved in setting their own purposes? 4. What choices or options are provided for learning experiences? The language arts program must involve the affective domain of students. 1. How are empathy and understanding of others encouraged? 2. How does the program help students become aware of beauty? 3. How does the program encourage students to expand their knowledge of the world? 4. How does the program increase the students' ability to understand themselves and the world in which they live? Provisions must be made for individual and group differences.	The language arts program must be based on how children learn language. 1. How does the program reflect the latest scientific knowledge about language? 2. In what ways do the activities planned for children reflect how language is acquired and developed? 3. What is done to assure that information about language which is presented to students is consistent with the latest scientific knowledge? The language arts program must be based on how students develop thought processes. 1. How does the program reflect the latest scientific knowledge about how thought processes develop in children? 2. In what ways do the activites planned for children reflect how students learn and acquire concepts? 3. In what ways does the program provide time for children's thought processes to develop? The language arts program must provide opportunity for application of learning. 1. In what ways is consideration given to	There must be continuous evaluation of the language arts program. 1. In what ways is the language arts program evaluated? 2. What provisions are there to evaluate on a periodic and regular basis? 3. In what ways is the evaluation related to objectives based on concern for individual and group differences? 4. In what ways is the evaluation related to objectives based on principles of language learning and the thinking process? 5. What is done to see that the objectives are clearly stated and understood by teachers? 6. How are the methods evaluated to see if they are suitable to the children? 7. How are teachers involved in the evaluation of the program and in setting significant and relevant objectives? 8. After evaluation, how are new objectives developed and current ones modified or dropped if they are no longer applicable?

1. How does the program take into consideration the ethnic, racial, and cultural differences of students?
2. How does the program take into consideration the social and economic differences among students?
3. How does the program take into consideration students' attitudes toward sex roles?
4. How does the program take into consideration the dialect and language background of students?
5. How does the program take into consideration differences in ability and interest of students?

Learning is accommodated best when there is an interrelationship among the various language arts of listening, speaking, reading, and writing.

1. How are speakers helped to become aware of their audience?
2. In what ways do student audiences recognize their roles in the speaking-listening exchange?
3. What opportunities are there for student writers to read their own products of writing as well as the composition of others?
4. What is done to help student writers produce with readers in mind?

the diversity of language experience?
2. In what ways is consideration given to the diversity of language development?
3. What provisions are made so all learning experiences are related to settings or concerns which children know and understand?

9. How are modifications and changes in in the program brought about to comply with new or changed objectives?
10. In what ways do objectives show concern for long-range goals as well as specific immediate needs and concerns?
11. How are students involved in the evaluation of their own work and in setting their own objectives?
12. How does evaluation consider both cognitive and affective domains?
13. How does the evaluation program relate to stated objectives?

There must be continuous evaluation of materials and packaged units.

1. What measurement devices are used to evaluate materials and packaged units?
2. How is the worth of commercial material determined?
3. In what way is there consideration of whether equally effective teaching can be done by less costly means?
4. In what ways have the materials proved to be worthwhile for the students?
5. In what ways do the materials contribute positively to the students' learning?
6. How do the materials encourage language development in children?
7. How do the materials encourage the

Continued

Concern for individual and group difference	Concern for principles of language learning	Concern for objectives and evaluation
Learning is accommodated when there is an interrelationship between the language arts and other areas of the curriculum such as science, social studies, mathematics, music, art, drama, physical education, and home arts. 1. In what ways are other subject matter areas involved in developing the programs for language arts? 2. How are the materials and texts of other subject matter areas used with understanding about language and thought development? 3. How are viewing experiences used to help develop language and thought? Children's literature must be an integral part of all the language arts. 1. In what ways through listening, reading, and viewing are children involved in knowing and enjoying children's books and their authors? 2. What provisions are made through speaking, writing, or other expressive forms for children's responses to literature? A variety of media must be used in the language arts curriculum.		development of thinking in students? 8. How do the materials encourage creativity in students? 9. How do the materials make provisions for individual needs, interests, and personal choices for the students? 10. How do the materials create curiosity in the students and encourage independent activity? 11. How do the materials encourage further exploration so the students will want to study various aspects in greater depth? 12. In what ways are the materials consistent with current knowledge in the field of language and language learning? 13. What evidence is there that the materials have been written with concern for growth and development? 14. How do the students show that they are interacting with materials? 15. In what ways are materials assessed on the basis of content, authenticity and accuracy? 16. In what ways are materials assessed to avoid stereotypes or misconceptions about ethnic, cultural, racial or sex groups?

1. How are media such as photographs, drawings, paintings, three dimensional objects, film strips and tape recorders used to enhance the curriculum?
2. What is done to assure that the media used is most appropriate for the activity?
3. How are libraries and learning centers used as focal points for small groups and individual learning activities?

17. What is done to make sure that a wide range and variety of materials is available?
18. What is done to make sure that trade books or multi-texts are used whenever possible in preference to a single text or program for all students?
19. How are the materials assessed to see that they are appropriate for the linguistic and cognitive development of the children who use them?

Listening

Listening activities must attract and involve students.
1. What is done to assure that an appropriate amount of time is given to listening activities?
2. What provisions are made for a variety of listening activities with one or two other children, in small groups, or in large groups?
   a. What provisions are made for listening to recorded materials that include both visual and non-visual experiences?
   b. What provisions are made for listening to selections read by the teacher, other adults, and other students?

Listening experiences must be based on how students learn language.
1. How does the curriculum present the target language or dialect as an alternative form without stressing its superiority?
2. In what ways are students provided with listening experiences which introduce a wide variety of language styles and dialects?
   a. Are experiences wih formal and informal language differences provided?
   b. Are various dialects provided?
   c. Are the language styles of different age groups provided?

A variety of means should be employed to assess listening.
1. In what ways are non-verbal responses used to assess listening?
   a. Through facial expressions and body language
   b. Through reactions to music, narrative records, and story telling
   c. Through peer conversations
   d. Through reactions to sounds of different intensity, pitch, and rhythm
   e. Through constructions based on oral instructions
   f. Through ability to play games or perform job responsibilities based on oral directions

Continued

Concern for individual and group difference	Concern for principles of language learning	Concern for objectives and evaluation

c. What provisions are made for listening to stories told by the teacher, other adults, and other students?
d. What provisions are made for listening during field trips, programs, or other audience settings?
3. How is listening outside of school encouraged and integrated into the instructional program?
  a. What opportunities are there for students to interview parents, siblings, community leaders, and others and to share what they have learned with classmates?
  b. What opportunities are there for students to report about games, trips, television shows, radio programs, plays, or concerts?
4. How are students involved in the selection of the musical records, narrative records, and tapes they wish to use?
A variety of experiences must be made available for listening related to the social, cultural, and economic differences.
1. In what ways are field trips and other
	3. If the language or dialect of the student is different from the language or dialect used by most teachers, what activities are provided to help the student gain receptive control over the target dialect or language before other kinds of performance are expected? For example:
	  a. Are musical and narrative records and tapes representing a variety of dialects available?
	  b. Are there varied listening experiences with peers who speak the target dialect or language?
	  c. Are there varied listening experiences with adults who speak the target dialect or language?
	Listening experiences must be based on how students develop thought processes.
	1. What opportunities are students given to learn through listening activities prior to the expectancy of achievement in other language arts areas?
	2. What opportunities are there for the student to learn to listen with an open mind?
		g. Through visual images which may accompany language
		2. In what ways are students' acquisition of concepts and meanings assessed?
		  a. Through interaction with peers
		  b. Through observation of large and small group discussions
		  c. Through students' graphic illustrations, art work, written work, science experiments, or other constructions
		3. In what ways are non-classroom experiences used to assess listening?
		  a. From the playground or street play
		  b. From reactions to television, radio, or movies
		  c. From related information by parents, siblings, peers
		  d. From stories about family experiences
		4. In what ways are verbal responses used to assess listening?
		  a. Through oral retellings
		  b. Through written reactions
		  c. Through dramatic activities such as role-playing and puppetry
		5. How are individual conferences with

investigative experiences planned to enhance awareness and understanding of others?

2. In what ways are books, stories, records, tapes, and films related to the backgrounds and experiences of the students?

Once students are comfortable in their learning environment, listening experiences should be planned to help them expand their background and experiences.

1. How are language differences introduced?

2. How are cultural differences introduced?

3. How are new concepts and ideas introduced?

a. Are group discussions encouraged in which positions may be questioned, compared, and evaluated whether they are stated by an authority in a particular field, a teacher, or a peer?

b. Are group discussions encouraged in which propaganda presented through various media (television, records, tapes, photographs, tape recorder, films, filmstrips, etc.) is evaluated and questioned, including reactions to loaded words, analogies, slogans, sarcasm, patriotic appeal, and status appeal?

students used to assess growth in listening?

Students must be involved in developing learning objectives.

1. How are students involved in setting new goals?

2. How are students involved in planning group experiences for listening?

3. How is the student involved in planning individual listening experiences?

Speaking

Speaking activities must attract and involve students.

1. In what ways are students who are not yet proficient in writing permitted to use speaking as the major medium for communication and learning?

2. What is done so that speaking experiences involve more time in the classroom than writing experiences?

3. What is done so that students have opportunities to select and plan various

Speaking experiences must be based on how students learn languages.

1. In what way does the program focus on the student developing language fluency rather than on concern for an arbitrary correctness?

2. How are students given the opportunity to interact frequently with their peers in speaking situations?

3. How is the legitimacy of language diversity recognized?

A variety of means should be employed to assess speaking.

1. What procedures are there to keep samples of students' oral language over a period of time to establish growth?

2. How are conferences with the individual student used to assess growth in speaking?

3. How are observations of the students' interaction with peers observed?

4. How is the use of oral language by stu-

Continued

Concern for individual and group difference	Concern for principles of language learning	Concern for objectives and evaluation

Concern for individual and group difference	Concern for principles of language learning	Concern for objectives and evaluation
kinds of oral language experiences and settings? a. Are students involved in their choice of audience? b. Do students choose their subject matter for speaking? c. Do students choose the time for their own speaking? d. Are a variety of settings provided for speaking? 4. What opportunities are there for students to talk to other students as much as they talk with adults? 5. How does the program encourage sharing of ideas, experiences, and activities among students? 6. Are role-playing and creative drama integral parts of all of the curriculum including language arts? Students should be encouraged to use with dignity a variety of dialects. 1. Are diverse dialects permitted in role-playing, folk singing, and story telling? 2. How are students helped to view all dialect differences with respect? 3. How are students whose speech represents one dialect given opportunities to	a. When students are talking, are they encouraged to use their own dialect without correction or rejection? b. What does the teacher do to understand children who speak a different dialect or language? 4. What opportunities are there for students to speak informally more often than formally in the classroom? 5. In what way does the teacher differentiate between speech problems and language difference? a. Are speech immaturities recognized and permitted to develop into adult forms without pressure? b. Are dialect differences and language differences due to foreign language influences recognized and respected as the student's home language and not treated as a speech problem? Speaking experiences must be based on how students develop thought processes. 1. How and when are students given time to consider the principles of effective discussion? 2. In what ways are they given opportunities to implement these principles?	dents observed? a. In front of the whole class b. With one other student c. Within a small group of students d. With an adult e. Behind a stage or puppet f. In play, game, or sport situations g. In formal learning situations Students must be involved in developing learning objectives. 1. How are students involved in setting new goals? 2. How are students involved in planning group experiences for speaking? 3. How is the student involved in planning individual speaking experiences?

talk with children and adults who speak other dialects?

Speaking activities should occur in curricular areas other than that of language arts.

1. How are speaking experiences provided in the areas of social studies, science, humanities, and literature?
2. What opportunities are provided for students to talk about viewing experiences they have had both in and out of the school setting?
3. How are students encouraged to plan questions which are appropriate for various situations?
   a. Are they given opportunities to ask questions about what they hear?
   b. Are they given opportunities to develop questions for interviews with peers and adults?
   c. Are they provided with opportunities to discover what kinds of questions are most appropriate for different settings?
4. What opportunities are there for vocabulary growth to be part of understanding concepts as opposed to learning meaningless labels?

Reading

There must be reading materials available for a range of reading abilities, interests, tastes, and racial and cultural backgrounds.

1. What materials or help are provided in selecting and purchasing a wide variety of materials?
2. How are students involved in selecting a variety of materials?
3. Are there textbooks available for resource material in content areas such as history, science, mathematics, music, and art?

Reading experiences must be based on how students learn language.

1. What provisions are made for more silent reading than oral reading as students progress through the grades?
2. Is oral reading used *only* for a specific purpose? For example:
   a. When a reader wishes to describe a situation or event?
   b. To interpret a character or a characterization?
   c. To support or elaborate on ideas

Students must be involved in developing learning objectives.

1. How are students involved in setting new goals?
2. How are students involved in planning group experiences for reading?
3. How is the student involved in planning individual reading experiences?

A variety of means should be used to assess reading.

1. What opportunities are there for students to read without the teacher's

Continued

Concern for individual and group difference	Concern for principles of language learning	Concern for objectives and evaluation
4. In what ways are trade books given as significant a role in the reading program as basal texts where the latter are built into the curriculum? 5. In what way is children's literature given a significant role in the reading program? Reading must be interesting and enjoyable to the individual student. 1. How are students involved in sharing their responses to reading with others to stimulate others to expand their reading? 2. In what ways does the teacher motivate students to broaden reading experiences? 3. How is sufficient time provided so each student can become involved in silent reading? 4. How are opportunities for sustained silent reading planned and carried out? 5. In what ways are magazines, newspapers, and other non-book reading materials used in the school curriculum to make reading a current and vital process? 6. How does the program provide for self-selection of both reading experiences and reading materials?	during discussion? d. To read words which are vivid in imagery? e. For diagnosis by the teacher? 3. When students read orally are they permitted to use their own dialect? 4. How are the reading materials selected so that they represent a variety of language styles and dialects? Reading experiences must be based on how students develop thought processes. 1. When informational materials are used, what non-reading experiences are provided as a basis for extending concepts and vocabulary prior to reading? 2. Is there opportunity to extend and expand on new concepts through many viewing experiences in addition to reading, such as films, filmstrips, television, taking pictures with a camera, and microscopes? 3. What experiences are provided to permit students to apply the knowledge acquired through reading to non-reading situations? 4. What experiences are provided to en-	help to discover what a reader can do independently? 2. What procedures are there to keep samples of students' reading over a period of time to establish growth? 3. How are individual conferences with students used to assess reading? 4. How is comprehension used as the main criterion for assessing reading? 5. In what ways are non-paper-pencil responses used to assess reading? a. Through ability to dramatize from reading b. Through following written directions c. Through carrying out experiments d. Through construction following written directions e. Through cooking following recipes f. Through sharing reading experiences with others 6. What variety of options do students have to share books with others? 7. How are reading experiences at home or in the library used in reading assessment?

7. How are materials written by students used as part of the classroom reading materials?
8. What opportunities are there for sharing what has been read?

A variety of reading opportunities must be provided.
1. What provisions are made so that plays, radio scripts, and other drama forms are part of the reading program?
2. How are choric reading and other kinds of unison or assisted reading part of the reading program?
3. What is done to assure a variety of audiences for oral reading?
4. How are televised productions planned to be a part of a reading-viewing program?

courage students to integrate previous knowledge with what they are reading?
5. What experiences are provided so that students can question, challenge, and criticize the authenticity and accuracy of written materials?
6. How are students helped to use reference materials, libraries, guides, signs, and other practical written material whenever they fit naturally into the learning experience or curriculum?

8. How are judgments about a child's reading made primarily from silent reading assessments?
9. What is done to consider errors in oral reading only if they disrupt the meaning of the text?
10. If oral reading is used to assess dramatic or expressive oral reading, what kinds of opportunities do the students have to read the material silently and to practice prior to the assessment?

Writing

Students must always write with a purpose in mind.
1. What efforts are made so that students always write with a purpose which they understand?
2. How are students involved in setting their own purposes for writing?
3. How are children introduced to a variety of appropriate writing styles to use at

A variety of means should be employed to assess writing.
1. What procedures are there to keep samples of students' writing over a period of time to establish growth?
2. What is done to focus the evaluation of writing so that teachers react mostly to students' ideas?
3. How are informal pupil-teacher confer-

Writing activities must attract and involve children.
1. In what ways are writing experiences built upon oral language activities?
2. What plans are there for many and varied writing experiences?
3. How is the program organized so that students are permitted to write when they want to?

Continued

Concern for individual and group difference	Concern for principles of language learning	Concern for objectives and evaluation
4. What provisions are made so that students have the right to keep their writing private if they wish to do so? 5. In what ways do students share their writing with others when they wish to do so? 6. How are students' responses to literature used for creative writing? 7. How are art and music used to stimulate or to accompany creative writing? 8. How are various media used in conjunction with creative writing? 9. What opportunities are there for children's writing to include both practical and creative expressions? 10. How are children involved in the editing process? 11. What opportunities are there for children to see their own writing published at least in classroom style? A variety of writing experiences must be provided. 1. How are student logs encouraged? 2. What time is provided so that teachers can respond to logs and other writing experiences?	times when they are needed to help achieve specific purposes? 4. What different kinds of writing experiences are encouraged? For example: a. Dictation b. Writing directions c. Reporting d. Story writing e. Letter writing Writing experiences must be based on how students learn language. 1. How is the time spent on writing activities related to the children's ability to write? 2. Is more time spent on writing as a process than on the mechanics of writing (handwriting, punctuation, spelling, grammar)? a. Are handwriting and spelling programs integrated and related to writing experiences? b. Are handwriting, spelling, punctuation and grammatical activities for practice of specific skills used only for students who provide evidence	ences used to encourage freedom of expression and to stimulate ideas? 4. What is done to assure that mechanics of writing are evaluated only in terms of a final copy? 5. How are initial baselines established for each child for continuous development in spelling, handwriting, punctuation, and other mechanics? Students must be involved in developing learning objectives. 1. How are students involved in setting new goals? 2. How are students involved in planning group experiences for writing? 3. How is the student involved in planning individual writing experiences?

Continued

3. What options or ideas are available for children to write about?
4. How are children encouraged to use their own ideas for writing even though a standard kind of assignment has been made?
5. Are products of children's writing not copied unless the students want to for the purpose of sharing?

When teachers have students with dialects different from their own, they must take this into account when thinking about the growth of the child in the areas of syntax, usage, mechanics, spelling, etc.

1. How does the teacher encourage children whose writing reflects a knowledge of the rules of their own dialect?
2. How are students encouraged to write in many styles and to use a variety of language structures?
3. How is discussion about language planned so students understand it as an area of discovery, exploration, and inventiveness, not as something which has a prescribed set of rules?
4. Are students who demonstrate they can spell the specified words or write in the appropriate style excluded from lessons related to such skills?

that they are having such specific problems?
c. In what way does the handwriting program focus on legibility for the sake of communication rather than on exact reproduction of models?
d. Are editing and rewriting encouraged only when there is a stated purpose for final copy?
3. Are students always encouraged to express their ideas in writing and not stifled by concern for mechanics?
4. Are students encouraged to use a variety of styles and structures and to experiment with forms as they write?

Writing experiences must be based on how students develop thought.

1. What opportunities are there for students to get feedback from peers and other adults, as well as teachers, in relation to the ideas written?
2. How is the student encouraged to use writing to express reactions to ideas—to criticize, to compare, and to question the ideas of others?
3. What opportunities are there for students to express themselves in writing in all areas of the curriculum?

Concern for individual and group difference	Concern for principles of language learning	Concern for objectives and evaluation
	4. How are students helped to write formal reports which are based on actual experiences?	
	5. What opportunities are there for students to talk about what they will write about?	
	Students should be encouraged to participate in creative writing frequently.	
	1. Are there opportunities for writing to take place daily?	
	2. Are students given opportunities to share their writing with others *only* if they wish to do so, and get reactions to their ideas?	
	3. What suggestions are provided to encourage students to write personal feelings and opinions?	

Committee Members

Alba Allard
  Westport, Connecticut
Inez Bishop
  DeKalb, Illinois
Naomi Chase
  Minneapolis, Minnesota
Yetta Goodman
  Tucson, Arizona
  Chairperson
Evelyn Luckey
  Columbus, Ohio
Dorothy Menosky
  Jersey City, New Jersey

Clara Pederson
  Grand Forks, North Dakota
Ruth Steinmetz
  LaMesa, California
Allaire Stuart
  Boulder, Colorado
DeWayne Triplett
  DeKalb, Illinois
Lois Williams
  Montebello, California

PART VI

APPENDICES

APPENDICES

Appendix A
Annotated List of Children's Books for Language Development

BOOKS FOR DEVELOPING CONCEPTS

Concepts of Color

Anglund, J. W. 1966. What Color Is Love? Haircourt Brace and World, New York.

J. W. Anglund shows the beauty in our world by introducing all the different colors and their place in nature. In the end she distinguishes between "outside" beauty, which we see, and "inside" beauty, which we feel.

Bright, R. 1955. I Like Red. Doubleday, Garden City, N.Y.

Janey, a red-haired little girl, tells of her encounters with other red things and finally another "redhead," which helps her decide that red is a nice color after all.

Macdonald Starters. 1974. Science, No. 14 Rainbow Colors. Macdonald and Co., London.

This book explores colors from a natural as well as a scientific angle. It involves the child in actual experimentation with colors and exposes him to the colorful world of nature.

O'Neill, M. 1961. Hailstones and Halibut Bones. Doubleday, Garden City, N.Y.

Mary O'Neill presents colors that can be heard, touched, and smelled as well as seen. In rhyming verse, each color is shown in various contexts and environments.

Concepts of Numbers

Carle, E. 1968. 1, 2, 3 to the Zoo. World Publishing Company, New York.

This is a delightfully illustrated book without text. It depicts a circus train carrying animals. Each double page has one of the numbers printed in large type and the corresponding numbers of animals in that particular car. It can be used for simple counting purposes, as well as for developing more involved arithmetic concepts.

Considine, K., and Schuler, R. 1963. One, Two, Three, Four. Holt, Rinehart and Winston, New York.

This book presents ordinal and cardinal numbers from 1 to 12 in a bit of a story line and illustrates both concepts with beautiful pictures.

Francoise (pseudonym). 1951. Jeanne-Marie Counts Her Sheep. Charles Scribner's Sons, New York.

The numbers from 1 to 10 are developed rather informally within the context of the story. The numbers are presented in numerals as well as words and are easily verified by the pictures.

Hoban, T. 1972. Count and See. Macmillan, New York.

The concepts of numbers from 1 to 100 (not proceeding one by one after 15) are demonstrated by exciting black and white photographs of things all around us. The numbers are represented as words, as numerals, and as model sets.

Jacobs, L. B. 1964. Delight in Number. Holt, Rinehart and Winston, New York.

Number concepts are explored in beautiful poems and verses and clarified by pertinent illustrations.

Kruss, J. 1965. 3 × 3, Three by Three. Macmillan, New York.

The concept of three is developed in verse form, using animals that are streaking in, out, and around "the little mouse-house."

Quackenbush, R. M. 1963. Poems for Counting. Holt, Rinehart and Winston, New York.

This book contains a collection of poems that emphasize counting and illustrate the different number concepts.

Reiss, J. J. 1971. Numbers. Bradbury Press, Scarsdale, N.Y.

This is primarily a counting book that presents the numbers 1 to 20 serially, depicts still countable objects to 100 (counting by tens) and closes with a less countable but nevertheless meaningful illustration of the concept of 1,000. Color groupings help facilitate the counting processes of the numbers 20 and above.

Tudor, T. 1956. 1 is One. Henry Z. Walck, Inc., New York.
T. Tudor has put the numbers 1 to 20 into original verse and accented each with one of her beautiful paintings.

Watson, N. D. 1954. What Is One? Alfred A. Knopf, New York.
The numbers from 1 to 10 are explored in the dialogue of two children, a little girl, Linda, and her older brother, Peter. Peter uses things they see on their walk to answer his sister's questions.

Wildsmith, B. 1965. 1, 2, 3. Oxford University Press, London.
B. Wildsmith uses geometrical shapes—rectangles, circles, and triangles—and a kaleidoscope of colors to make this counting book. A section at the end tests the child's assimilation of the different concepts developed.

Concepts of Shape

Borten, H. 1959. Do You See What I See? Abelard-Schuman, Toronto.
H. Borten shows how different combinations of lines, shapes, and colors can evoke emotional responses. The imaginative illustrations together with the vivid word-pictures accompanying them are sure to arouse responses from the young reader.

Martin, J. 1965. Round and Square. Platt and Munk, New York.
J. Martin introduces the basic geometric shapes and shows their presence in our daily surroundings. The discoveries are made by a little boy named Nick, whose background and curiosity about things parallel those of the beginning reader.

Sullivan, J. 1963. Round Is a Pancake. Holt, Rinehart and Winston, New York.
This book explores the many kinds of "roundness" from a pancake to an owl eyes' view of the world.

Concepts of Size

Froman, R. 1971. Bigger and Smaller. Thomas Y. Crowell, New York.
This book explains the relativity of the concepts big and small using interesting examples from the world around us.

Krasilovsky, P. 1969. The Very Tall Little Girl. Doubleday, Garden City, N.Y.
P. Krasilovsky relates the happy and often unhappy experiences of

a girl who is a bit taller than average. At the same time relativity of size is brought into focus.

Kraus, R. 1949. The Big World and the Little House. Harper and Row, New York.
This book talks about the big world and a little, deserted, bare house and how a family manages to make that little house into a warm home by bringing some of the outside world into it.

Walter, M. 1971. Make a Bigger Puddle Make a Smaller Worm. Andre Deutsch, Ltd., London.
This book invites a child to experience spatial relations using a mirror. Ingeniously it gets children to change the shape, size, and number, using this added dimension.

Wing, H. R. 1963. What is Big? Holt, Rinehart and Winston, New York.
The little boy Tommy compares himself in size to several animals bigger than himself and then to as many animals that are smaller than himself; thus the relativity of size is brought into focus.

Multiple Concepts

Macdonald Series. 1973. Starters Maths. Macdonald and Co., London.
The books effectively deal with concepts such as number, shape, size, and other mathematical ideas in contexts familiar to the child.

1: Kitchen Maths	5: Playground Maths
2: Garage Maths	6: Toyshop Maths
3: Circus Maths	7: Farm Maths
4: Seaside Maths	8: Building Maths

BOOKS FOR VOCABULARY DEVELOPMENT

Brown, M. 1961. Once A Mouse ... Charles Scribner's Sons, New York.
A hermit employs magic to increase a mouse's size to protect him from threatening predators.

Carrick, C., and Carrick, D. 1970. The Pond. Macmillan, New York.
This is a book of poetry about a turtle dozing in the sun, a dragonfly casting a giant shadow on the water, fish darting and flashing while looking for food, and more. Carol Carrick's poetry evokes the changing moods of the pond and the creatures that depend on it.

Eastman, P. D. 1964. The Cat in the Hat Beginner Book Dictionary. Random House, New York.
This is a funny book of words, full of ridiculous alligators, foolish bears and giraffes' uncles, all racing around and getting involved in nonsensical adventures.

Frith, M. 1973. I'll Teach My Dog 100 Words. Beginner Books, New York.
A very funny dog acquires an even funnier vocabulary. Eastman's illustrations make this a most delightful vocabulary adventure.

Funk, T. 1962. I Read Signs. Holiday House, New York.
This book explores all possible signs city children could come into contact with. It has very suitable illustrations.

Hefter, R., and Moskof, S. 1971. Everything. Parents' Magazine Press, New York.
An alphabet, number, reading, counting, and color-identification book.

Holl, A. 1970. Adventures with Words. Western Publishing Co., Racine, Wisc.
This book actively involves children in the recall and production of nouns, verbs, adjectives, and number words. It is an excellent book for increasing vocabulary.

Hurd, E. T., and Hurd, C. 1971. Wilson's World. Harper and Row, New York.
Wilson likes to paint pictures and write stories to go with them. One day he paints a big round world, a big bright sun, green grass, flowers, animals, and people. Then, slowly, Wilson's world begins to change: too many people, too many cars, too much smog. What can Wilson do now?

Langstaff, J. 1955. Frog Went A-Courtin'. Harcourt Brace and World, New York.
This Caldecott Award winner presents a delightful parade of wild-life characters who make their contribution to the wedding feast for Frog and Miss Rat.

Lenski, L. 1938. The Little Airplane. Oxford.
Pilot Small owns a little airplane, which on fine days he rolls out of the hangar and flies. This book tells all about one of his trips, including a forced landing.

Lenski, L. 1940. The Little Train. Oxford.

Engineer Small has a little train. The engine is black and shiny and with help of Fireman Shorty and Conductor Little, Engineer Small drives the little train from one end of his run to the other. He passes farms and woods, grade crossings, and drawbridges; he goes through tunnels and stops at stations on the way.

McGinley, P. 1948. All Around the Town. J. B. Lippincott, Philadelphia.

This is a gay and entrancing picture book of city sights and sounds, feelings and fun, from Airplane and Buses to Your House and the Zoo. The witty and charming city verses for city lovers of any age are arranged in alphabetical order.

McNaught, H. 1973. 500 Words to Grow on. Random House, New York.

This book contains pictures of 500 things and their graphic representations.

O'Neill, M. 1961. Hailstones and Halibut Bones. Doubleday, New York.

Using colors as base, new words are explained in delightful verse that belong to each color category.

Piatti, C. 1964. The Happy Owls. Atheneum, New York.

This is an old legend retold in vivid word pictures. The text abounds with colorful descriptive verbs and adjectives and the story can be a good basis for an oral discussion.

Reed, M., and Osswald, E. (n.d.). My First Golden Dictionary. Golden Press, New York.

This book represents hundreds of everyday objects in words and pictures. Beneath each word is a short sentence that is easy for the beginning reader to read and that repeats the object word and tells something about it.

Reid, A. 1958. Ounce, Dice, Trice. Little, Brown and Co., Toronto.

Reid has collected sounds and made words with them—squishy words, grumpy words, counting words, etc. This book shows children that playing with sounds and words can be fun.

Ward, L. 1952. The Biggest Bear. Houghton Mifflin Co., Boston.

Another Caldecott Award winner documenting the "biggest bear" ever for the zoo.

Watson, A. A. (n.d.). Very First Words. Holt, Rinehart and Winston, New York.

This is a dictionary of sentences and phrases of words to help children write and spell independently. Children will enjoy pondering both the escapades of Little Mouse and his family and the language patterns relating to those escapades.

Wildsmith, B. 1967. Birds. Oxford University Press, London.
Brian Wildsmith has combined the most attractive birds with group names that aptly and wittily sum up the character or ideosyncrasy of the bird, e.g., a party of jays, a rafter of turkeys, etc.

BOOKS FOR LETTER KNOWLEDGE

Alexander, A. 1956. A B C of Cars and Trucks. Doubleday, New York.
This is a very special A B C book, from A is for AUTO TRAILER'' to "Z is the ZONE TRUCK."

Baskin, L., Baskin, T., and Baskin, H. Hosie's Alphabet. Viking Press, New York.
Hosie was three when he asked his father to draw this alphabet for him. He helped choose the creatures in the book, and his mother and brother helped him with the big words. This is a Caldecott Honor Book.

Deasy, M. 1974. City A B C's. Walker and Company, New York.
Striking black and white photographs of city life enliven this A B C book that describes words such as "alley" and "laundromat"—a real alphabet book that will bring the city alive for both urban and rural children.

Duvoisin, R. 1952. A for the Ark. Lothrop, Lee & Shepard, New York.
R. Duvoisin ingeniously combined the much-loved Old Testament story of Noah with the sequence of the alphabet.

Eastman, P. D. 1964. The Cat in the Hat Beginner Book Dictionary. Random House, New York.
This is a funny book of words, full of ridiculous alligators, foolish bears, and giraffes' uncles, all racing around and getting involved in nonsensical adventures.

Fife, D. 1971. Adam's A B C. Coward, McCann and Geoghegan, New York.
Meet Adam and his friends Arthur and Albert. They live in the city in the same apartment house. What they like to do every day at home, in school, and after school is followed through each letter of the alphabet.

Hefter, R., and Moskov. M.S. (n.d.). The Great Big Alphabet Picture Book with Lots of Words. Grosset & Dunlap, New York.
This is an alphabet book that gives several words for each letter and illustrates them in the most comical pictures.

Mendoza, G. 1972. The Alphabet Boat. American Heritage Press, New York.

With lyrical, seagoing lines and strongly nostalgic pictures, the author and artist together create a wonderfully poetic evocation of all it means to be at sea in a boat.

Miller, E. 1972. Mousekin's A B C. Prentice-Hall, Englewood Cliffs, N.J.
This is an alphabet book that introduces words from the everyday life of a fieldmouse. Not only are the words ordered alphabetically, but they are further explored in delightful verse.

Munari, B. 1960. Bruno Munari's A B C. World Publishing Company, New York.
This is an alphabet book that cleverly combines the written form of object with the most functional prepositions. Both are clarified through pictures.

Ogle, L., and Thoburn, T. 1973. A B See. McGraw-Hill, New York.
This alphabet book goes well beyond the scope of conventional alphabet books in helping children learn about the shapes and sounds of letters. In addition, a charming variety of letter forms are presented.

Oxenbury, H. 1971. A B C of Things. Franklin Watt, N.Y.
Besides being a typical alphabet book, the illustrations make starting points on which parent, teacher, or the child himself can build a story.

Reed, M., and Osswald, E. (n.d.). My First Golden Dictionary. Golden Press, New York.
This book represents hundreds of everyday objects in words and pictures, and beneath each word is a short sentence that is easy for the beginning reader and that repeats the object word and tells something about it.

Scarry, R. (n.d.). Find Your A B C's. Random House, New York.
This alphabet book tells a story of the two detectives Sam and Dudley, who wear the most deceiving disguises. They go on an alphabet hunt and involve the reader actively in the search for words containing the different letters of the alphabet.

Schmiderer, D. (n.d.). The Alphabeast Book. Holt, Rinehart and Winston, New York.
This is an alphabet book of animals. It is a wonderfully whimsical menagerie in which each letter is graphically transformed into an animal. Thus "A" becomes an anteater and "Y" becomes a yak.

Watson, A. A. (n.d.). Very First Words. Holt, Rinehart and Winston, New York.
This is a dictionary of sentences and phrases of words to help children write and spell independently. Children will enjoy pondering both the escapades of Little Mouse and his family and the language patterns relating to these escapades.

BOOKS FOR SENTENCE PATTERNS

Burningham, J. B. 1963. The Adventures of a Goose with no Feathers. Jonathan Cape, London.
This story is about the Plumpster goose family, and especially about Borka, the gosling that was born without feathers, and the problems Borka had because she was different.

Burton, V. L. 1942. The Little House. Houghton Mifflin Co., Boston.
V. L. Burton tells the story of the little country house that was first encrouched upon and then slowly but surely swallowed up by the city. The author establishes the stark contrast between country and city life and imparts the feeling of "out-of-placeness" of the little house to the reader. However, in the end, the little house is compensated.

Hurd, E. T. 1965. The Day the Sun Danced. Harper and Row, New York.
Perfectly accompanied by Clement Hurd's stunning woodcuts, Edith Hurd's poetic text leads the bear, the fox, and the deer through the bleakness of winter to a final burst of color, warmth, and spring. This beautiful book will be loved by readers of all ages.

Ipcar, D. 1955. World Full of Horses. Doubleday, Garden City, N.Y.
When grandfather was a little boy, the world was full of horses. In fact, they were everywhere you looked. When children look at this book, they will see them again, as they were used in the old days and as they are used today.

Krasilovsky, P. 1957. The Cow Who Fell in the Canal. Doubleday, Garden City, N.Y.
This is the story of Hendrika, a fine Dutch cow, who lived on Mr. Hofstra's farm. Hendrika was very unhappy until the great day when she fell into the canal and floated right down to the city. At last she could see all the exciting city things that Peter the horse

had told her about. It was a real adventure, especially when she got to running through the cheese market.

Lewis, R. (ed.). 1965. In a Spring Garden. The Dial Press, New York.
This book speaks directly to the heart and the imagination. This collection of Haiku demonstrates the warmth, vigor, and simplicity of a form at once demanding and subtle. A single image perfectly caught is the stuff of Haiku.

McCloskey, R. 1957. Time of Wonder. Viking Press, New York.
In simple rhythmic prose, which does not need the occasional rhymed words to made it pure poetry, the author-artist tells of a Maine island that is home.

Mizumura, K. I See the Winds. Thomas Y. Crowell, New York.
As the seasons turn, so does the wind: playful in the spring, cooling in the heat of summer, raging in the snows of winter. In delicate free verse and beautiful illustrations Kazue Mizumura captures these many forms of the wind.

Potter, B. (n.d.). The Tale of Peter Rabbit. Frederick Warne & Co., New York.
This is Beatrix Potter's timeless tale of the little bunny, called Peter, who got into all kinds of trouble because he did not heed his mother's warning.

Schick, E. 1970. City in Winter. Macmillan, New York.
No school today! Jimmy's mother has to go to work, blizzard or no blizzard. But Jimmy and Grandma have a snow holiday. Being snowbound is different from just being inside. Everything is somehow new and exciting; but until he and Grandma go outside, it is hard to imagine what a blizzard really is.

Titus, E. 1956. Anatole. McGraw-Hill, New York.
Anatole lived in a small mouse village with his wife and six children. Every evening he bicycled into the city to find food for his family. One evening he heard a man say very unkind things about mice, and he decided right then and there to do something to prove to people that mice did have some worth after all.

Tresselt, A. 1948. Johnny Maple-Leaf. Lothrop, Lee & Shepard, New York.
This book shows the cycle of the seasons told from the point of view of a little maple leaf, from the time it first breaks out of its tight brown bud in the spring until it finally falls to the ground for its winter sleep.

Tresselt, A. 1957. Wake Up, City! Lothrop, Lee & Shepard, New York.

With his customary ease in evoking atmosphere and mood, Alvin Tresselt describes the way a big city wakes up—from the first chirping of the city sparrows to the honking of the bus that picks the children up for school.

Watson, A. A. (n.d.). Very First Words. Holt, Rinehart and Winston, New York

This is a dictionary of sentences and phrases of words to help children write and spell independently. Children will enjoy pondering both the escapades of Little Mouse and his family and the language patterns relating to those escapades.

Zion, G., and Graham, M. B. 1951. All Falling Down. Harper and Row, New York.

"Snow falls down on heads and hats, on dogs, on cats who look out of the window ..." Leaves fall down, and nuts, and sand castles by the sea. Shadows fall; night falls, and sometimes even stars. In fact, almost everything in this book comes falling down! But not quite everything—and that's the surprise of the book.

Zolotow, G. 1952. The Storm Book. Harper and Row, New York.

Here is a picture book that is so real, so alive, you can almost hear the thunder as a summer storm sweeps over the countryside, the city, and the seashore, and almost feel the fresh clean air when the storm has passed and a lovely rainbow arches splendidly across the sky.

Zolotov, C. 1975. When the Wind Stops. Harper and Row, New York.

This book deals with the question and answer dialogue of a little boy and his mother. The little boy is curious where the sun goes and where the wind goes. As the mother answers question after question about the end of things, the little boy begins to understand that nothing really ends, only changes into the beginning of something else.

BOOKS FOR PHONOGRAM PRACTICE

Blakely, P. 1966. Sounds. A. & C. Black, London.

Sounds of everyday life are related in sometimes free and often rhyming verse.

Cole, W., and Ungerer, T. (n.d.). Limerick Giggles. Joke Giggles. The Bodley Head, London.
All kinds of jokes and limericks are presented to tickle a child's fancy.

Cole, W., and Ungerer, T. (n.d.). Rhyme Giggles. Nonsense Giggles. The Bodley Head, London.
Rhymes, nonsense, and such.

Crow, E. (n.d.). Speck the Brownie Here and There. Manuscript. Direct Process Lithography Home Workshop Ed., Victoria, B.C. This is the story of the three Brownies (miniature people) and their adventures in the basement of a people house.

DeRegniers, B. S. 1968. Willy O'Dwyer Jumped in the Fire. Atheneum, New York.
A cry in the night and Willy O'Dwyer is off. Where? To the fire, to the pot, to the moon, to the sun ... But where is not nearly so important as why and how and what happens. That's what this book is really about. That and the girl who gave the cry in the first place.

Emberley, B. 1967. Drummer Hoff. Prentice-Hall, Englewood Cliffs, N.J.
B. Emberley presents this folk verse in a delightfully illustrated form.

Fontane, T. 1969. Sir Ribbeck of Ribbeck of Havelland. (Freely translated from German by Elizabeth Shub.) Macmillan, New York.
This is a delightful poem that tells how Sir Ribbeck outwitted his miserly son and made sure that all the village would be supplied with pears from his tree even after his death.

Galdone, P. 1970. Little Tom Tucker. McGraw-Hill, New York.
Being whipped and scolded and put into chains and made to wear the dunce's cap did not bother Tom. He was much more afraid he would learn how to spell. One special event changed all that. This change of heart is only the beginning of Tom Tucker's story.

Hopkins, L. B. 1974. Hey-How for Halloween. Harcourt Brace Jovanovich, New York.
L. B. Hopkins has selected a delightful sampling of verses to pay tribute to the spine-tingling season of Halloween.

Lear, E. 1968. The Scroobious Pip. Harper and Row, New York.
The Scroobious Pip is one of Lear's most engaging poems, in

which all the animals gather around a strange, inscrutable creature that is part bird, beast, insect, and fish and calls himself the Scroobious Pip.

Leichman, S. 1972. The Wicked Wizard & the Wicked Witch. Harcourt Brace Jovanovich, New York.
When a wicked wizard meets an equally wicked witch, their fierce competition to determine who is more wicked reaches outrageous heights of absurdity. As the witch bestows measles and athlete's foot on the wizard, he in turn counters with mumps and a case of giggles until both the wizard and the witch disappear altogether. This strange contest continues through the night until the frazzled sorcerer's rage gives way to reason.

McCord, D. 1967. Every Time I Climb a Tree. Little, Brown and Co., Boston.
Here are some of David McCord's youngest verses riotously illustrated. Listen to them, look at them, recite them. The sounds and the sight to be found in this book will prick the ears, light the eyes and goad the imagination of all who handle it.

Parkin, R. 1948. The Red Carpet. Macmillan, New York.
This is a very funny account of a run-away carpet from a posh hotel.

Peet, B. 1970. The Whingdingdilly. Houghton Mifflin Co., Boston.
This is a look on the positive side of accepting what you've got. Scamp, a very unhappy dog, is transformed into a hodgepodge of animal parts by a zany witch. His adventures are related in hilariously funny verse.

Preston, E. M. 1969. Pop Corn and Ma Goodness. Viking Press, New York.
A lot of nonsense, but herein lies the fun, particularly with the pleasure afforded through silly words "skippety, skoppety, chippety, choppety, mippety, moppety."

Reid, A. 1959. Ounce, Dice, Trice. Little, Brown and Co., Boston.
This is a book of words. Some are funny, some are serious and beautiful, some are rude, and some are old. Alastair Reid has collected sounds and made words grow from them.

Rounds, G. 1968. Casey Jones. Golden Gate Junior Books, Los Angeles, Calif.
Mr. Rounds has captured not only the spirit of the song but the

very essence of a bygone era when the trains that criss-crossed our land were the pride and joy of the nation.

Zemach, M. 1969. The Judge. Farrar, Straus and Giroux, New York. "A horrible thing is coming this way." Anxious prisoner after anxious prisoner echoes and embellishes this cry, but each time in vain. The fiery old judge, impatient with their foolish nonsense, calls the prisoners scoundrels, ninnyhammers, and throws them all in jail. In the end, though, justice is done. . . .

BOOKS FOR RECURRING PATTERNS

Brooke, L. 1903. (Artist). Johnny Crow's Garden. Frederick Warne & Co., London.
A delightfully illustrated version.

Burton, V. 1939. Mike Mulligan and the Steam Shovel. Houghton Mifflin Co., Boston.
This is the story of a faithful steam-shovel artist and his steam shovel—the beguiling Mary Anne—that he would not desert even though competition from gas Diesel-motored shovels is ruining him. The solution of Mike's problem is classic in its simplicity. Under pressure to show Mary Anne at her very best, Mike digs the foundations of the town hall of Popperville, and in his haste forgets to leave a way out. This suggests to the ingenious townspeople that Mary Anne could easily be remodeled as a furnace and Mike, her master, retained to keep her heart and boiler warm.

Clifton, L. 1970. Some of the Days of Everett Anderson. Holt, Rinehart and Winston, New York.
This book tells all about six-year-old Everett Anderson who lives in Apt. 14 A. Who is Everett Anderson? He could be any child who has ever played in the rain, been afraid of the dark, felt lonely, or wondered about the stars.

Cohen, C. 1975. Wake Up, Groundhog. Crown Publishers, New York.
When Mrs. Pigeon uses an alarm clock to wake up Groundhog, he keeps on sleeping. She then borrows Mouse Brothers' grandfather clock, Rabbit's pocket watch, Frog's cuckoo clock, and soon every clock in town is bonging, ticking, cuckooing, and dingdonging, and still Groundhog sleeps. It is not until an hourglass is tried and fails that Miss Pigeon humorously learns what wakes up the Groundhog.

Gordon, G. 1974. Walter and the Balloon. Heinemann, London.
Walter's balloon flies out of reach and Walter and his cat, Freddie, go through the town asking a policeman, a soldier, a clown, and a string of strange and wonderful people to catch it for him. This is a satisfyingly simple, rhythmical cumulative story for young children.

Heilbroner, J. 1962. This is the House Where Jack Lives. Harper and Row, New York.
This story starts, of course, with the house where Jack lives. A dog lives there, too. The dog and the boy are going for a walk when the boy is surprised by a falling pail, which was held by a man who is bumped by a mop, etc.

Holl, A. 1970. Listening for Sounds. Rev. Ed. Western Publishing Co., Racine, Wisc.
This book explores sounds within a child's daily environment and expands from there to a wider circle of experience, e.g., sounds of the ocean, in the woods, etc. The sounds are spelled phonetically and incorporated artistically into free verse.

Lefevre, F. (n.d.). The Cock, the Mouse, and the Little Red Hen. Macrae-Smith.
The delightful classic tale is gaily illustrated.

McGovern, A. 1964. Zoo Where Are You? Harper and Row, New York.
There is no zoo in Josh's town. But he wants one so badly that he decides to find one of his own. He gets together everything he needs: a wild-animal-catching bag, a hunter's gun, heavy ropes, and a whistle for calling animals. Then he sets out.... .

Martin, Jr., B. (n.d.). A Ghost Story. Holt, Rinehart and Winston, New York.
A very eerily illustrated version of "In a dark, dark woods...."

Martin, Jr., B. (n.d.). Sounds of Home. Holt, Rinehart and Winston, New York.
Simple selections of stories and poems.

Pomerantz, C. 1975. The Ballad of the Long-tailed Rat. Macmillan, New York.
Who caught the elegant, long-tailed rat? The landlady, the landlord, the cat, and even the cheese all take credit for capturing him. But did they? The verses are irresistibly repeatable and sure to be quickly chorused by story-time listeners.

Preston, E. M. 1969. Pop Corn and Ma Goodness. Viking Press, New York.
A book of rhythmical nonsense on marriage, birth and death, summer and winter, tears and laughter. Exquisitely illustrated and filled with tongue-tripping words that demand to be read aloud.

Preston, E. M. 1969. The Temper Tantrum Book. Viking Press, New York.
This book explains the most fervent dislikes of different types of animals and the reason for their frustrations.

Saxe, J. G. 1963. The Blind Men and the Elephant. McGraw-Hill, New York.
The first blind man found the elephant "very like a wall," the second said he was "very like a spear," and each other man in his turn had an opinion as surprising—but different. All of which might go to show that even the shape of an elephant depends on how you look at it.

Seuss. 1957. The Cat in the Hat. Random House, New York.
A very mischievous cat entertains two children one afternoon and gets them into all kinds of trouble, which he rather magically clears up at the end of the story.

Seuss. 1960. Green Eggs and Ham. Random House, New York.
Using a vocubalary of only 50 different words, Seuss concocts a little masterpiece that delights beginning readers.

Simon, N. 1974. I Was So Mad! Albert Whitman & Company, Chicago.
In this book a child's very basic and honest feelings are expressed as she learns to cope with every-day problems.

Appendix B
Reading Checklist

	Seldom or never	Usually	Always
A. WORD RECOGNITION			
I. Sight vocabulary			
1. Recognition			
a. Recognizes most words taught	____	____	____
b. Recognizes interesting content words	____	____	____
c. Recognizes polysyllabic words	____	____	____
d. Recognizes function words (articles, conjunctions, prepositions, etc.)	____	____	____
2. Identification			
a. Identifies most words taught	____	____	____
b. Identifies interesting content words	____	____	____
c. Identifies polysyllabic words	____	____	____
d. Identifies function words (articles, conjunctions, prepositions, etc.)	____	____	
B. WORD ANALYSIS			
I. Phonic			
1. Recognition—integrates auditory and visual skills in recognizing.	____	____	____
a. Beginning consonants	____	____	____
b. Final consonants	____	____	____
c. Beginning consonants clusters			
i. Double	____	____	____
ii. Triple	____	____	____
d. Rhyming elements	____	____	____
e. Lax vowel sounds	____	____	____
f. Tense vowel sounds	____	____	____
g. Consonant digraphs	____	____	____

Continued

	Seldom or never	Usually	Always
2. Identification—integrates auditory and visual skills in identifying			
a. Beginning consonants	___	___	___
b. Final consonants	___	___	___
c. Beginning consonants clusters			
i. Double	___	___	___
ii. Triple	___	___	___
d. Rhyming elements	___	___	___
e. Lax vowel sounds	___	___	___
f. Tense vowel sounds	___	___	___
g. Consonant digraphs	___	___	___

II. Structural
   1. Recognition—integrates visual and auditory skills in recognizing:

	Seldom or never	Usually	Always
a. Compound Words	___	___	___
b. Base words and inflectional endings (number, tense, degree)	___	___	___
c. Number of structural elements in a word (word part families)	___	___	___
d. Base words and affixes	___	___	___
e. Contractions	___	___	___
f. Possessives	___	___	___

   2. Identification—integrates visual and auditory skills in identifying:

	Seldom or never	Usually	Always
a. Number of structural elements in a word	___	___	___
b. Base words and inflectional endings (number, tense, degree)	___	___	___
c. Base words and affixes	___	___	___
d. Compound words	___	___	___
e. Contractions	___	___	___
f. Possessives	___	___	___

III. Semantic—Associational context clues
   1. Identifies words from associations of surrounding meaning clues:

	Seldom or never	Usually	Always
a. Comparison or contrast	___	___	___
b. Synonyms	___	___	___

	Seldom or never	Usually	Always
c. Summary	——	——	——
d. Mood	——	——	——
e. Familiar Expression	——	——	——
f. Classification	——	——	——
g. Familiar Experience	——	——	——
h. Appositives	——	——	——
i. Simile	——	——	——

IV. Syntactic—graphic context clues
   1. Identifies words from their syntactic—graphic clues:

	Seldom or never	Usually	Always
a. Position in sentence	——	——	——
b. Function of word	——	——	——
c. Punctuation (intonation in oral language)	——	——	——
d. Typographical aids	——	——	——

   2. Recognizes function words as organizational clues   —— —— ——

V. Phonic-structural-context integration
   1. Identifies words by combining semantic, syntactic and phonic-structural elements   —— —— ——

C. COMPREHENSION SKILLS

I. Literal
   1. Recognizes

	Seldom or never	Usually	Always
a. Details	——	——	——
b. Main Ideas	——	——	——
c. Relationships	——	——	——
i. Cause-effect	——	——	——
ii. Space/place	——	——	——
iii. Sequence	——	——	——

   2. Identifies:

	Seldom or never	Usually	Always
a. Details	——	——	——
b. Main ideas	——	——	——
c. Relationships	——	——	——
i. Cause-effect	——	——	——
ii. Space/place	——	——	——
iii. Sequence	——	——	——

Continued

	Seldom or never	Usually	Always

II. Inferential—uses implied information to:
1. Predict outcomes ___ ___ ___
2. Identify cause/effect relationships ___ ___ ___
3. Identify space/place relationships ___ ___ ___
4. Identify time relationships ___ ___ ___
5. Identify sequence ___ ___ ___

III. Evaluative—uses information to:
1. Distinguish fact from fiction ___ ___ ___
2. Make judgments ___ ___ ___
3. Recognizing author's purpose ___ ___ ___
4. Recognizing propaganda techniques ___ ___ ___

IV. Interpretive—uses information to:
1. Draw conclusions ___ ___ ___
2. Identify emotional tone ___ ___ ___
3. Identify character traits ___ ___ ___

D. STUDY SKILLS
  I. Locational—is able to:
    1. Arrange words in alphabetical order ___ ___ ___
    2. Apply alphabetic knowledge in locating information in dictionaries, indexes, etc. ___ ___ ___

  II. Organizational—is able to:
    1. Recognize that headings and sub-headings reflect organization ___ ___ ___
    2. Apply knowledge of main idea and detail relationships to outline ___ ___ ___
    3. Apply knowledge of main idea and detail relationships to summarize ___ ___ ___
    4. Apply knowledge of main idea and detail relationships to take notes ___ ___ ___
    5. Synthesize information from two sources ___ ___ ___

	Seldom or never	Usually	Always
III. Table-graphic skills—is able to:			
1. Identify purposes	——	——	——
2. Identify details	——	——	——
3. Make summary statement	——	——	——
IV. Skimming-scanning—is able to:			
1. Set purposes for reading	——	——	——
2. Skim a passage	——	——	——
3. Scan a passage	——	——	——

Appendix C

Language Skills Checklist

Language Skills Checklist

Composition skills	Needs work	Has been introduced	Student has attempted	Student is proficient	Mechanics, usage, etc.	Needs Work	Has been introduced	Student has attempted	Student is proficient	Group process	Needs work	Has been introduced	Student has attempted	Student is proficient
A. Narrative skills														
Incidents					Dialogue without quotation marks					Getting acquainted				
Jokes, personal experiences					Possessives					Organizing for action				
Plot					Use of colon					Dramatization				
Setting					Parentheses					Discussion: using other peoples' responses				
Character														
Stories					Writing titles									
News stories					Direct quotations									
Tall tales					Interjections									
Legends and fables					Unity									
Plays					Sentence expansion									
Songs														
B. Description					Tense					Responsibility for all to contribute				
Factual description					Conjunctions					Taking roles				
Imaginative description					Adjectives									

Mood

C. Exposition
Direction and explanation
Directions
Announcements
Advertising
Giving information

Acronyms
Adverbs
Pronouns
Basic sentence patterns
Coherence

Reaching a consensus
Sharing information
Brainstorming
Tutoring an individual
Using information sources

Hyphen
Roots and affixes
Sentence combining
Common signs and symbols
Abbreviations
Alphabetization
Documenting books and articles
Limiting a topic

D. Reporting
Notetaking
Outlining
Report preparation
Editing
Proofreading

Using the colon
Abbreviations
Using capitals
Subject of sentence
Predicate

Dividing duties in research groups
Presenting a report

Continued

Composition skills	Needs work	Has been introduced	Student has attempted	Student is proficient	Mechanics, usage, etc.	Needs work	Has been introduced	Student has attempted	Student is proficient	Group process	Needs work	Has been introduced	Student has attempted	Student is proficient
E. Letters and forms Friendly letter Invitation and reply Business corres- pondence Addressing envelopes					Abbreviations of weights, sizes, etc. Coding systems used on forms Subordination					Making an introduction Asking for assistance in bussinesses and letters.				
F. Poetry Experimenting with words Extemporaneous poetry Visual poetry Unrhymed verse Senryu/Haiku Cinquain Diamante Rhymed verse Couplets/ Triplets/ Quatrains Jingles Limericks Clerihews Worksongs					Using repetition Using rhythm Participles Semicolon Antonyms Homonyms Apostrophe					Group planning Presenting a poem to a group or class Bookbinding Choral reading				

InDex